Statistical Process Control

DeMYSTiFieD®

DeMYSTiFieD® Series

Accounting Demystified
Advanced Calculus Demystified
Advanced Physics Demystified
Advanced Statistics Demystified
Algebra Demystified
Alternative Energy Demystified
Anatomy Demystified
Astronomy Demystified
Audio Demystified
Biology Demystified
Biophysics Demystified
Biotechnology Demystified
Business Calculus Demystified
Business Math Demystified
Business Statistics Demystified
C++ Demystified
Calculus Demystified
Chemistry Demystified
Circuit Analysis Demystified
College Algebra Demystified
Corporate Finance Demystified
Data Structures Demystified
Databases Demystified
Differential Equations Demystified
Digital Electronics Demystified
Earth Science Demystified
Electricity Demystified
Electronics Demystified
Engineering Statistics Demystified
Environmental Science Demystified
Everyday Math Demystified
Financial Planning Demystified
Forensics Demystified
French Demystified
Genetics Demystified
Geometry Demystified
German Demystified
Home Networking Demystified
Investing Demystified
Italian Demystified
Java Demystified
JavaScript Demystified
Lean Six Sigma Demystified
Linear Algebra Demystified
Logic Demystified

Macroeconomics Demystified
Management Accounting Demystified
Math Proofs Demystified
Math Word Problems Demystified
MATLAB® Demystified
Medical Billing and Coding Demystified
Medical Terminology Demystified
Meteorology Demystified
Microbiology Demystified
Microeconomics Demystified
Minitab Demystified
Nanotechnology Demystified
Nurse Management Demystified
OOP Demystified
Options Demystified
Organic Chemistry Demystified
Personal Computing Demystified
Pharmacology Demystified
Philosophy Demystified
Physics Demystified
Physiology Demystified
Pre-Algebra Demystified
Precalculus Demystified
Probability Demystified
Project Management Demystified
Psychology Demystified
Quality Management Demystified
Quantum Mechanics Demystified
Real Estate Math Demystified
Relativity Demystified
Robotics Demystified
Signals and Systems Demystified
Six Sigma Demystified
Spanish Demystified
SQL Demystified
Statics and Dynamics Demystified
Statistical Process Control Demystified
Statistics Demystified
Technical Analysis Demystified
Technical Math Demystified
Trigonometry Demystified
UML Demystified
Visual Basic 2005 Demystified
Visual C# 2005 Demystified
XML Demystified

Statistical Process Control
DeMYSTiFieD®

Paul Keller

New York   Chicago   San Francisco   Lisbon   London   Madrid   Mexico City
Milan   New Delhi   San Juan   Seoul   Singapore   Sydney   Toronto

The McGraw·Hill Companies

Cataloging-in-Publication Data is on file with the Library of Congress

Statistical Process Control DeMYSTiFieD®

1 2 3 4 5 6 7 8 9 0   DOC/DOC   1 7 6 5 4 3 2 1

ISBN 978-0-07-174249-8
MHID 0-07-174249-2

Sponsoring Editor Judy Bass	**Project Manager** Shruti Vasishta, Cenveo Publisher Services	**Indexer** Robert Swanson
Editorial Supervisor Stephen M. Smith	**Copy Editor** Eina Malik, Cenveo Publisher Services	**Cover Illustration** Lance Lekander
Production Supervisor Pamela A. Pelton		**Art Director, Cover** Jeff Weeks
Acquisitions Coordinator Michael Mulcahy	**Proofreader** Namita Panda, Cenveo Publisher Services	**Composition** Cenveo Publisher Services

*To Mom and Dad, for their endless encouragement, love, and support;
and to my brother Dave, whose generosity and advice have
always been there for me.*

About the Author

Paul Keller is President and Chief Operating Officer of Quality America, Inc., and has developed and implemented successful Six Sigma and quality improvement programs in service and manufacturing environments. He is the bestselling author or coauthor of several books, including *The Six Sigma Handbook* and *Six Sigma DeMYSTiFieD*.

Contents

Preface

Welcome to the exciting world of statistical process control! I am very pleased to write this book, as I have had passion for the subject for many years. I was first introduced to SPC over 25 years ago, as a graduate student intern at a leading computer products manufacturer. Although I had a bachelor's degree in engineering, and had worked for several years in industry, I had not been exposed to this particular type of statistical analysis. The manufacturing engineers I worked with had only limited experience, and together we persevered our way through implementing control charts on a key process. Along the way, we made what I later determined were several fundamental errors. We learned the hard way that our process suffered from issues that hadn't been discussed in our textbook examples.

I took these hard lessons back to graduate school and learned as much as I could on the techniques. I applied them myself as a quality director in a couple of manufacturing organizations. In the early 1990s, I had the chance to become the technical services director for a company that developed SPC software. In that capacity I oversaw the technical support group, working with customers as they implemented SPC in a wide variety of industries including healthcare, aviation, banking, insurance, chemical processing, and manufacturing. Our customers had seemingly varied needs; in reality there were many common threads. As much as each industry felt theirs was unique, in fact they had much in common. As might be expected, the tools of SPC have application across many types of processes, with only subtle differences in use.

As I write these pages, I am now president and chief operating officer of the company. Over the past 20 years I have applied these tools internally to our key processes, to learn, improve, and predict the dynamics of our internal sales and support processes, as well as our marketing and product development efforts. SPC is an integral part of what we do, and how we remain competitive in a sometimes crowded market. It provides the fundamental backbone to our systems, to consistently meet the needs of a demanding yet appreciative audience of quality professionals. I am indebted to many of these clients, who over the years have shared their problems and experiences with me, through their technical support issues, sales inquiries, or training sessions. I feel quite fortunate to have worked with so many professionals who work diligently to service their customers and seek the truth that only data can provide. I have tried to encapsulate as much of their collective experiences in this book as possible.

Examples are provided throughout this book from a wide variety of applications, including general service (aka transactional) processes, healthcare processes, chemical processing and manufacturing. The book's topics build on each other, so it is recommended to read each chapter in the order provided. There are a number of critical and fundamental concepts discussed in earlier chapters that are required for later chapters.

Calculations and statistical assumptions are provided as needed, with emphasis on chart application and interpretation. Examples are provided for each chart, which may be downloaded from the author's Web site at www.qualityamerica.com/downloads/SPCDemystified.htm. Given the commercial availability of inexpensive SPC software, students are expected to use statistical software to quickly calculate the statistics and draw the chart. A time-restricted license of an easy to use MS Excel add-on for SPC is available for free via the above link for users of this textbook. This commercially available SPC software package has been confidently used by thousands of organizations worldwide to quickly perform SPC analysis.

This text may be used for training groups of SPC practitioners within an organization, or for self-study to master the tools and methodology of statistical process control.

I hope you enjoy it and have the opportunity to realize the full potential of these powerful tools.

Paul Keller

Statistical Process Control

DeMYSTiFieD®

chapter **1**

Analyzing Process Data

Statistical process control is a fundamental analysis tool for business processes. If that comes as a surprise, then your business can surely benefit from its use.

CHAPTER OBJECTIVES

After completing this chapter, you will be able to

- Explain the difference between analytical and enumerative statistics
- Describe the general characteristics of a control chart
- Demonstrate the advantage of statistical control chart in detecting process shifts
- Illustrate the misuse of process data in process tampering
- Explain the interpretation of statistical control charts

The Application of Statistics to Processes

Many organizations strive to achieve data-driven decision making. In today's electronic world, data is often readily available. With proper analysis, data becomes information; with action, knowledge. Unfortunately, improper analysis leads to misinformation, and reaction to misinformation can lead to disastrous results. Samuel Clemens (aka Mark Twain) popularized the notion of the misuse of statistics as the worst of three possible types of mistruths: "lies, damned lies, and statistics." It should be clear that Twain was referring to the misuse of statistics, and not the general use of statistics to define an issue or assist in problem-solving.

Yet, even the proper application of statistics, when used to support unpopular conclusions, can lead to bemoaning of the statistics themselves, particularly amongst those ignorant in the use of statistics. The often-cited refrain "You can prove anything with statistics" enforces this notion, even as it lacks the clarity to differentiate between proper and improper uses.

Many applications of statistics in popular use employ the principles of *enumerative statistics*. Enumerative statistics are designed to quantify and compare populations. The weatherman notes the average temperature, where the population in question is the specific day for a particular geographic region; the housing expert quotes a median price, where the population includes all homes within a specific town, county, state, or country; a political pundit delivers his or her projection of an election outcome based on sampling, where the population includes all expected voters in the election.

The notion of populations is a simplification employed by statisticians to reduce the complexity of the real world: If the world from which we sample can be reduced to a universe of fixed properties, then enumerative statistics are useful. Yet, many of these so-called populations are really processes which are repeatable over time. They are influenced by a collection of known (and perhaps unknown) factors, which themselves may vary over time. This system of causal factors influenced the past behavior of the process in some relatively consistent manner, unless and until the system itself changes. The past behavior of the process provides some indication of its future behavior: The local weather results from an environmental process influenced by climate, wind patterns, relative humidity and so on; its responses to these factors are experienced on a daily basis, and are relatively consistent over some period of time, indicative of the consistency of the system of causes that influence the outcome.

There is information in this prior data that is lost, or not used, in the enumerative analyses. There are inherent differences between the analysis of processes, which occur over time, and populations, which are static snapshots.

A Process Defined

Deming says simply, "Every activity, every job, is part of a process" (Deming, 1986). A process consists of repeatable tasks, carried out in a specific order (Keller, 2011). While many processes are defined to satisfy the demands of different products, services, or even customers, for example, the manner in which they meet these challenges should be relatively consistent to constitute a process. Alternatively, a purely random manner of producing outcome is certainly evidence of a lack of process: An element of repeatability or consistency is lacking.

Pure consistency of process delivery is not necessarily desirable. Rather, processes are considered *robust* when they can meet the challenges of varied input to achieve consistent, predictable output. In this way, a robust process will not require adjustment to achieve consistent results in spite of sometimes severe changes in the inputs. The fast service restaurant that seamlessly meets the increased demand of lunch hour traffic does so not by abandoning its process, but by executing it: The process is equally capable of meeting the varied demands placed on it.

A repeatable process is one in which the actions undertaken within the process are basically the same for a given set of inputs. The process is designed with forethought of the influence of the varied input. Yet, since most processes include some level of human interaction, there remains a natural source of variation *within the process delivery mechanism itself* that contributes to variation in process delivery. The rate at which humans can perform even simple tasks, and their ability to replicate their own actions consistently, vary from individual to individual, or from day to day or hour to hour for a specific individual. If not, most of us could make free throws and sink 10-foot putts 100% of the time! Obviously, even the best- skilled athlete achieves less than 100% repeatability on even relatively simple mechanical tasks. When process tasks involve perception, reasoning or experience, variations in human behavior are to be expected. While some may choose to minimize these activities to achieve consistency, robust processes are designed to allow for some level of fluctuation in delivery methods to achieve optimal delivery outcomes. That is, the best process designs may allow for some level of improvisation, in order to provide opportunity for elevated perceptions in the customer experience. The process that anticipates the need for personnel to meet the varied expectations of clients, while maintaining the other necessary outcomes of the process, is ultimately the optimal process. Note that the process retains elements of consistency in process design, so as to satisfy the sometimes competing demands of other process "customers" including shareholders and downstream processes.

Likewise, consistent outcome does not imply that all output has exactly equal numerical value for a given metric. Rather, variation in outcome exists in most, if not all, processes. Process output that appears exactly or nearly identical may reflect an inability to measure actual differences in output because of inexact measurement methods or measurement imprecision. Variation in process output reflects the complexity of the process: the variations in inputs and process delivery that influence the output. Statistics provide the means to quantify the expected output, including its expected variation.

Population versus Process Statistics

Consider for example the conversion rate for a sales process. A *point estimate* of the conversion rate is obtained by dividing the number of actual sales by the number of potential sales in a given time period. For example, if 300 sales prospects in September resulted in 98 sales, then the conversion rate is calculated as 98 divided by 300 or 32.7%.

While the point estimate itself is useful, it lacks context: Is this 32.7% better than expected, or worse? Comparisons using *statistical inference* can be constructed to evaluate the sample data relative to prior experience.

A *confidence interval* for the proportion can be calculated as the range 27.4% to 38.3% (assuming normality), using confidence interval for proportion techniques, such as described in Keller (2011). Since this interval includes the historical estimate of 33.0%, there is no evidence the sample differs significantly from the past experience.

Similarly, a *hypothesis test for two proportions*, such as found in Minitab, can be used to determine if September's conversion rate is equivalent to the historical conversion rate. In this case, the historical data consisted of approximately 9000 prospective clients over 30 months, of which nearly 3000 were converted into sales. The hypothesis test yielded a p-value of 0.91, suggesting that samples this extreme would occur 91% of the time if the conversion rates were equal. In other words, there is no evidence that the conversion rates are different. (Note: We would typically look for a p-value of 0.05 or less to suggest the conversion rates were different.)

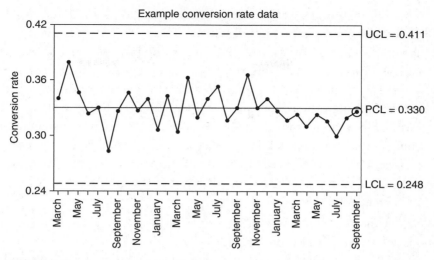

FIGURE 1.1 · Example control chart of sales conversion process.

A *control chart* of these 31 months of data is shown in Figure 1.1. This particular control chart is referred to as a *p chart*, where p refers to *percent*. It is the preferred chart when plotting percentages, and will be discussed in more detail later in the book.

All control charts have the following properties, which are evident in Figure 1.1:

1. The x-axis is a time-ordered sequence, with earlier data on the left and the most recent data at the far right of the chart. Note in Figure 1.1 the x-axis is scaled by months, where each plotted point represents the summarized data for a sample taken that month.

2. The y-axis is scaled to the statistic charted for each point in time. Figure 1.1 charts the conversion rate.

3. Statistical *control limits* are defined for the plotted statistic based on process data. The limits are never determined using customer specifications or management goals. In Figure 1.1 the upper control limit (labeled UCL*)* is calculated as 0.411; the lower control limit (labeled LCL*)* is calculated as 0.248. (The calculation methods for these statistics are dependent on the type of chart, as discussed later in the book for each chart type.)

4. The statistical control limits are determined by estimating the "short-term" variation in the process. Statistical process control is synonymous with stability and is achieved when the short-term variation provides a good model (or estimate, or prediction) of the longer-term variation.

5. The calculated statistical control limits provide an indication of the expected bounds of the plotted statistic. This expected variation (between the control limits) is intrinsic (built-in) to the process. This inherent process variation is usually referred to as *common cause variation*, since the sources of variation are common to all plotted points within the control limits. Although the actual sources of variation (and their relative contribution) may be unknown, their effect on the process is systematic and consistent over time, allowing prediction of the future performance of the process. If the control limits defined in Figure 1.1 are representative of the conversion rate process, the conversion rate is expected to vary between 24.8% and 41.1%.

6. When plotted points exceed the control limits, they are influenced by *special causes* of variation. This is evidence that the process has shifted or changed, at least for the time period evidenced by the points beyond the control limits. When special causes exist, the process is *out of control*. A key value of the control chart is to identify the occurrence of special causes so that the process knowledge can be gained concerning the sources of special causes and corresponding corrective and preventative action taken for process improvement.

7. In the absence of special causes, the process is *in control*. The control limits are calculated such that the chance of plotted points exceeding the upper or lower control limit is very small unless the process has changed.

8. In addition to the control limits, statistical *run test rules* can also be applied as appropriate to test for unlikely conditions indicative of a special cause. These run test rules enhance the sensitivity of the control chart by looking for unnatural data patterns within the control limits. In Figure 1.1, note how the last plotted point (September's data) is circled, which this software uses to indicate a violation of one of the run test rules. In this case, the chart detected that nine points in a row were beneath the center line of the process. The chance of this happening if the process had not been subject to a special cause of variation is extremely rare (less than 2/10 of 1%). The implication is that the process has changed, perhaps as early as January (the first of the nine plotted groups in a row beneath the center line). When a sustained process shift is identified and confirmed in process terms, the control limits can be adjusted as shown in Figure 1.2 to reflect the new process conditions.

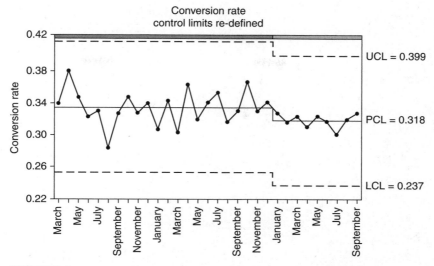

FIGURE 1.2 · Example sales conversion process with sustained process shift.

It should be clear that the control chart identified a process shift that was undetected by the classical statistical methods. These classical methods, including statistical inference tools of confidence intervals and hypothesis testing as well as histograms, ignore the sequencing of the process data which in many cases provide valuable additional information. The classical statistical tools are developed for fixed populations and not for processes.

The confidence intervals and hypothesis tests cited earlier in the example pooled the data and ignored their sequence. Process control charts add the element of time to the analysis: This additional dimension takes advantage of the inherent time sequencing of data produced by a process.

Similarly, process histograms have become the graphical equivalent of the damned lies and statistics. The histogram is an enumerative tool: Even when process data is properly collected for analytical use, its time sequence is lost as the data is collapsed into the histogram cells. Consider the histogram shown in Figure 1.3. Note the well-defined bell-shaped curve, and its positioning well within the customer's upper specification limit (USL) and lower specification limit (LSL). Obviously this process is well-controlled, stable, and capable of meeting the customer requirements.

Or perhaps not. The processes shown in Figures 1.4 and 1.5 contain the identical data used to construct the histogram. Clearly, even with limited understanding of control charting, it is apparent that the processes associated with

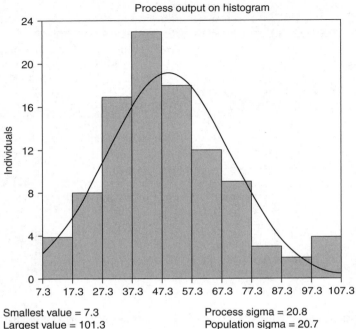

Smallest value = 7.3
Largest value = 101.3
Average = 49.2
Skewness = 0.6
Kurtosis = 0.1
Standard error of mean = 2.1
K-S test: 0.4
Curve fit: normal

Process sigma = 20.8
Population sigma = 20.7
Sample sigma = 20.8
USL = 120
LSL = 0

FIGURE 1.3 · Histogram with the intent to show a stable and capable process.

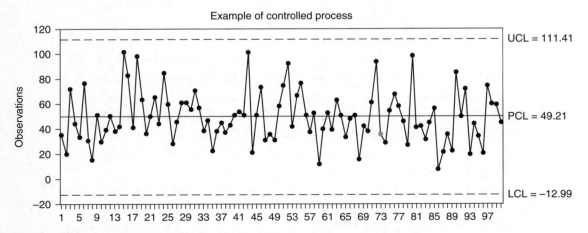

FIGURE 1.4 · One of many possible processes producing the histogram of Figure 1.3.

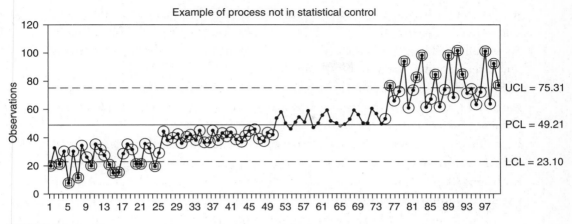

FIGURE 1.5 • A less favorable process producing the histogram of Figure 1.3.

Figures 1.4 and 1.5 are quite different. Figure 1.4 shows a stable process operating within its statistical control limits; Figure 1.5 shows a process trending in a positive direction. Will its next sample be even larger? Or perhaps the cycle will start over again? Or something else? There is no way to know, since the process is out of control! By definition, it is unpredictable.

Histograms can never be used to show process stability, or even conformance to requirements. The control chart is the only tool that can serve those purposes. Unlike the histogram, confidence intervals and hypothesis tests, only the control chart is capable of predicting future process behavior. Generally, a histogram should not be used without a control chart, unless the data used to construct the histogram is census data (i.e., 100% of all possible units in the study). When there is no time sequence to the data, such as when data is sampled from a supplier's shipment, a histogram can be used to graphically show the distribution *of the sample*, whose interpretation is subject to the limitations of sampling statistics. Those limitations include 100% sampling (i.e., all output is measured and verified) if the process has not been shown to be in statistical control.

Statistical Process Control Concepts

Statistical process control (SPC) is a primary analysis tool of process evaluation and improvement. Developed by Walter Shewhart in the 1920s to evaluate production processes, its application to a wide variety of industries and market sectors was perhaps most influenced by W. Edwards Deming. His seminal text, *Out of the Crisis*, resulted from his years of postwar training and consulting in Japan followed by general apathy toward these methods by the Japanese man-ufacturers' counterparts in the United States.

Shewhart defined statistical control as follows: "*A phenomenon is said to be in statistical control when, through the use of past experience, we can predict how the phenomenon will vary in the future.*"

SPC uses the element of time as one of its principle axes. Data is collected over a short period of time: Each of these samples is referred to as a *subgroup*. Each subgroup tells us two things about the process: its current location and its current amount of variation.

When enough subgroups have been collected over a longer period of time, the short-term estimates are used to predict where the process will be (its loca-tion), and how much the process is expected to vary over a longer time period. Thus, rather than pooling the data to calculate the average and standard devia-tion, the time component of the process is retained and used to calculate the average and standard deviation of *each* subgroup separately. The collective properties of the short-term estimates (i.e., the subgroups) are used to predict the longer-term properties of the process.

Process variation may be due either to causes that are persistent, or to causes that come and go. Potential sources of variation include the five Ms and an E: Our *Methods*, the *Materials* used in the process, the *Manpower* or personnel involved in the process, the *Machines* or equipment that are used, our *Measure-ment* techniques, and the surrounding *Environment*.

Deming's red bead experiment is a classic teaching demonstration of the principles of SPC. In Deming's seminars, students were enlisted as process workers, who would dip into a bucket of beads to collect the "daily production" of 50 white beads. Since the bucket had a small percentage of red beads, the production workers would naturally have several red beads in each sample. An inspector counted the number of white beads in each sample, which repre-sented usable output that could be sold to customers; red beads could not be "sold" and were thus considered scrap. A manager would observe the sample results, counsel the production workers who had high numbers of red beads, and congratulate those with fewer red beads. Improvement on subsequent samples would bring reward; an increase in red bead count would be indicative of a worker's degrading performance.

A control chart of the typical red bead "error rate" is shown in Figure 1.6. Notice the variation in the process observations: Each 50-bead sample yields a

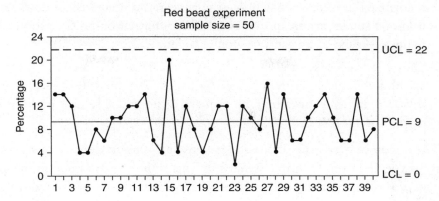

FIGURE 1.6 · Example control chart of Deming's red bead experiment.

different count of white beads. The process itself has not changed, since *no one has changed the bucket.* The control limits indicate that between 0 and 11 red beads (0% and 22%) should be expected on each sample of 50 beads.

Process variation is quite natural, and each process has a unique level of variation that is inherent (or built-in) to this process. If a particular sample observation seems large (such as a count of 9 red beads), is it unnaturally large or should it be expected? The control limits remove the subjectivity from this decision, and define the level of natural process variation.

Samples that occur beyond the control limits are the result of a *special cause of variation:* Something occurred at this point in time (or just prior to this point in time) to influence the process differently than seen in the past. The statistical control limits provide the *operational definition* of the special cause: The existence of a special cause can be determined only through use of a statistical control chart. While process personnel are often tempted to categorize particular sources of variation as special causes of variation, perhaps because of the perceived spontaneity of their occurrence, that is an improper use of the terminology. Only the properly defined statistical control limits can differentiate a special cause of variation from common causes of variation.

Process changes are manifested in one of two ways:

1. A *process shift* redefines the location (or numerical center point) of the process metric. For example, if we add enough red beads to the bucket, we would detect a process shift such as shown previously in Figure 1.2. Process shifts may result in process improvement (e.g., cycle time reduction) or process degradation (e.g., an increased cycle time). The ability to

recognize the variation as a process change, rather than just random variation of a stable process, provides valuable information on the process dynamics, leading to overall variation reduction.

2. Short-term process variation may also increase or decrease, indicative of an inherent change in the process dynamics. For example, the short-term variation in cycle time may be reduced systematically by simplifying a complicated process.

The region between the upper and lower control limits define the variation that is expected from the process statistic. This is the variation due to *common causes*: causes common to all the process observations. If we want to reduce this level of variation, we need to redefine the process, or make fundamental changes to the design of the process.

When a process is subject to only sources of common cause variation, the process is considered *in statistical control*, or simply *in control*. When the process is in control, the control limits can be used to predict the future performance of the process. For example, if the process variable is related to a customer specification, the chart can predict the defect levels, influencing estimates of the cost to produce the product or deliver the service. If the process variable is the time to deliver the product or service, the control chart is useful for planning resources, such as in a doctor's office, or deliver product, such as in a warehouse.

As data is collected and analyzed for a process, it seems almost second nature to assume that we can understand the causes of this variation. In Deming's red bead experiment, the manager invariably congratulates workers with a relatively low number of red beads, and counsels those with a high number of red beads. This interaction is comical to the seminar audience, since the worker had no control over the number of red beads in each sample. Yet, this same experiment happens daily in real business environments.

Suppose, for example, that an Order Processing Supervisor, being unfamiliar with statistical process control, expected all orders to be processed at a certain pace, say within 15 days. In the supervisor's experience, the process could obviously perform this well, since it had processed orders at or below this level many times in the past. Perhaps some or even most orders can be processed within that time period. Yet, if unknown to the supervisor the upper process control limit is above that level, then a percentage of the orders will not (predictably) be processed within that time period. If the supervisor expected that all orders should be processed within the 15 days, he will look for special causes that don't exist. He may blame the order processors, their suppliers, or the equipment that was used in the process. Instead, if the natural process control limits exceed the 15-day specification limits, then a better use of his resources is in redesigning the system (i.e., changing the fundamental nature of the bucket of red beads).

Requirements versus Control

Many processes are dictated by customer requirements, also known as specifications, or even management goals. Each of these terms refers to the *voice of the customer*, where the customer may be internal (either within the organization or the process, depending on context) or external (outside the organization or process).

Requirements, specifications, or goals are often expressed as fixed constants. For example, the customer requires delivery in 5 days, or the part must be between 3.5 and 3.55 inches. The implication is that any value within the specifications is of equal value to the customer: If the customer receives the product in 4 days, he is equally as happy as receiving the product in 2 days.

In reality, it's often the case that the voice of the customer is not a constant, but varies. In other words, a 5-day delivery is undesirable, but a 2-day delivery is preferred over the 4-day delivery. Taguchi expressed this notion in terms of a loss function, where the loss to society (the inverse of the customer satisfaction) is minimized at some value within the customer requirements, then maximized outside the range of acceptable values, as shown in Figure 1.7.

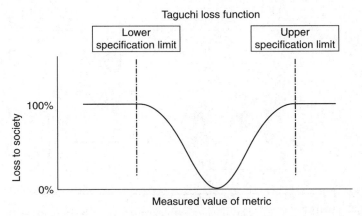

FIGURE 1.7 • Taguchi loss function.

The *voice of the process*, on the other hand, represents the natural tendency of the process. It is determined statistically, defined by control limits, and unique to each process. When the natural tendency of the process is undesirable, the process must be redesigned, as discussed above.

Consider a process whose distributional properties are unknown, as happens quite frequently when process personnel don't use SPC to understand the natural tendency of the process. A typical response to an out of specification condition is to adjust the process. It is assumed that the process has shifted off target by the amount of deviation between the current process sample and the target, so the operator adjusts the process by this amount and takes a second sample to confirm the new process location.

But did the process ever shift off target in the first place?

It is quite possible that the process was properly centered on the specifications before the operator's first adjustment, as shown by the leftmost distributional curve in Figure 1.8 from which the first sample was obtained. When the operator adjusted the process, the effect was to move the process distribution to a new level, as shown by the second distribution labeled "After adjustment #1" in Figure 1.8.

Subsequent samples from this new process distribution would ultimately yield an observation toward the lower tail of the distribution, causing another adjustment by the well-meaning operator. This adjustment would again move the process distribution in the direction of the target by the amount of the deviation of the current sample from the target.

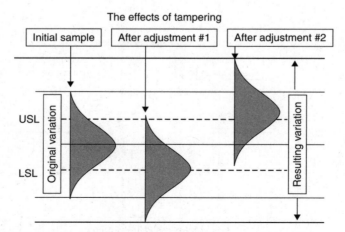

FIGURE 1.8 · Unnecessary process adjustments and the increased process variation that result.

When processes are adjusted because observations are arbitrarily treated as special causes, the process has been tampered with. The effect of the tampering is shown by comparing the two sets of solid horizontal lines in Figure 1.8: The narrow set of solid lines shows the original process variation; the wider set of solid lines results from the process operator's adjustments. The resulting process variation due to the tampering is much larger than the original process variation. It should be clear that

1. The process variation is increased by tampering.
2. The process operator's adjustments represent special causes of variation that should be eliminated to reduce the process variation.

The underlying problem in this example is that the process distribution is not well-suited to meet the specifications (shown by dashed lines in the figure). Notice that the initial distribution has significant area in its tails that extend beyond the process specifications. The best remedy for this process is to reduce the inherent (i.e., common cause level of) process variation. Until this common cause variation in the process is sufficiently reduced, the operators must inspect 100% of the output and sort the good product from the bad as the only way to ensure only good product reaches the customer. This will likely be much more costly than a process improvement effort to reduce the variation.

Deming (1986) offered the following comments on tampering, which he demonstrated through his funnel experiment example:

> If anyone adjusts a stable process to try to compensate for a result that is undesirable, or for a result that is extra good, the output that follows will be worse than if he had left the process alone (attributable to William J. Latzko).
>
> A common example is to take action on the basis of a defective item, or on complaint of a customer. The result of his efforts to improve future output (only doing his best) will be to double the variance of the output, or even to cause the system to explode. What is required for improvement is a fundamental change in the system, not tampering.

Since tampering increases process variation, and any adjustment to a process that is influenced by only common cause variation is tampering, the control chart is an essential tool for every process. Only a properly designed control chart can distinguish between common causes and special causes of variation. The control chart provides the *operational definition of a special cause*: A special cause is defined as a special cause only when the control chart indicates it is a special cause. In practice, tampering occurs when we respond to common cause variation as if it were special cause variation. Underlying reasons for this include:

- We try to control the process to specifications, or goals. These limits are defined externally to the process, rather than being based on the statistics of the process.
- Rather than using the suggested control limits defined at 3 standard deviations from the center line, we instead choose to use limits that are tighter (or narrower) than these (sometimes called Warning Limits). We might do this based on the faulty notion that this will improve the performance of the chart, since it is more likely that subgroups associated with a process shift will plot outside of these limits. For example, using limits defined at 2 standard deviations from the center line would produce narrower control limits than the 3 standard deviation limits. However, you can use probability theory to show that the chance of being outside of a 3 standard deviation control limit for a normally distributed statistic is 0.27% if the process has not shifted. On average, you would see a false alarm associated with these limits once every 370 subgroups (=1/0.0027). Using 2 standard deviation control limits, the chance of being outside the limits when the process has not shifted is 4.6%, corresponding to false alarms every 22 subgroups!

When action is taken on false alarms, the process location (i.e., centerline) is shifted. Over time, this results in process output that varies much more than if the process had just been left alone. In spite of good intention, it should be clear this is just another form of process tampering.

Still Struggling

The notion of tampering is difficult for many to accept. It seems second nature to react when a process seem erratic. Action is certainly necessary: The issue is the type of action needed to respond to process variation.

First, accept that all processes have some level of variation. There is some level of variation (referred to as the common cause variation) that is built-in to the process. That is, the design of the process has allowed that amount of variation, whether it is an acceptable amount or not. The actual sources of this variation (in terms of the 5Ms and E), and their relative contribution to variation, are unknown. The only way to change this level of variation is to make fundamental changes to the design of the process, which requires some level of understanding of the relative sources of common cause variation.

There are times when the process is influenced by an inordinate or uncommon level of variation, which is termed special cause variation. For the moment, avoid trying to differentiate between common and special causes in process terms. A given source of variation (such as manpower, for example) may contribute to common cause variation day in and day out, yet also be responsible for special cause variation at a specific point in time (perhaps due to an untrained worker, or someone having an exceptionally bad day, for example). The presence of a special cause merely indicates that the level of variation is statistically different at that point in time: For some reason, the variation associated with one or more source has increased so that the process is now operating at a new level.

So a primary difference between a common and special cause is timing: Process variation is considered special cause variation because, at a specific point in time, it is larger than expected based on the past performance of the process.

When we react to process variation as if it were special cause variation, without proof it is special cause variation, then we are incorrectly asserting that the process is different now than in the past, and any action taken that are limited to the conditions present at the time are unfounded. If the variation is in fact common cause variation, we need to understand the more complex process dynamics that influence the day to day variation (i.e., the common cause variation), as discussed further in Chapter 7.

Control Chart Interpretation

A key rationale for using statistical control charts is to detect the existence of special causes of variation. Control charts are designed to detect shifts with a minimal chance of a *false alarm*. That is, there is a negligible chance that the process has not changed when a special cause has been identified. Conversely, a special cause provides overwhelming evidence that the process has changed, and by removing this special cause, we will reduce the overall variability of the process. Therefore, whenever a special cause is present, we must not ignore it but learn from it.

Referring to Figure 1.9, the leftmost distribution is indicative of a process that is in control. Notice that there is only a small portion of the distribution that exists beyond either the upper or lower control limit, indicating that samples from this process distribution have only an extremely small chance of being outside the control limits. If a sample from this leftmost distribution exceeded one of the control limits then we would incorrectly assert that the process has shifted due to a *false alarm*. The chance of a false alarm in a properly constructed control chart is about 1 in 370: For every 370 subgroups plotted, on average one subgroup would be falsely estimated to be out of control. Since real changes to process often occur more frequently than that, this error rate is considered to be appropriately insignificant.

When the process does undergo a shift, such as is shown in the three distribution curves on the right of Figure 1.9, then the process shift is detected as a special cause if a sample is taken from the tail region of the process distribution that exceeds the control limit. As shown in the figure, the larger the process shift (as shown by the rightmost distribution), the more tail area is beyond the lower control limit, so the greater chance the shift is detected.

An important consideration is that a control chart will not detect all shifts, or necessarily detect shifts as soon as they occur. Notice in Figure 1.9 that even though there was a large tail area outside the lower control limit, the majority of the subgroup samples are within the control limits. For this reason, samples taken close in time to the detected special cause, even those within the control limits, should be evaluated to consider if they too are influenced by the special cause of variation.

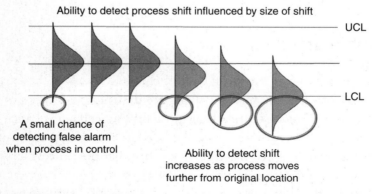

FIGURE 1.9 · Control chart's ability to detect process shifts influenced by size of shift.

Furthermore, the detection of special causes can be often improved through proper selection of the type of control chart, its options, and the method and frequency by which samples are drawn from the process. These practices will be discussed in more detail in Chapter 2 and relative to each control chart in Chapters 4 though 6.

Another means of improving the sensitivity of many control charts is through the use of run test rules. Standard run test rules were developed by Western Electric in the 1950s, and subsequently published in their seminal *Western Electric Handbook*. With some improvement by statistician Lloyd Nelson (1984), the run test rules are recognized as useful tests to detect patterns of unnatural behavior within the control limits.

The run tests increase the power of the control chart, that is, the likelihood that shifts in the process are detected with each subgroup. They also increase the false alarm rate, but are designed specifically with the intention of only minimally increasing the false alarm rate.

The Western Electric *Statistical Quality Control Handbook* defined zones using the sigma levels of the normal distribution, as shown in Figure 1.10. Most SPC software will automatically apply these zones so there is no need to memorize the zone placements.

Run test number 1 (see Figure 1.11): Developed by Western Electric, tests whether a subgroup is beyond the three sigma value. It is synonymous with the control limits, and provides an indication that the process mean has shifted.

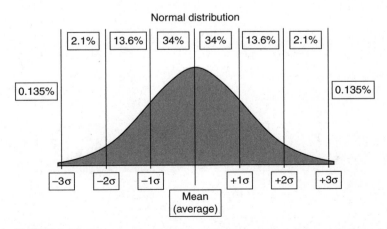

FIGURE 1.10 • The normal distribution with Western Electric run test zones corresponding to sigma levels of the distribution.

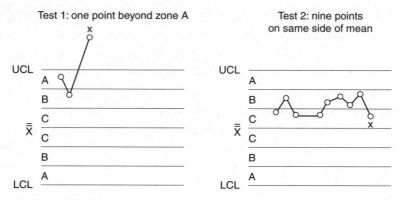

FIGURE 1.11 · Run test rules 1 and 2.

Run test number 2 (see Figure 1.11): Developed by Nelson, tests for nine consecutive subgroups on the same side of average, indicative that the process mean has shifted. Note that Western Electric used eight consecutive points on the same side of average, but Nelson changed it to nine points to decrease the false alarm rate.

Run test number 3 (see Figure 1.12): Developed by Nelson, tests for six consecutive points increasing or decreasing. This test indicates the process mean has shifted by result of a trend within the control limits.

Run test number 4 (see Figure 1.12): Developed by Nelson, tests for fourteen consecutive points alternating up and down. This test indicates sampling from multi-stream process, as alternating subgroups are sampled from separate processes.

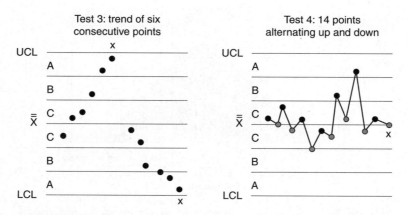

FIGURE 1.12 · Run test rules 3 and 4.

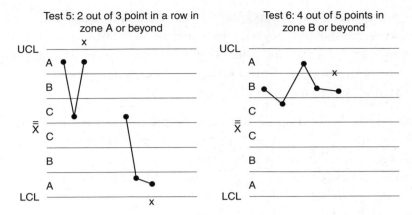

FIGURE 1.13 • Run test rules 5 and 6.

Run test number 5 (see Figure 1.13): Developed by Western Electric, tests for two out of three consecutive points beyond two sigma. This test indicates the process mean has shifted.

Run test number 6 (see Figure 1.13): Developed by Western Electric, tests for four out of five consecutive points beyond one sigma. This test indicates the process mean has shifted.

Run test number 7 (see Figure 1.14): Developed by Western Electric, tests for fifteen consecutive points between plus one sigma and minus one sigma. This test provides an indication of decreased process variation, or of stratification in sampling, as discussed in Chapter 5 with regard to X-bar charts.

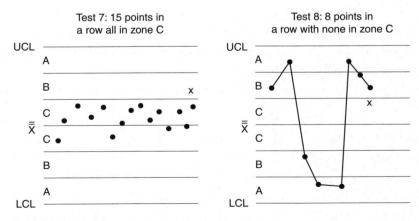

FIGURE 1.14 • Run test rules 7 and 8.

Run test number 8 (see Figure 1.14): Developed by Western Electric, tests for eight consecutive points beyond plus one sigma and minus one sigma (on both sides of center). This test indicates sampling from a mixture. The subgroups on one side of the mean are from a different process stream than the subgroups on the other side of the mean.

Examples of these run test rules will be provided in the relevant chart-specific chapters. The presence of run test violations indicative of a shift in the process mean should be treated as a special cause of variation with the same response as out of control subgroups, as discussed in the next section.

Reaction to Special Cause Variation

When special causes of variation are detected, determine (in process terms) the cause of the process shift. Similarly, when processes are improved, such as resulting from the efforts of Six Sigma project teams, the control chart should provide evidence of a special cause resulting from that change. For this reason, Six Sigma teams always use statistical control charts in the Measure stage of the Define-Measure-Analyze-Improve-Control (DMAIC) methodology to first baseline the existing process, then again in the Control stage to verify the process improvement. For example, if the Six Sigma team had revised the method of customer service by routing clients to more experienced personnel in an attempt to reduce service times, the control chart in the Control stage should indicate that current service times are identified as a special cause (below the lower control limit or a run test violation) relative to the control limits established during the Measure stage. This special cause would be indicative of an actual sustained improvement in service time resulting from the process change. If special causes are not detected between the pre-project Measure stage data and the post-project Control stage data, the project would be presumed to have little or no effect on improving service time.

Once special causes are identified, the total process variation can be reduced by proper action:

- Isolate the instances of variation due to special causes using the time-ordered nature of the control chart to understand what happened (in process terms) at each point in time represented by special causes.
- To reduce the variation due to common causes, look to all elements of the system for clues to variation. Ignore the point to point variation, since it represents a combination of factors that is common to all the subgroups.

Chapter 7 includes a number of techniques to aid in this investigation, including the use of designed experiments and multivariate regression analysis to understand the significance and relative effects of these sources of variation.

When special causes have been identified on a control chart, the statistical control limits and center line should be recalculated to exclude their effect. Since special causes represent a different process distribution than that defined by the common cause level of variation, their numerical impact on the calculation of the common cause centerline and control limits represents a *statistical bias* in the estimates.

If control limits were calculated manually, this would obviously be burdensome; however, most practical applications of SPC nowadays are conveniently done using computer software designed for the purpose. Most credible SPC software allows for convenient *remove from analysis* right mouse menu features for a selected subgroup on a control chart. Some even include so-called *autodrop* features which automatically remove subgroups that are out of control from the calculations. Sophisticated logic within the automatic subgroup dropping will exclude the data only where bias is present:

1. When subgroups are out of control with respect to variation, remove their impact from both estimates of variation and process location.
2. When subgroups are out of control with respect to process location, remove their impact only from process location estimate, allowing the maximum possible number of subgroups to estimate variation.

These features are most useful for sporadic occurrences of special cause variation. When special cause variation is persistent, such as resulting from a fundamental change to the process dynamics (or even a planned change intended to optimize the process), the control limits should be recalculated for the region influenced by the special cause such as shown previously in Figure 1.2.

Interpretation Relative to Requirements

As discussed in the prior sections, it is inappropriate to consider the process observations relative to customer specifications or management goals. Reacting to common cause variation as if it were special cause variation is process tampering, which increases process variation. Instead, processes should be monitored relative to their statistical control limits using the control chart, to ensure that adjustments are only made when warranted by introduction of special cause variation into the process.

If the process shows control relative to the statistical limits and run tests for a sufficient period of time (see Chapter 2), then its capability relative to requirements can be evaluated as discussed further in Chapter 3. Process capability provides the means to *predict* the future performance of the process. It cannot be overly stressed that *process capability is only meaningful when the process is stable* (i.e., in statistical control) because the outcome of an unstable process cannot be predicted.

Process capability indices provide an indication of whether a process can consistently meet internal or external customer requirements. Process capability indices are only meaningful if the data is from a controlled process. The process capability estimate uses the location, spread, and shape of the process distribution, which, by definition, are changing in an out of control process.

The process performance indices offer an alternative when the process is out of control; however, they only indicate the properties of the sampled data. While the process capability indices use the *process sigma* statistic (from the control chart) to estimate variation, process performance indices use the *sample standard deviation* statistic (an enumerative statistic) to estimate variation. The process performance index is valid only for the sample in question, telling us whether the sampled units meet the customer requirements.

Summary

SPC can help you understand and reduce the variation in any business process. Greater consistency in fulfilling your customer's requirements leads to greater customer satisfaction. Reduced variation in your internal processes leads to less time and money spent on rework and waste. Predictable processes are manageable: budgetary estimates become reliable; processes flow. SPC is an essential tool to maintain an advantage in today's competitive marketplace.

As part of an ongoing cycle of continuous process improvement, SPC can help you fine-tune your processes to the virtually error-free Six Sigma level. SPC is a necessary tool for Six Sigma and Lean. Lean practices such as *Just in Time*, with its reliance on reduced inventory, require statistically controlled processes to ensure predictability and stability.

- Control charts demonstrate how consistently your process is performing, and whether you should, or should not, attempt to adjust it.

- SPC chart output is used to compare the process behavior to customer or management requirements, providing a process capability index as an ongoing, accurate direction for quality improvement.

- Control charts and their resulting process capability indices quickly evaluate the results of quality initiatives designed to improve process consistency.

Whether you track metrics related to operational processes such as billing or medication errors, service times in transactional or manufacturing processes, dimensions of manufactured components, or business-level metrics related to cash flow, revenue or profitability, SPC can help you measure, understand, and control the variables that affect your business processes.

QUIZ

1. **The difference between control limits and confidence intervals is mainly that:**
   A. the control limits are analytic statistics applied to process data while confidence intervals are enumerative statistics applied to populations.
   B. the control limits are based on the average and standard deviation.
   C. the control limits indicate the expected bounds of the population.
   D. there is no difference: They can each be applied to the same types of problems with equal results.

2. **The variation within the statistical control limits define:**
   A. all variation the process can experience.
   B. common cause variation in the process.
   C. special cause variation in the process.
   D. All of the above.

3. **A control chart will generally detect:**
   A. all shifts in the process mean as soon as they occur.
   B. all shifts in the process mean, but not necessarily immediately after they occur.
   C. some process shifts, and oftentimes also indicate the process mean has shifted when it hasn't.
   D. some process shifts, and are designed to rarely indicate the process mean has shifted when it hasn't.

4. **When customer specifications are used in place of statistical control limits:**
   A. the control chart is more sensitive to detecting meaningful shifts in the process.
   B. the amount of variation in the process can be effectively reduced.
   C. unnecessary adjustments are often made to the process.
   D. the customer is assured of receiving consistent products and services.

5. **Enumerative statistics:**
   A. assume the data come from a single population.
   B. properly analyze the data in consideration of the time at which a process generated the data.
   C. provide similar results to that found in a statistical control chart.
   D. All of the above.

6. **Before adjusting a process, a current sample should be compared to:**
   A. customer requirements.
   B. the most recent sample.
   C. a confidence interval based on historical data.
   D. calculated bounds of the process statistic based on statistical estimates of process variation over time.

7. **When a process is in statistical control, the control limits aid the analyst to:**
    A. predict the future outcome of the process.
    B. avoid unnecessary process adjustments.
    C. plan and budget the process resources.
    D. All of the above.

8. **Each subgroup on the control chart:**
    A. reflects the short-term process variation at the time the data was generated by the process.
    B. should contain a random sample of data obtained over a longer period of time.
    C. has properties dependent on the prior subgroup.
    D. provides an accurate prediction of the longer-term process behavior.

9. **An out of control subgroup on a control chart indicates that:**
    A. the process is different from what has been seen in the past.
    B. the process influenced by a special cause of variation.
    C. the process distribution has changed.
    D. All of the above.

10. **A bell-shaped distribution in a process histogram is evidence that:**
    A. the process is in statistical control.
    B. the process has the properties of a normal distribution.
    C. the sample has the properties of a normal distribution.
    D. All of the above.

chapter 2

Data Collection

The critical precursor to any relevant statistical analysis is data collection. The adage *garbage in, garbage out* certainly applies: if data is not intelligently collected for the specific purpose, the analysis may be fundamentally flawed and its results meaningless.

CHAPTER OBJECTIVES

After completing this chapter, you will be able to

- Describe the types of process data and the requirements for data
- Understand the selection and use of metrics for organizational and process level dashboards
- Select the proper subgroup size and implement a meaningful data collection scheme

Data Properties

There are two basic types of data that can be analyzed on a control chart:

- *Attribute data:* Also known as "count" data, where the count refers to the number of times a condition (often something undesirable, such as a defect or an error) is observed in a given sample from the process.
- *Variables data:* Also known as measurement data. Variables data is continuous in nature, generally capable of being measured to enough *resolution* to provide at least 10 unique values for the process being analyzed.

Attribute data has less resolution, by definition, than variables data, since the count is based on the presence or absence of a condition. As such, it has a resolution of two possible values (yes, no; present, not present; green, not green; and so on). Attribute data for a manufacturing process might include the number of items in which the diameter of a ground rod exceeds the specification, whereas variables data for the same process might be the measurement of the rod diameter.

Attribute data provides less information than variables data for the same process. Attribute data would generally not allow prediction if the process is trending toward an undesirable state, since it is already in this condition. As a result, variables data is considered more useful for defect *prevention*.

A banking operation, for example, might count of errors in a given sample of deposits to estimate the error rate of the deposit process. The error count is incremented only when an error is observed in one of the deposit records. Attribute data have less resolution than measurement (*variables*) data because a count is registered only if an error occurs. In a health care process, an attribute count of the number of patients with a fever would provide less information than a variables measurement of the patients' temperatures: The variables data indicates a level of acceptability rather than just acceptable or unacceptable. This lack of resolution in attribute data prevents detection of trends toward undesirable process conditions.

Error counts are also intrinsically linked to the specification criteria from which they were based. All samples that are not counted as error are considered equally valuable to the customer, while all samples exceeding the specifications have zero value to the customer. Recall from the discussions of the Taguchi loss function in Chapter 1 that this rarely is justified from a customer's perspective.

TABLE 2.1 Example of how rounding of data affects results (Keller, 2011, by permission).

	Measure *A*	Measure *B*	Measure *C*
Observation 1	9	9.4	8.6
Observation 2	10	9.8	10.4
Observation 3	9	9.3	9.3
Observation 4	10	10.1	10.1
Observation 5	10	9.7	9.6
Standard deviation	0.548	0.321	0.704

For control charting of variables data, adequate resolution is required to reliably estimate process variation. Poor resolution effectively "rounds" the data, biasing the estimate of standard deviation. Consider the data in the "Measure *A*" column of Table 2.1, which has been rounded up or down owing to poor resolution of the measurement system. The data in the "Measure *B*" and "Measure *C*" columns represent two possible sets of data that, when rounded, would result in the "Measure *A*" data. In one case, the estimate from "Measure *A*" is inflated; in the other case it is underestimated. Inaccuracies like this disrupt the ability of the control chart to estimate common cause variation and distinguish special cause variation from common cause variation.

A good rule of thumb is to have at least 10 unique data values within the data set for proper application of the control charts for variables data (see *Chart Selection* section below). Inadequate resolution must be addressed through better measurement equipment, or improved measurement methods, to measure the process to a higher degree of accuracy. Alternatively, a different metric may prove to be more useful.

Metrics

Business-Level Metrics

Metrics provide a quantitative means to assess the state of the process or organization relative to a critical criteria. At the business level, metrics provide feedback to stakeholders in terms consistent over time and relevant to the business strategy.

Appropriate metrics for tracking performance at the business level have the following characteristics (Keller, 2011):

- *Customer-centered:* Indicators that are significant to the customer are many times significant to your operations. These indicators typically drill down to processes with a direct impact on customers. Conversely, operational indicators with little value to the customer essentially waste resources. A proper understanding of the flow-down functions (big Y, little y) for defining process-level metrics that meet business-level customer requirements is shown below.

- *Linked to organizational strategy:* Metrics clearly linked to each of the main stakeholder groups (customers, shareholders, and employees) provide high visibility within the organization and help steer the organization toward achievement of their goals.

- *Developed collaboratively to ensure buy-in:* A means of communicating the rationale, application and interpretation of the metric is needed to build organizational buy-in.

- *Measures performance over time:* As discussed in Chapter 1, the control chart provides the proper means of analyzing process statistics.

Dashboards, just like gauges in a car, are used to provide a "heads up" display of business conditions to avoid unpleasant surprises. Business-level dashboards provide input for data-driven decision making and communicate the performance of the business relative to key goals and objectives. Control charts are used to provide historical context and statistical significance of the observed variation. Drill-down capability to subsets of the data or to the operations or process levels of the organization provides further understanding of the key drivers influencing trends.

In practice, metrics can be considered as big Ys and little y's, where the little y's provide the systematic variation that drive the performance of the big Ys. Mathematically,

$$Y_1 = \text{function of } \{y_1, y_2, \ldots, y_n\}$$

$$Y_2 = \text{function of } \{y_1, y_2, \ldots, y_n\}$$

$$\rightarrow$$

$$Y_m = \text{function of } \{y_1, y_2, \ldots, y_n\} \qquad \text{for } m \text{ big } Y\text{s}$$

These transfer (or flow-down) functions define the relationships between process and business-level metrics. Little y's at the business level become big Ys for operational metrics; little y's for operational metrics become big Ys for process metrics. While big Ys are intuitively more meaningful to the stakeholders at that organizational level and generally more useful for tracking, the little y's provide the detail for controlling and improving processes. In practice, the transfer functions are determined through regression and correlation analyses using designed experiments, data mining, surveys, focus groups, and critical-incident techniques as described in Keller (2011).

Figure 2.1 shows a dashboard developed for a software company, where metrics were established at the business level (ovals), operations level (diamonds), and process level (rectangles). At the business level, for example, the client retention rate is monitored monthly for trends in overall existing-customer satisfaction. An organizational Six Sigma project developed the operational predictors of retention rate: the percent of customers engaged by staff; and a defect rate relative to an established baseline for responsiveness to each type of customer inquiry. Process metrics were defined for each operational metric: Engagement is influenced by the number of instructional demonstrations provided by sales, service, and support staff for existing customers, as well as the number of quotes provided for additional products and services (data suggested that engaged customers purchased more software more frequently).

These analyses are facilitated by software that allows filtering by operating unit or product family and drill down to the lower-level drivers at the operations and/or process levels. Figure 2.2 shows an example of meaningful drill-down and analysis available by right-mouse menus for rapid feedback. The software links to operational data within quality management, customer resource management (CRM), accounting, and human resources software, so there is no need for costly reentering of data into the dashboard reporting software. The reporting software filters and groups the data as necessary for the monthly (or real-time) business- and operations-level analyses. Once defined, these charts are available in real time to all relevant stakeholders to provide transparency of key operations to facilitate appropriate reaction.

Operational and Process Metrics

At the operational level, indicators of performance must be established to baseline and monitor key processes. These process indicators must provide information useful to *achieve* process improvement and not just recognize the success

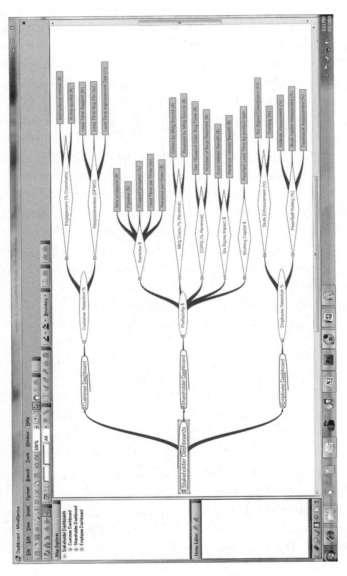

FIGURE 2.1 • Example deployment dashboard metrics from the Green Belt XL/MindGenius application (from Keller, 2011, by permission).

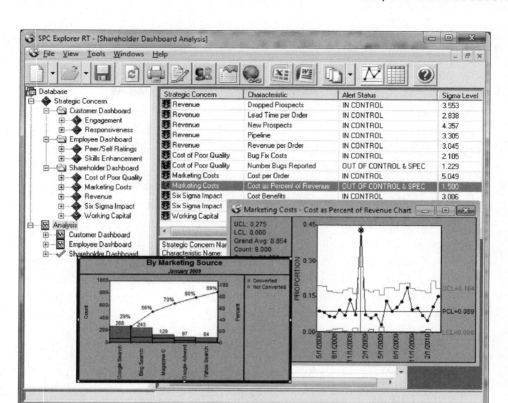

FIGURE 2.2 · Example dashboard displays with filtering and drill down to lower levels using Quality America's *SPC Explorer* software (from Keller, 2011, by permission).

of the efforts. As discussed in Chapter 1, the control chart provides the means of distinguishing between special and common causes of variation, which is essential precursor to process improvement.

There are several key reasons a given process indicator may be unable to detect true shifts in the process. Consider the food preparation service of a hospital that monitors customer satisfaction through quarterly surveys sent to a random sampling of recent patients at the hospital. The survey asks a number of questions, about many different aspects of the patients' experience at the hospital. Among the questions is a question devoted to the quality of the food service. The hospital's quality assurance department analyzes the survey results via a control chart in the hopes of detecting statistically significant changes in the level of service delivered over time. This analysis will likely not produce the feedback they desire.

Consider first the time lag of the survey. Poor quality would not have been prevented, merely detected. Furthermore, since the data is nearly 3 months old when plotted, it would be difficult to ascertain the underlying conditions of the process that lead to the process shift so much later in time.

In addition, relevant information for process improvement was not obtained. If surveys indicate the quality of food service is poor, what can be done to improve it? The quality of the food service may be judged by many underlying factors, including food temperature, texture or taste; selection options; wait time; and so on. Since there are many components of food service quality, there are many potential areas of improvement. Which is most critical?

The control chart itself is also unlikely to detect anything but dramatic shifts in process performance, since pooling of these factors dampens the overall response. Even a significant change in one factor is unlikely to cause a significant change in the whole score, unless its contribution to the pooled rating is large relative to the other factors. The single factor, or the critical few, with the largest effect on the customer response would provide the best indication of process changes.

An example of the impact of pooling is shown by the control chart of the satisfaction rating for a telephone support line in Figure 2.3. The u chart used in the figure (discussed in detail in Chapter 4) shows the overall satisfaction rating to be stable at approximately 9.1 out of 10, an excellent score by most standards. If we consider the Pareto diagram of Figure 2.4, however, we see that the survey respondents' calls were related to varied interests: price (59%), product features (19%), shipping status (16%), and a relatively insignificant "other"

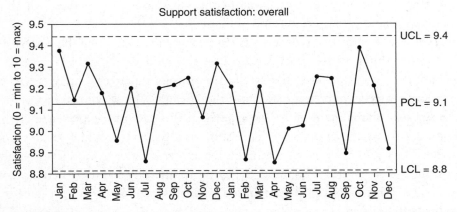

FIGURE 2.3 · Control chart of phone support satisfaction rating is insensitive to changes in its components.

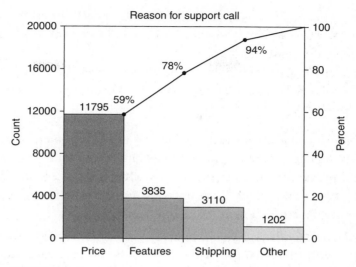

FIGURE 2.4 · Pareto diagram of issue types for phone support example.

category (6%). Since questions on pricing comprise the lion's share of the calls, its satisfaction rating will heavily skew the overall rating. If, as in this case, the telephone support process is properly designed to address questions of this type, customers are likely to be largely satisfied with this aspect of the service. If we look at the other types of calls, satisfaction may not be evident, nor stable, as shown by the u chart for product features in Figure 2.5. In this case, the instability was related to the introduction of new product which the phone staff were not well-trained to handle. This is another example of sampling from

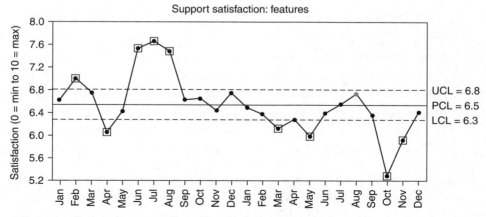

FIGURE 2.5 · Control chart of call satisfaction for product feature issues.

a multistream process: Each aspect of service delivery is its own unique process. By pooling the three aspects of service into one indicator, valuable information on improvement potential is lost.

Clearly, considerable thought must be given to metrics before meaningful data can be collected. In general, process metrics should possess the following characteristics:

- *Easy and economical to measure:* The cost of measurement should always be kept at a minimum and never exceed its value for improvement. Measurements taken later in the process, or after the process has achieved its result, have diminished return since loss may already be realized through customer dissatisfaction or internal process "rework."

- *Provide rapid feedback to process personnel:* Indicators should have close association with the dynamics of the process. Broad-based measures such as customer satisfaction provide little usable feedback. Metrics should provide direct focus on the particular aspect of the process that needs attention.

- *Prevent poor quality:* Metrics internal to the process, rather than which result from the process, can prevent poor quality. For example, analyzing the number of customer complaints on an attribute control chart will only detect a change in the number of unhappy customers and not prevent customers from having something to complain about. If waiting time is a critical cause for customer dissatisfaction, poor service could possibly be prevented by monitoring wait time; if time between arrivals and number of support staff heavily influences customer wait time, monitoring time between arrivals and diverting support staff to accommodate a heavy influx of customers will prevent poor quality. Six Sigma projects are often useful for understanding the factors contributing to resultant metrics.

- *Sensitive to process change:* Use an indicator that provides a large (i.e., detectable) change for small, yet meaningful changes in the process outcome. Stated differently, a small change in the indicator should NOT produce a large change in the response (process outcome). For example, if the typical variation in food temperature produces little variation in the customer satisfaction, then it would not be a very good indicator of process shifts, even if customers consider it important.

Note that these criteria lead to similar conclusion: The external process outcome is often not the best choice for process control. Rather, determine the internal process characteristics that drive the outcome, and use those as your process indicators. Start with a simple cause and effect diagram to brainstorm the potential internal factors and then quantify each potential factor's contribution to the effect using regression analysis. For example, monthly sales figures (the effect) might be compared to the number of leads generated by particular marketing efforts, to see which marketing effort has the largest influence on sales. When the causes have interdependence between them, such as the number of leads and the conversion rates for the leads, the multiple regression analysis features of most Design of Experiment (DOE) software will come in handy. These software packages also provide contour plotting to determine the conditions resulting in maximum or minimum responses. For example, we might find the optimal level of sales personnel and marketing expenditures which result in maximized sales. These concepts are discussed in more detail in conjunction with Six Sigma projects in Keller (2011). An overview of this approach is provided in Chapter 7.

Chart Selection

The SPC selection diagram shown in Figure 2.6 is useful for choosing the correct chart for particular data types and sample sizes. Start by determining the type of data that will be collected as either attribute data (for counting occurrences

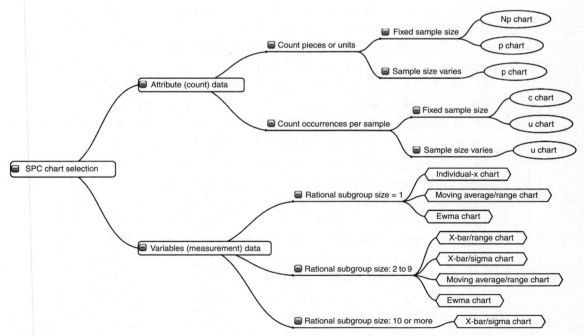

FIGURE 2.6 • SPC selection diagram.

or units) or variables data (for measured process parameters), as discussed above, then review the *Sampling Requirements* section below. The charts themselves are discussed in further detail in Chapters 4 through 6.

Sampling Requirements

Rational Subgroups

The key to successful control charts is the formation of *rational subgroups*. Control charts rely upon rational subgroups to estimate the short-term variation in the process. This short-term variation is then used to predict the longer-term variation defined by the control limits, which differentiate between common and special causes of variation.

A rational subgroup is simply "a sample in which all of the items are produced under conditions in which only random effects are responsible for the observed variation" (Nelson). Another way to express this is that a rational subgroup is one in which the system of causes influencing *within* subgroup variation is equivalent to the system of causes influencing *between* subgroup variation.

A rational subgroup has the following properties:

1. The observations within the subgroup are collected from a single, stable process. If subgroups contain data of multiple process streams, or if other special causes occur frequently within subgroups, then the within subgroup variation will be large relative to the variation between subgroup averages. This large within subgroup variation forces the control limits to be too far apart, resulting in a lack of sensitivity to process shifts. Run test 7 (15 successive points within one sigma of center line), introduced in Chapter 1, is helpful in detecting this condition.

2. The subgroups are formed from observations taken in a time-ordered sequence. Subgroups cannot be randomly formed from a set of data (or a box of parts); instead, the data comprising a subgroup must be a "snapshot" of the process over a small window of time, and the order of the subgroups would show how those snapshots vary in time (like a movie). The size of the "small window of time" is determined for each process to minimize the chance of a special cause occurring in the subgroup.

3. The observations within the subgroup are *independent*, implying that no observation influences, or results from, another. If observations are dependent on one another, the process has autocorrelation (also known

as serial correlation). In many cases, the autocorrelation causes the within subgroup variation to be unnaturally small and a poor predictor of the between subgroup variation. The small within subgroup variation forces the control limits to be too narrow, resulting in frequent out of control conditions, leading to the tampering discussed in Chapter 1. Many examples of autocorrelation exist in business processes and nature itself including:

- *Chemical processes:* Samples drawn from liquids in batches are often influenced by prior samples if the time between the samples is small. The batch is essentially homogenous throughout, and its properties change slowly so that the measurement at one point in time is influenced by the state of the process in an earlier state of time.

- *Service processes:* The wait time of a person in a queue is influenced by the wait time of the person in front of him/her. Recall your wait time at the supermarket check out line when you're behind a chatty customer: You cannot be serviced until their service is completed; likewise for the person behind you, and so on.

- *Discrete part manufacturing:* Feedback controls used to adjust processes based upon past observations cause autocorrelation in data observed closely in time.

Examples of irrational subgroups will be shown in Chapter 5.

Subgroup Size Considerations

For either variables or attribute data, a sample of n items is taken from the process over a relatively short time frame. The parameter n is the sample size, also known as the subgroup size; the collection of n samples constitutes a *subgroup*. The subgroup size influences the statistics of the data, and thus the type of chart used (as shown in Figure 2.6).

Variables Data

Larger subgroup sizes are more sensitive to process shifts. Referring to Figure 2.7, the distribution of a set of process observations is shown in the bottom distribution curve; the distribution of the subgroup averages for the same set of data is shown in the top distribution curve. Notice that the distribution of averages is much narrower than the distribution of observations. The width of the distribution of averages is inversely proportional to the square root of the subgroup size: As subgroup size increases, the width of the distribution of subgroup averages decreases.

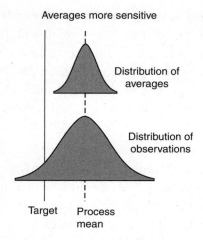

FIGURE 2.7 • Distribution of averages detects shift from target more reliably than the distribution of observations.

Mathematically, for a given process standard deviation σ_x, the standard deviation of the averages is calculated as:

$$\sigma_{\bar{x}} = \frac{\sigma_x}{\sqrt{n}}$$

For a subgroup of size 5, the above formula shows that the distribution of the averages will be approximately 45% of the width of the distribution of the observations. The impact of this is seen if the process shifts away from an original target line such as in Figure 2.7: As the process distribution drifts away from the target, there is much less chance of sampling data from the distribution of the average that would make one think the process is still close to target. The larger the subgroup size, the narrower the distribution, the further away the closest tail is to the original target line.

Another issue with analyzing the observations using a subgroup size of one concerns the distribution of the observations, as will be discussed in Chapter 6. Subgroups of size 2 or more allow for charting of the subgroup average on an X-bar chart. The normal distribution may be assumed for the distribution of the subgroup averages, based on the central limit theorem. The averages will tend to follow a normal distribution even for heavily skewed distributions with subgroup size as small as 3 or 4.

Table 2.2 shows the average number of subgroups necessary to detect the shift of size k (in standard deviation units), based on the subgroup size n over

TABLE 2.2	Average number of subgroups of size n needed to detect shift of k standard deviations.					
n/k	0.5	1	1.5	2	2.5	3
1	155	43	14	6	3	1
2	90	17	5	2	1	1
3	60	9	2	1	1	1
4	43	6	1	1	1	1
5	33	4	1	1	1	1
6	26	3	1	1	1	1
7	21	2	1	1	1	1
8	17	2	1	1	1	1
9	14	1	1	1	1	1
10	12	1	1	1	1	1

a long period of sampling (i.e., a large number of subgroups). For example, the average number of subgroups of size $n = 3$ needed to detect a one sigma shift in the process average is 9 subgroups. A small subgroup of size $n = 2$ will readily detect relatively large shifts of two or three sigma, but is less capable of quickly detecting smaller shifts.

While larger subgroups are better at detecting smaller shifts in the process, there is diminishing return in larger samples even for moderate shifts in the process mean. Note in Table 2.2 that a sample of size $n = 4$ is equally likely to detect a 1.5 sigma shift in the mean on the first sample as a subgroup of size $n = 10$.

A good rule of thumb is the use of subgroups of size $n = 4$ or $n = 5$ whenever possible. These provide reasonable protection for moderate shifts in the process, which should be the focus for most applications. To detect smaller shifts in the process (0.5 sigma or less), the EWMA and moving average charts discussed in Chapter 6 are recommended.

Larger subgroup sizes also increase the risk that special causes will be prevalent within the subgroups. That likelihood is dependent on the process dynamics, and the time needed to acquire the observations within each subgroup. The longer the time period, the more opportunity there is for special causes to be introduced within the subgroup. A special cause introduced into the subgroup represents a different process distribution from that intended to be estimated by the common cause variation in the subgroup. This violates the first property of rational subgroups noted above (a single stable process), and the subgroups will then provide an inflated estimate of the process common cause variation: These irrational subgroups will prove detrimental to the chart's ability to detect process shifts.

On the other hand, if the process has autocorrelation over short time periods, then a longer time period is required *between observations* to collect independent observations for the subgroup (see property 3 of the rational subgroup above). To avoid the risk of special causes being introduced into the subgroup (as in the last paragraph), a subgroup size of one is often required. This happens frequently with service processes where autocorrelated time estimates (cycle time, wait time, etc.) are the metrics of interest. This is discussed further in Chapters 5 and 6.

In some cases, it seems desirable to use a variable sample size, such as when grouping by batch: If some batches have 4 pieces and others 5, 6 or 7 pieces, why not use all the pieces within a batch to constitute a sample? One problem with this approach is in the calculations of the control limits, which are based on a constant subgroup size. There are algorithms to adjust for missing data, such as proposed by Burr (1969); most credible SPC software will allow for this adjustment in calculations. The resulting control limits are staggered to reflect the varying subgroup size, which detracts somewhat from the simplicity of the control chart. While this is particularly useful when data values must be discarded, a review of Table 2.2 suggests little advantage in the regular use of a varying subgroup size. There is also risk that the subgroup is not rational, since time (rather than batch size) is the overriding consideration to creating a rational subgroup. Note also that some batches created over a short time interval, such as in bottling or injection molding, are irrational for being multiple stream processes. This is discussed further in Chapter 5.

Attribute Data

Larger subgroups also tend to increase the sensitivity of the attribute control charts, but again there is risk that special causes will dominate the larger subgroups. It's not uncommon to see attribute control charts constructed so that each group represents a month or even a year of activity. While this seems convenient for the analyst, it often disregards the requirements for rational subgroups. Are there no opportunities for special causes to arise within a month? Or a year? That seems unlikely for many processes.

A general rule of thumb for attribute data is that the average count of items in each group is 5 or more. This provides sufficient level of variability in the data to meet the data resolution requirements for meaningful control charts.

For counts of errors or defects, if the process has a low error rate then this usually requires fairly large samples. For example, a process with an error rate of 1% would require a minimum sample size of 500 to ensure an average count of 5 errors per subgroup. Clearly, as processes are improved to meet requirements, the lower error rates which result require larger samples. Given the general limitations of attribute data discussed above, it seems reasonable to move toward variables data whenever possible. When lower rates of occurrence are the issue, try measuring the time between occurrences as variables data. This is a common practice when analyzing safety-related metrics (e.g., time between accidents) and is easily extended to other processes (e.g., time between errors; time between calls; time between patients; etc.).

Frequency of Subgroup Collection

The frequency of collecting subgroups is based on the process dynamics. Brainstorm with process experts, especially those operating the process, to consider the types of issues that might upset process stability. Sample frequently enough to capture all sources of variation.

The general rule is to collect smaller subgroups more often. Since the smaller groups tend to estimate variation fairly well (as shown in Table 2.2), it's best to spend data collection dollars/resources on periodic checks to detect the introduction of special causes into the process. Consider the control chart a learning tool for the process: Start by collecting subgroups frequently, then reduce frequency once knowledge is gained regarding the types and occurrences of special causes. Check at each sample frequency to ensure the observations within subgroups are not autocorrelated using the techniques described in Chapters 5 and 6.

Number of Subgroups Needed

An ample history of the process is needed to estimate the common cause operating level of the process. This implies that all sources of common cause variation for the process must be included in the analysis. The control chart, in effect, needs to experience the complete range of process inputs. For example, if process data is collected over only one shift of production, using one operator and a single batch of material from one supplier, it's likely that some elements of common cause variation have not been experienced, and thus excluded from the estimates. Control limits defined under these limited conditions may later detect natural variation in one or more of these factors as special causes. This is an expected outcome for any set of statistical trials: The probability of detecting data toward the center of a normal distribution (for example) is much greater than in the tails of the distribution. It takes many trials to gain a complete picture of the distribution. So it is with common cause variation.

In practice, the sources of common cause variation and their relative impact are unknown. The control chart defines the common cause variation for the process, based on the data presented. As more data is accumulated, this estimate can be refined to reflect additional sources of variation included in the newer data. In some cases, the wealth of new data provides evidence that the process was influenced by special causes of variation at earlier times in the process that were previously undetected.

There are two standard approaches to defining control limits:

1. Conduct a detailed study (sometimes called a process capability study) to measure process output over a defined period, often trying to control as much of the inputs as reasonably possible. Collect 35 to 100 subgroups and calculate the control limits. If the process is in control and statistically capable of meeting the requirements for process output, then set the control limits at these levels to determine if future output of the process is stable relative to the initial study. When special causes are identified, investigate and correct the process as necessary. This approach is often used when intending to meet the demands of customers who require controlled and capable processes from their suppliers. The initial study data is deemed acceptable by the customer, and the intent is that future output will closely resemble this approved output. Long-term process stability is achieved through responding to special causes as they arise, where a special cause is defined (based on the preset control limits) as a level of variation exceeding that found in the initial study.

2. Collect data from the process on an on-going basis, and recalculate control limits as each new subgroup is added.

There is an additional statistical consideration for variables control charts: The statistical "constants" used to define control chart limits (such as d_2, d_3, and c_4, discussed in Chapter 5) are actually variables, and only approach constants when the number of subgroups is "large." For a subgroup size of five, for instance, the values approach constants for 25 or more subgroups (Duncan, 1986).

When a limited number of subgroups are available, short run techniques may be used. Short run analysis combines data from several "runs" into a single analysis, where a given run refers to data collected for a given product or service classification. Short run is typically used to analyze processes with an insufficient amount of data available from each product or service to adequately define the characteristics of the process.

Short run standardizations are useful in many applications, including piece production, service or transactional processes, and chemical or process industries.

A manufacturing site may produce only a limited number of a given part number, then reset the machine for a different part number. Although the process is fundamentally the same (if it is acted upon by the same causal system), the part numbers may have very different nominal (i.e., target) dimensions. For example, if Part A is meant to be ground to a 1 inch diameter, plus or minus 1/8 inch, and Part B has a nominal diameter of 2 inches, plus or minus 1/8 inch, then the parts cannot be plotted directly on the same control chart because of the difference in nominal size: One part is out of control relative to the other.

Likewise, in a service application, the amount of time to resolve a customer complaint may be influenced by the type of complaint, such as 1 day for incorrect item shipped versus 5 days for incorrect billing.

In either case, we are interested in statistically significant changes to our system, relative to either a nominal value (which we define) or an average value (which the system defines).

Standardization and stabilization techniques for using short run charting are discussed in Chapters 5 and 6 for each chart type. The key assumption for use of the short run technique is that each run is inherently influenced by the same system of common causes. In other words, the *process* is the same, regardless of whether the *parts* are the same. Recall that the letter p in SPC refers to *process* and not *parts*.

Still Struggling?

There are many opportunities to analyze data that was not collected specifically for use in control charts. The business metrics presented in Figures 2.1 and 2.2, for example, are derived from CRM and order processing databases, which exist primarily to facilitate customer interaction and the sales process. Nearly all organizations use software ubiquitously; each software stores pertinent data which in many cases provides useful insight into the organization's fundamental processes. The ability to access this data and generate meaningful analyses is a tremendous opportunity that should not be ignored.

Yet, it is critical to provide *meaningful* analysis of this process data. While the statistical control chart is uniquely qualified for the purpose of analyzing process data (as discussed in Chapter 1), its requirements for rational subgrouping noted above must be maintained. While data collected solely for the purpose of a control chart can easily be obtained in consideration of these general rules, data generated by the process may not be so accommodating. (See also the concerns regarding any retrospective analysis discussed in Chapter 5). It is not uncommon to see autocorrelation between observations (due to queuing theory) or multiple stream processes. Fortunately, the wealth of data usually provides some advantages: Data can be easily filtered by a key field in the database to remove the multiple stream effect, sorted to maintain its time-ordered sequencing, and filtered or grouped by an element of time to form rational subgroups without the influence of autocorrelation. Advanced SPC software easily provides this level of functionality. Control charts can be linked to these external data sources, filtered by one or more fields, and easily analyzed in a variety of what-if scenarios to understand the process dynamics.

Summary

The usefulness of any control chart is fundamentally based on the data collection process: What data is collected and how it is collected. In deciding on the metric and its sampling plan, consider the actions that would result from statistically significant changes: Does the metric provide information useful for process improvement?

QUIZ

1. Nursing staff at a hospital count the number of pharmacy errors, which is considered:
   A. variables data.
   B. attribute data.
   C. preventive data.
   D. enumerative data.

2. Counting errors as a process metric is not ideal because:
   A. it is not preventive since the error has already occurred.
   B. each occurrence of the error is treated equally in the count, regardless of the extent of the error.
   C. the definition of an error may be subjective at times, such as when consistent customer requirements cannot be determined.
   D. All of the above.

3. Adequate data resolution for variables data suggests the analyst collect:
   A. subgroups of two or more observations.
   B. 25 or more subgroups.
   C. at least 10 unique data values within the data set.
   D. two or more unique data values within each subgroup.

4. Effective dashboards metrics at the business level:
   A. often provide direct information useful for process improvement.
   B. often provide an indication of issues that must be analyzed in more detail.
   C. are defined exclusively by management.
   D. are dictated by customer requirements.

5. Effective process level metrics:
   A. should relate to an organization's strategic objectives.
   B. provide information useful for gaining process knowledge and achieving process improvement.
   C. make information available in a timely fashion to process personnel.
   D. All of the above.

6. Metrics that include the effects of multiple sub-processes:
   A. are useful to control many aspects of the process in one chart.
   B. provide a means of detecting subtle shifts in each of the sub-processes.
   C. risk a lack in ability to detect process shifts in any single sub-process.
   D. All of the above.

7. **A u chart is useful for:**
   A. variables data.
   B. attribute data when the sample size varies.
   C. attribute data when the sample size is constant.
   D. choices B and C.

8. **On average, a control chart using a subgroup size of 1 will detect a two sigma shift in the process in:**
   A. 17 subgroups.
   B. 43 subgroups.
   C. 6 subgroups.
   D. 1 subgroup.

9. **Large subgroup sizes of 25 or more observations:**
   A. are most often recommended since they provide better sensitivity to process shifts.
   B. are not recommended because of the risk of special causes within the subgroups.
   C. are often needed for autocorrelated processes.
   D. often provide an ideal size to capitalize on the central limit theorem.

10. **An order may be processed by any of five similarly designed process lines. A subgroup formed from the output of each of the five process lines will likely:**
    A. be rational since the process lines were designed to accomplish the same purpose.
    B. be irrational since any one of the five processes may have process properties distinct from the others.
    C. detect subtle changes to the process, since it uses the average of the five observations.
    D. provide a reliable estimate of the common cause variation in the process output.

chapter 3

Determining Suitability to Requirements

As discussed in Chapter 1, a control chart provides an indication of the stability or consistency of a process over time. It does not directly address how well the process meets the needs of internal or external customers. Furthermore, neither the control chart nor any other tool should be used to adjust the process relative to requirements due to the risk of tampering with the process, which results in increased process variation. Process capability estimates have been developed to predict the ability of a process to consistently meet the requirements of internal or external customers.

CHAPTER OBJECTIVES

After completing this chapter, you will be able to

- Discuss the use and application of process capability indices for estimating the suitability of a process in meeting requirements
- Describe the methodology for determining appropriate statistical distributions, and demonstrate their impact on the capability estimates
- Demonstrate the impact of error in capability estimates, and show recommended strategies for minimizing the error
- Discuss issues governing process performance indices for out of control processes

Overview

Process capability is a prediction of future performance, which is only practical (and meaningful) if the process is in a state of statistical control: Only stable processes are predictable. Process capability analysis can only be applied if the process is in control for an extended period of time.

When a process is not in statistical control, predictions cannot be made of its capability to meet requirements. A given sample can be evaluated; however, the ability to estimate the properties of the sample (and its ability to meet customer requirements) is greatly influenced by the sampling. The process performance index is valid only for the sample in question, indicating whether the sampled units meet the customer requirements.

Capability Indices Assuming Normality of Process Data

C_p for Bilateral Specifications

A number of capability indices have been developed assuming normality of the data. The simplest is the C_p index, which compares the tolerance to the spread of the distribution, expressed as plus and minus three sigma, where sigma$_x$ is the *process sigma*, calculated using the control charts.

$$C_p = \frac{\text{high spec} - \text{low spec}}{6\sigma_x}$$

For example, consider a grinding process with an upper specification of 1.02 inches and a lower specification of 1.00 inch. A control chart of the process indicates the process is in control over the last several months, with a process sigma value (calculated from the control chart) of 0.003 inch. When the normal distribution can be assumed for the process data, the capability index C_p is calculated as:

$$C_p = \frac{1.02 - 1.00}{6 \times 0.003} = 1.11$$

The C_p index is only useful for bilateral specifications; that is, when there is both an upper specification limit and a lower specification limit. This is a common case in manufacturing and process industries, where products must be delivered to customers within often tightly controlled upper and lower limits to ensure suitability of raw product for assembly into a finished product or use as a chemical agent in a processing line. Service or transactional processes often have only a single bound; for example, a delivery time within 5 days of order placement (i.e., an upper specification of 5) where delivery time as close to 0 days from order placement as possible is preferred. In this case, there is no lower specification, although the process has a natural lower bound at 0 days.

For bilateral specifications, the optimal condition for the customer occurs when the process average is situated exactly at the midpoint of the specification limits. The C_p index does not consider the process location, and considers only the process variation (as expressed by the process standard deviation). This limitation restricts its usage, and leads to the development of the C_{pk} index which has wider application and usage.

C_{pk} Index for Bilateral or Unilateral Specifications

The C_{pk} statistic is the most commonly used capability index. Unlike the C_p index, it includes both process dispersion and the process location relative to the specifications. While C_p can only be calculated when there is both an upper and lower specification, C_{pk} can be used when there is either one or the other. When there are both upper and lower specifications, C_{pk} is calculated separately for each of the specifications, with the lower (or worst case) estimate reported as the process capability.

When the normal distribution can be assumed for the process data, the capability index C_{pk} is calculated as:

$$C_{pk} = \min(C_{pl}, C_{pu})$$

$$C_{pl} = \frac{Z_l}{3}$$

$$C_{pu} = \frac{Z_u}{3}$$

$$Z_l = \frac{\bar{\bar{x}} - \text{low spec}}{\sigma_x}$$

$$Z_u = \frac{\text{high spec} - \bar{\bar{x}}}{\sigma_x}$$

Using the data from the earlier example, if the process average from the control chart is 1.014:

$$Z_l = \frac{\bar{\bar{x}} - \text{low spec}}{\sigma_x} = \frac{1.014 - 1.00}{0.003} = 4.67$$

$$C_{pl} = \frac{Z_l}{3} = \frac{4.67}{3} = 1.56$$

$$Z_u = \frac{\text{high spec} - \bar{\bar{x}}}{\sigma_x} = \frac{1.02 - 1.014}{0.003} = 2.0$$

$$C_{pu} = \frac{Z_u}{3} = \frac{2.0}{3} = 0.67$$

$$C_p = \min(C_{pl}, C_{pu}) = 0.67$$

Interpretation

Historically, practitioners have considered a process to be capable when it has attained a C_{pk} of 1.33 or better. A process operating between 1.0 and 1.33 is considered "marginal." Refer to Table 3.1 for conversion between a given C_{pk} value and an error rate, expressed in percent. (Note: The percent error can be easily calculated in MS Excel for a given C_{pl}, C_{pu} using the equation "=(1-NORMSDIST(A2*3))" where the cell A2 contains the C_{pl}, C_{pu} value.)

Many companies now suggest that even higher levels of C_{pk} should be maintained by their suppliers. Six Sigma organizations expect that processes over the long term should have capability index of at least 1.5, whereas their short-term estimates would exceed 2.0. This reflects the organizational concerns for error rates in the single digits per million opportunities, or near-zero error rates for practical purposes.

A C_{pk} exactly equal to 1.0 would imply that the plus and minus three sigma process variation exactly meets the specification requirements. Unfortunately, if the process shifted slightly, and the out of control condition was not immediately detected, then the process would produce output that did not meet the requirements. The 0.33 buffer or margin of error is required to accommodate small process shifts that might be undetected even with the use of statistical control charts.

A negative C_{pk} indicates that either the process mean is less than the lower specification or greater than the upper specification, both of which are undesirable.

C_{pl}, C_{pu}	Percent Error
0.5	6.681%
0.6	3.593%
0.7	1.786%
0.8	0.820%
0.9	0.347%
1	0.135%
1.1	0.048%
1.2	0.016%
1.3	0.005%
1.4	0.00133%
1.5	0.00034%
1.6	0.000079%
1.7	0.000017%
1.8	0.0000033%
1.9	0.0000006%
2	0.0000001%

TABLE 3.1   Error rate for C_{pl}, C_{pu} (each side).

Consider the distributional curves shown in Figure 3.1. The upper distributional curve in Figure 3.1a is an example of a normally distributed process where both C_p and C_{pk} equal 1. That is, the plus and minus three sigma levels of the process distribution exactly coincide with the specifications.

The lower distributional curve in Figure 3.1a depicts an example where the process is again centered between the specifications, but the variation is excessive. In this case, the upper and lower specification limits coincide with the two sigma levels of the process.

If the process distribution is not exactly centered relative to the specifications (as shown in the two distribution curves of Figure 3.1b), C_{pk} will diverge from C_p. Recall that the equation for C_p included only an estimate of process variation, and did not include an estimate for process location. This is a shortcoming of C_p; however, when used in conjunction with C_{pk} then C_p can be helpful in problem solving the process improvement requirements.

Referring to the earlier example, C_p is marginal at 1.11. If the process were perfectly located at the midpoint of the specifications, the C_p value provides

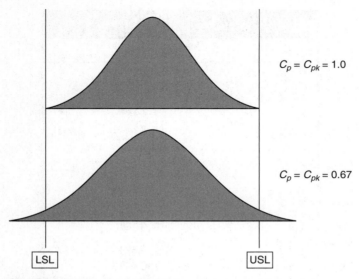

$C_p = C_{pk} = 1.0$

$C_p = C_{pk} = 0.67$

LSL   USL

FIGURE 3-1a · Example C_p and C_{pk} for processes centered within specifications.

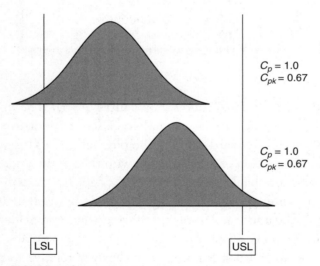

$C_p = 1.0$
$C_{pk} = 0.67$

$C_p = 1.0$
$C_{pk} = 0.67$

LSL   USL

FIGURE 3.1b · Example C_p and C_{pk} for processes not centered within specifications.

the optimal level of capability that can be expected of the process given the estimated process variation. For data that follows a normal distribution, C_p will always be larger than C_{pk}. (Note that this is not necessarily true for non-normal data, depending on the methodology used for analysis.) Since the process is not perfectly located at the midpoint of the specification (i.e., 1.010 in this example), the actual process capability is much lower (calculated as C_{pk} of 0.67), reflective of its location above the midpoint of the specifications.

Referring to Table 3.1, the example error rate associated with defects larger than the upper specification limit of 1.020 is found using the C_{pu} value of 0.67 as approximately 2.22%; the error rate associated with defects smaller than the lower specification limit of 1.00 is found using the C_{pl} value of 1.56 as approximately 0.00014%; the total error is the summation of the two estimates, which in this case is dominated by the error associated with the upper specification.

Estimating Process Variation

The calculations for C_p and C_{pk} provided above require an estimate of the process standard deviation σ_x. There are a number of methods available to calculate standard deviation, each with different implications. Many statistical spreadsheets or calculators will calculate sample or population sigma, while SPC software will also calculate process sigma based on the control charts.

Sample standard deviation is conveniently calculated using Excel's STDEV function, or as follows:

$$\sigma_{sample} = \sqrt{\frac{\sum_{i=1}^{n}(x_i - \overline{\overline{x}})^2}{n-1}}$$

The sample standard deviation is not useful for prediction, since it can include the effects of trends and shifts: It pools the data as discussed in Chapter 1. Since a process can only be predicted if it is in statistical control, process capability must always be based on the process standard deviation obtained from a statistical control chart. Process standard deviation σ_x is calculated using the range or sigma charts for variation, as discussed in Chapters 5 and 6 for variables data.

Most importantly, the process must be in control for the capability index to have any meaning whatsoever. If the process is not in a state of statistical control, it is not stable and cannot be predicted. In these cases, the process performance indices discussed below can be used, subject to their inherent limitations.

Still Struggling

Process capability is designed as a prediction of the process output. A process that is instable cannot be predicted: Who knows what it will do next? The concept of stability is necessarily time-based: Does the process operate now as it has in the past?

A control chart is used to verify that a process is stable. The control chart uses the past behavior of the process, viewed over time, to verify that the process output is essentially repeatable over time, within some level of error (i.e, common cause variation).

The sample standard deviation calculation does not consider the time-ordered nature of the process data. It includes both common and special causes of variation, without distinction, so is not useful for calculating process capability.

Errors in Estimating Process Capability

Even when all assumptions are valid, a capability index is a statistic, subject to statistical error. Just as each plotted subgroup in a control chart varies somewhat from the other plotted groups even for a controlled process, each estimate of process capability is also subject to sampling error that affects its result. As such, statistical confidence limits may be developed for each of the capability indices, which may be added and subtracted from the calculated capability index to indicate the range of values expected from random samples of a stable process.

The confidence interval for C_{pk} may be expressed as follows (Pigantiello & Ramberg):

$$C_{pk} \pm k \left[\frac{C_{pk}^2}{2(n-1)} + \frac{1}{9n} \right]^{1/2}$$

In the example above, C_{pk} was estimated as 0.67. If the estimate had been based on a sample of 300 observations, the true value of C_{pk} would lie somewhere in the range 0.57 to 0.77; if based on a sample of only 50 observations, the true value of C_{pk} would lie somewhere in the range 0.42 to 0.92. Clearly, the range of possible estimates varies widely!

A Monte Carlo simulation (Pigantiello & Ramberg) involving 1000 different trials of 30-piece samples showed that when the true capability equaled 1.33, nearly 20% of the trials indicated a capability less than 1.2; 5% of the trials had capability estimates less than 1.10. Similarly, if the true capability was a marginal 1.0, more than 10% of the trials indicated that the capability was 1.2 or greater, and 4% indicated a capability of 1.3 or greater.

Recognizing the errors inherent in these estimates of process capability provides a lesson in how the index should be treated: Point estimates of capability indices are misleading! Customers who demand updated capability estimates *based on each shipment* are grossly misusing and misunderstanding the capability estimates. Notice how the estimate for error is reduced as larger data sets are used. In other words, the estimate becomes more reliable with additional data. If the process is in control, there is absolutely no justification (and increased error) in recalculating the capability index for specific time periods. A controlled process implies the process distribution and its calculated parameters (its mean and standard deviation) do not change over time.

For these reasons, capability indices should not be recalculated for specific data or time periods unless the process has undergone a sustained shift (evidenced by a control chart shift). The random variation within a controlled process will otherwise result in meaningless, random variation of the calculated process capability index.

Identifying Non-Normality in Process Data

Statistical distributions are characterized by up to four parameters:

- *Central tendency:* For symmetrical distributions (see "Skewness" below), the average (or mean) provides a reliable description of the central tendency or location of the process. For skewed distributions, such as incomes, housing prices, or instances of cycle times where the median is near a zero bound, the median is a much better indicator of central tendency.

- *Standard deviation:* The standard deviation provides an estimate of variation. In mathematical terms, it is related to the second moment about the mean. In simpler terms, it is related to the average distance of the process observations from the mean.

- *Skewness:* The skewness provides a measure of the location of the mode (or high point in the distribution) relative to the average. In mathematical terms, it is related to the third moment about the mean. Symmetrical distributions, such as the normal distribution, have a skewness of zero. When the mode is to the left of the average, the skewness is negative; to the right, it is positive.

- *Kurtosis:* The kurtosis provides a measure of the "peakedness" of a distribution. In mathematical terms, it is related to the fourth moment about the mean. The normal distribution has a kurtosis of 1. Distributions that are more peaked have higher kurtosis.

The binomial and poisson distributions discussed in Chapter 4 require only a known (or reliably estimated) average to define the distribution. These are one-parameter distributions, meaning that the remaining parameters (standard deviation, skewness, and kurtosis) are defined solely as a function of the mean, or a function of the distribution itself. The normal distribution requires two parameters (the mean and the standard deviation) because the skewness and kurtosis are defined to produce its characteristic bell shape.

When the convenience of known distributions such as the normal distribution cannot be applied, more advanced curve-fitting techniques can be used to model the process. There are various techniques available in SPC software packages in today's market. An older technique uses the Pearson distribution, which was particularly popular in academic textbooks of the 1950s era because of its use of tables for estimating process parameters. Since the widespread use of computers, the Johnson translation system (Johnson & Kotz, 1983) has become more popular. It is an iterative approach to curve fitting, which provides a fitted distribution based on one of four possible transformation types: bounded distributions; unbounded distributions; the log normal distribution; and the normal distribution. A key advantage of its application toward quality improvement is that it essentially transforms the data into a normal distribution, allowing the standard process capability assumptions to be applied (Pyzdek, 1992).

The basic assumptions required to model distributional curve fits for a set of data include (Keller, 2011):

1. The data are representative of the process during the period when the data were collected (i.e., measurement error is negligible, and the sampling process produced data reflective of the process conditions). This

implies that the data have sufficient resolution to estimate variation among the data and that there are sufficient data to represent the common cause variation in the process.

2. The data can be represented by a single, continuous distribution. A single distribution can be sensibly fit to the data only when the process is stable (in statistical control), without any influences that may shift the process in time (special causes).

Many practitioners are familiar with the use of process histograms for determining the distribution of a set of process data. This is a risky practice which is not recommended.

A histogram is a graphic tool used to visualize data. It is a bar chart where the height of each bar represents the number of observations falling within a range of rank-ordered data values. The number of bars influences the shape of the perceived distribution and should not be based on convenience or data resolution. Instead, the number of bars is approximately equal to the square root of the number of data values, with exact formula calculated within statistical software.

When the data are not evenly distributed about the center of the histogram, the process is skewed. When skewness exists, the practitioner should seek to understand the cause of this behavior. Some processes naturally have skewed distributions and also may be bounded, such as the concentricity data in manufacturing and cycle time data in transactional processes. Concentricity and cycle time have natural lower bounds at zero because no measurement values can be less than zero. As the process is improved by moving its location closer to zero, the lower bound is encountered. As more of the data accumulate just above zero, a sharp demarcation at the zero point develops, highlighting this lower bound, such as shown in the histogram in Figure 3.2.

If double or multiple peaks occur, look for the possibility that the data are coming from multiple sources, such as different suppliers or machine adjustments.

The histogram provides a view of the process as measured. The actual output over a larger sample period may be much wider, even when the process is in control. As a general rule, 200 to 300 data observations are preferred to provide a realistic view of a process distribution, although it is not uncommon to use a histogram when you have much fewer data. Bear in mind that fewer data generally imply a greater risk of error.

One problem that novice practitioners tend to overlook is that the histogram provides only part of the picture. A histogram with a given shape may

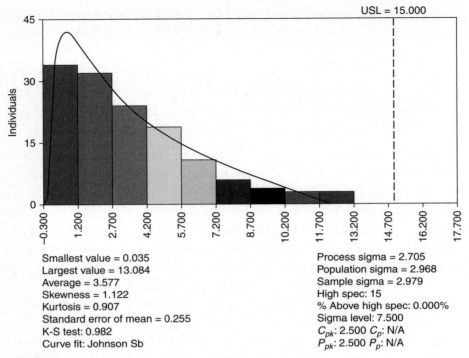

Smallest value = 0.035
Largest value = 13.084
Average = 3.577
Skewness = 1.122
Kurtosis = 0.907
Standard error of mean = 0.255
K-S test: 0.982
Curve fit: Johnson Sb

Process sigma = 2.705
Population sigma = 2.968
Sample sigma = 2.979
High spec: 15
% Above high spec: 0.000%
Sigma level: 7.500
C_{pk}: 2.500 C_p: N/A
P_{pk}: 2.500 P_p: N/A

FIGURE 3.2 · Example histogram from *SPC IV Excel* software.

be produced by many different processes, the only difference in the data being their order. Recall the two processes with identical histograms shown in Figures 1.4 and 1.5. When a process is out of control, then, by definition, a single distribution cannot be fit to the data. Therefore, *always use a control chart to determine statistical control before attempting to fit a distribution or interpret a histogram.*

Similarly, once process control has been established, a probability plot can be used to graphically confirm fit of the data to an assumed distribution. The assumption of normality is applied for many statistical tests, including the use of the standard process capability indices discussed above. The cycle time data shown in the histogram of Figure 3.2 is analyzed in the normal probability plot of Figure 3.3. Note its lack of fit to the projected line of normality, particularly at each end.

A useful graphic technique for determining whether there are too much or too little data in the tail regions of the distribution is to look for patterns near the far-left and far-right portions of the line. Excessive data in the tails

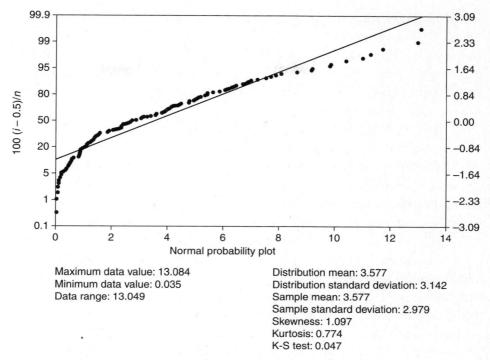

FIGURE 3.3 · Example probability plot based on cycle time data from Figure 3.2.

would group data above the confidence interval on the left side (small probabilities) and below the confidence interval on the right side (high probabilities). Likewise, a lack of data in the tails would produce the opposite effect.

When normal-distribution plots are analyzed and the data reasonably fit the distribution, the mean of the population can be estimated as the value of the line as it crosses the 50th percentile. The distribution standard deviation may be estimated as the difference between the x values corresponding to the points at which the normal line crosses the $y = 50$th ($z = 0$) and $y = 84$th ($z = 1$) percentiles.

A more objective means to assess goodness-of-fit is based on the statistical goodness-of-fit tests. While the Chi-square test is perhaps the most frequently referenced goodness-of-fit technique in general application statistical textbooks, its popularity in academic circles may indeed lie in its simplicity: Authors can easily describe and demonstrate the test without the need for computer software. In practice, however, data is almost exclusively analyzed using computer software, allowing the use of more sophisticated techniques which are better suited for most applications, particularly in testing continuous distributions (Massey). Two of these techniques are the Kolmogorov-Smirnov test (often referred to simply as the K-S test) and the Anderson-Darling test. Each of these techniques may be used to compare the fit of assumed distributions to sample data.

In both the K-S and the Anderson-Darling test, the null hypothesis is that the data follows the specified distribution. Most statistical software reports a p-value, where the null hypothesis, H_0, is rejected (i.e., the distribution is a poor fit) if the p-value is less than a predetermined alpha value (typically 0.05 or 0.10). Distributions can also be compared: The distribution with the larger p-value is the more likely distribution.

The K-S criterion is based on the expectation that there is likely to be a difference between a discrete distribution generated from data and the continuous distribution from which the data were drawn, caused by step difference and random error. As n increases, the size of the difference is expected to decrease. If the measured maximum difference is smaller than expected, then the probability that the distributions are the same is high.

The K-S criterion is very demanding as n becomes large because the K-S criterion is scaled by the square root of n, reflecting an expected decrease in the step-size error. The random error and outliers then dominate, with outliers having a strong effect on the reported p-value (because K-S is a measure of maximum deviation).

The histogram of Figure 3.2 fits a non-normal Johnson distribution to the data. The software permitted the entry of a lower bound value, which in this case is zero, since cycle time values less than zero could not physically exist for the process. With the specified lower bound of zero, the fitted distribution provides a K-S value of 0.982 (as shown in the figure); without a lower bound specified, the curve fit extended to just below zero (a lower bound of −0.3 was predicted), with a comparable K-S estimate. Obviously the curve fit shown in the figure is preferred, since it predicts a lower bound at or above the physical lower bound of zero.

A normal distribution curve fits this data poorly, as indicated by the K-S value of 0.047 shown in Figure 3.3. Values less than 0.05 are statistically significant in asserting the distribution is a poor match for the data. As noted above, the process must be in statistical control for any of these distributional tools (the curve fit, the K-S values, the probability plot, and the histogram) to be relevant.

Still Struggling

When a process is in a state of statistical control, it can be represented by a single distribution. If the in-control process is influenced by a special cause, it is driven out of control, and the new state of the process would be represented by a different distribution. The out of control condition thus provides evidence that more than one distribution is present.

Therefore, it is critical to establish that the process is in control before any meaningful analysis can be done with regard to the distribution, including a process capability analysis. Likewise, when a histogram is used to visualize the process distribution, or show how the process compares to requirements, then statistical control must first be established. Without control, the histogram provides information only for the data included in the histogram, whose results cannot be extended to the overall process or to items whose data are not included in the plotted histogram.

Once statistical control has been established, a distribution may be fit to the data. A large K-S value indicates a good curve fit; K-S values less than 0.05 indicate an extremely poor fit, which can sometimes be improved with additional data.

Capability Estimates for Non-Normal Processes

For capability analysis, the process data, from a controlled process, is first fit with a distribution. Once the distributional properties have been defined, the capability estimate C_p can be determined by estimating the process values coinciding with the 99.865 and 0.135 percentiles of the fitted distribution. These percentile values correspond to the plus and minus three sigma values of the normal distribution, providing 99.73% of the predicted output within the stated percentiles.

Similarly, the C_{pk} index for a non-normal distribution can be estimated by first estimating the percentiles of the fitted distribution corresponding to the upper and lower specifications. The Normal distribution tables are then used to determine the comparable z-value coinciding with these percentiles. When the lower specification is less than the 50th percentile, it coincides with a negative z-value, so they are multiplied by a negative one.

For non-normal distributions, the capability indices are calculated from

$$C_p = \frac{\text{high spec} - \text{low spec}}{\text{ordinate}_{0.99865} - \text{ordinate}_{0.00135}}$$

$$Z_l = |Z_{\text{normal}, pl}| \qquad Z_u = |Z_{\text{normal}, pu}|$$

where $\text{ordinate}_{0.99865}$ and $\text{ordinate}_{0.00135}$ are the values of the non-normal cumulative distribution curve at the 99.865 and the 0.135 percentage points, respectively; $Z_{\text{normal}, pl}$ and $Z_{\text{normal}, pu}$ are the z-values of the normal cumulative distribution curve at the pl and the pu percentage points, respectively, where pu is the percentile of the fitted distribution corresponding to the USL and pl is the percentile of the fitted distribution corresponding to the LSL. Z_l and Z_u are used as in the normal distribution calculations to obtain C_{pl} and C_{pu}, respectively. The actual calculations used for these estimates are not shown here, given the iterative nature of the curve-fitting algorithms.

Note that while the algebraic equations used in the normal distribution calculations can be meaningfully expressed even for large values of C_p and C_{pk}, there is a risk of excessive error in interpolation of a fitted curve when the z-value is large (7.5 or more, corresponding to C_p or C_{pk} of 2.5 or greater). In the extreme tail regions of the fitted distribution the percentiles (which can be inferred from Table 3.1) are too small to reliably estimate given the accuracy of the curve-fitting methodology. For this reason non-normal estimates for capability would not reliably exceed values of 2.5 or so. Note the C_{pk} value of 2.5 in Figure 3.2.

Since two distinct methods are used to estimate C_p and C_{pk}, it is possible to estimate values of the non-normal C_{pk} which exceed the estimated value of the non-normal C_p. While this is mathematically impossible for the case of the normal distribution, it is practically possible for non-normal cases because of the differences in the tail regions of the normal and non-normal curve fits. Note that the non-normal C_p uses the precise percentile values associated with the normal distribution, while the non-normal C_{pk} estimates a percentile associated with each specification, subject to the adequacy of the fitted non-normal distribution.

When both the normal and non-normal estimates for capability are available, compare the indices and test which assumption (normal or not) fits the data better. Assuming normality is always easier, but when the data is severely non-normal, significant error will occur in the estimate, as shown via example in Chapter 6.

Process Performance Indices

A common misuse of process capability indices is their applications to out of control processes. The process capability indices use the process sigma value, obtained through use of a control chart (as described in Chapters 5 and 6). The process sigma value provides the common cause level of variation expected from the process if it remains in statistical control. If the process is out of control, the calculated process sigma value provides only the variation that *could be attained if control is established* rather than the current level of process variation. That is, while the current level of process variation for the out of control process includes both common and special causes of variation, the control chart estimate of process sigma includes only the common cause variation.

When a process is not in statistical control, the prevalent and often recommended strategy is to use process performance indices. The process performance indices P_p and P_{pk} are similar to the corresponding capability indices C_p and C_{pk}, respectively, except the performance indices use the sample standard deviation estimate of variation (shown above in the "Estimating Process Variation" section). The rationale is that the sample standard deviation includes both common and special cause variation (without distinction), obtained by random sampling from a given batch or shipment of product.

There are several problems with this approach, not the least of which is that the calculations for process performance rely upon the assumption of a normal distribution with known (or estimated) average and standard deviation. Since the process is out of control, there are (by definition) *multiple process distributions*, so it is a fundamental mistake to assume that the parameters of a single distribution are reliable indicators of the data. Furthermore, there is no evidence that a normal distribution is warranted for the data; unfortunately, it would be near impossible to realistically model any one of the multiple distributions represented by the out of control process with a normal or non-normal distribution since the process is out of control! While software could certainly fit a distributional curve to the data, the curve is meaningless.

Similarly, any sample of data less than 100% of the total batch or shipment is not likely to be representative of the entire batch. Consider a simple case with only two distributions contained within the batch: The process was in control (distribution 1), then (unknown to the process personnel) the process was influenced by a persistent special cause (resulting in distribution 2). Assuming the probability of selecting each item in the batch is equal (i.e., the samples are independent and random), the probability of sampling from distribution 2 equals the percent of the batch that was influenced by the special cause. The most likely samples to be selected from distribution 2 are those close to its mode (the high point in the distribution), with decreasing chance of selecting samples further from the mode based on the specific shape of the distribution. For example, a symmetric distribution would provide (perhaps exponentially) decreasing chance of selecting samples as you move from the mode in either direction; a skewed distribution would provide higher probability of selecting samples in the direction of the shorter tail than in the direction of the longer tail. The ability to select samples representative of each distribution is thus dependent on many factors, including the differences between the distributions' medians, the shape of each distribution, the number of samples within each distribution, and so on. Without the use of a control chart, and being ignorant of the time-ordered sequence of the data, it would be difficult to identify an outlier or a multimodal process without making fundamental assumptions of the distribution, which would be unwarranted.

It should be clear that a process performance index based on anything but a 100% sample is a risk. Deming (1986) quantified the risk using his *all or nothing rule*. If k_1 is the cost to inspect one piece and k_2 is the total cost associated with failing to detect a defective piece, then k_1/k_2 is the point of break-even quality. Deming's all or nothing rule dictated 100% sampling for batches whose fraction defective exceeded the break-even point, and no inspection otherwise. Whereas this rule applied only for processes in statistical control, Deming suggested the use of Joyce Orsini's modification for processes in chaos: 100% sampling for processes where $k_2 > 1000k_1$; no sampling if $k_2 < 10k_1$; sample size of 200 for other cases, with 100% sampling required if any defect is found in the sample of 200 pieces.

While these rules provide economical justification for 100% sampling, their "no sampling" condition does little to placate a customer demand for process performance indices as a condition of shipment. As such, when a performance index is required, then 100% sampling is the only viable alternative.

Of course, the cost of 100% sampling cannot be ignored. The remedy is process control, which permits much smaller sampling rates over time, with the economic benefit of decreased sampling and improved quality. In the absence of process control, 100% sampling should be required of your vendors for any significant process characteristic.

Summary

Process capability and performance indices, while widespread in use, are often misapplied. Adherence to the fundamental assumptions governing the estimates reduces the error associated with their use.

QUIZ

1. **Which of the following is the best method for determining if a set of data fit a particular distribution?**
   A. Kolmogorov-Smirnov test.
   B. Histogram.
   C. Probability plot.
   D. Once statistical control has been established for the process data, each of the above tools should be used in conjunction with one another to determine the distributional fit.

2. **The cycle time of a process (the time taken from beginning to completing the process) is in statistical control, with an average of 7 days and a process standard deviation of 0.75 day. Assuming a normal distribution, if the customer requires the process be completed in 10 days, then process capability C_p is approximately:**
   A. 2.22.
   B. 1.33.
   C. 4.0.
   D. Cannot be determined with the information provided.

3. **When using process capability estimates:**
   A. C_p may be acceptable and C_{pk} unacceptable.
   B. C_p tells us how the actual variation compares to the acceptable variation.
   C. C_{pk} is better to use than C_p since C_{pk} considers process location.
   D. All of the above.

4. **Histograms are useful because you can look at their shape and get a general feel for:**
   A. the range of data values in the sample.
   B. whether the process is in control.
   C. the distributional shape of the process.
   D. All of the above.

5. **Histograms:**
   A. give us a graphical view of sample location and variation.
   B. provide a quick means of checking process control.
   C. detect subtle trends in the process.
   D. All of the above.

6. **Process performance indices P_p and P_{pk} provide an indication of:**
   A. how well the process will perform relative to customer requirements in the future.
   B. how well a given sample meets the customer requirements.
   C. if the process is in control.
   D. All of the above.

7. **A customer requires that inventory replenishments be received within 10 days of due date, but no earlier than the due date. The number of days from due date to shipment receipt is in statistical control, with an average of 7 days and a process standard deviation of 0.75 day. Assuming a normal distribution, the process capability C_{pk} is approximately:**
   A. 2.22.
   B. 1.33.
   C. 4.0.
   D. Cannot be determined with the information provided.

8. **When reporting how well we meet our customer requirements:**
   A. a histogram showing a sample of process data, with specification limits, allows the customer to verify a shipment will meet their requirements.
   B. outliers observed in a random sample of the process should be removed from the analysis if they were removed from the shipment.
   C. we should use C_{pk} if the process is in control, and P_{pk} based on 100% sampling if the process is not in control.
   D. All of the above.

9. **Before calculating the process capability indices C_p and C_{pk}:**
   A. the customer requirements should be verified.
   B. the process stability should be evaluated on a control chart.
   C. the process distribution should be evaluated.
   D. All of the above.

10. **If C_p is larger than C_{pk}, then:**
    A. the process variation is too large.
    B. C_{pk} can be improved by relocating the process.
    C. something is wrong with the calculation since C_p can never be larger than C_{pk}.
    D. None of the above.

chapter 4

Attribute Control Charts

Attribute charts are a set of control charts specifically designed for count data, as described in Chapter 2.

CHAPTER OBJECTIVES

After completing this chapter, you will be able to

- Differentiate between the four charts useful for attribute data
- Understand the construction and use of each chart
- Apply and interpret the charts

Description and Use

Typically, a condition of interest is defined, and the process is observed for a period of time during which a sample (or subgroup) is collected. As the sample is collected (or sometimes after the entire sample is collected), the number of instances (i.e., the count) of the condition of interest is recorded. The condition of interest is often an undesirable process state, such as an error or defect, but in other cases it may be something desirable, such as the number of orders.

As discussed in Chapter 2, attribute data has less information content than variables data: A count is obtained only when a condition occurs. Variables measurement data permits understanding of how close an item is to meeting the condition, even when it does not meet the condition. For example, attribute data for patient monitoring in a health care process might include the number of patients with a fever, whereas variables data for the process might be the measurement of the patients' temperature. The variables data can detect if the process is trending toward an undesirable state, permitting prevention of the undesirable condition, whereas attribute data only recognizes the condition's occurrence.

Attribute charts monitor the process location and variation over time in a single chart. The family of attribute charts includes the following:

- *p chart:* For monitoring the percent of samples having the condition, relative to either a fixed or varying sample size, when each sample can either have this condition, or not have this condition.
- *Np chart*: For monitoring the number of samples having the condition, relative to a constant sample size, when each sample can either have this condition, or not have this condition.
- *u chart*: For monitoring the number of times a condition occurs per sample unit, relative to either a fixed or varying sample size, when each sample can have more than one instance of the condition.
- *c chart*: For monitoring the number of times a condition occurs per sample unit, relative to a constant sample size, when each sample can have more than one instance of the condition.

The following example for an accounting process demonstrates the differences between the various attribute charts. Table 4.1 provides the following columns of data for a 12-month period:

TABLE 4.1	Example of order processing attribute data.						
Month	Orders	Orders with Errors	p_j	Total Errors	u_j	Sample Orders with Errors	Sample Errors
January	268	14	0.052	48	0.179	6	16
February	342	24	0.070	42	0.123	5	14
March	321	25	0.078	53	0.165	7	18
April	287	17	0.059	38	0.132	7	13
May	258	17	0.066	50	0.194	6	17
June	306	12	0.039	42	0.137	9	14
July	329	27	0.082	45	0.137	12	15
August	299	26	0.087	61	0.204	6	20
September	332	22	0.066	52	0.157	5	17
October	292	24	0.082	64	0.219	5	21
November	286	18	0.063	40	0.140	5	13
December	349	26	0.074	38	0.109	8	13
SUM	3669	252		573	u_j	81	191

- *Orders:* The total number of orders processed in the month.
- *Orders with errors:* The number of orders with one or more errors in that month, as found by inspection of all orders processed that month.
- *Total errors:* The number of errors detected on all orders processed that month.
- *Sample orders with errors:* The number of orders with one or more errors detected on a random sample of 100 of the total orders processed that month.
- *Sample errors:* The number of errors detected in a random sample of 100 orders (the same random sample as prior column).

The p Chart

The p chart monitors the percent of samples having a condition of interest, relative to either a fixed or varying sample size, when each sample can either have this condition, or not have this condition. The *binomial* distribution is assumed for the data.

Using the example data in Table 4.1, the "Orders" column contains the sample size for each month. Each order either has or does not have one or more errors associated with it. The count of orders that contained one or more errors is contained in the "Order with Errors" column.

Plotted statistic

The percent of items in the sample meeting a criterion of interest.

$$p_j = \frac{(\text{count})_j}{n_j}$$

where n_j is the sample size (number of units) of group j.

For example, the plotted percent for the first subgroup (January) is calculated as 14/268 or 5.2%. The column labeled p_j in Table 4.1 contains the calculated percent for each subgroup. This is provided only for reference, as most SPC software will calculate this value using the input counts and sample sizes. Note below that the sample size is required for calculating the control limits. While most SPC software will allow entry of the percents rather than the count, the sample size is needed in either case to allow calculation of the control limits.

Centerline

$$\bar{p} = \frac{\sum_{j=1}^{m}(\text{count})_j}{\sum_{j=1}^{m} n_j}$$

where n_j is the sample size (number of units) of group j, and m is the number of groups included in the analysis.

In the example:

$$\bar{p} = \frac{\sum_{j=1}^{m}(\text{count})_j}{\sum_{j=1}^{m} n_j} = \frac{252}{3669} = 6.87\%$$

UCL, LCL (upper and lower control limit)

$$\text{UCL} = \bar{p} + 3\sqrt{\frac{\bar{p}(1-\bar{p})}{n_j}}$$

$$\text{LCL} = \max\left[0, \bar{p} - 3\sqrt{\frac{\bar{p}(1-\bar{p})}{n_j}}\right]$$

where n_j is the sample size (number of units) of group j, and $\bar{p}$ is the average percent.

When the samples size varies from subgroup to subgroup, as in this example, the control limits will vary as well: The control limits are narrower for larger sample sizes, reflecting the improved ability to estimate the true percent for larger samples. In the example, the control limits for the **last** subgroup (i.e., December) is calculated as follows:

$$UCL = \bar{p} + 3\sqrt{\frac{\bar{p}(1-\bar{p})}{n_j}} = 0.0687 + 3\sqrt{\frac{.0687(.9313)}{349}} = 0.1093$$

$$LCL = \max\left[0, \bar{p} - 3\sqrt{\frac{\bar{p}(1-\bar{p})}{n_j}}\right] = \max\left[0, 0.0687 - 3\sqrt{\frac{.0687(.9313)}{349}}\right] = 0.0281$$

Figure 4.1 displays the completed control chart based on Table 4.1 data.

The Np Chart

The Np chart monitors the number of samples having the condition, relative to a constant sample size, when each sample can either have this condition, or not have this condition. When the sample size is the same for each sample, the Np chart will show an identical pattern to the p chart, the only difference being the unit of measure (a count rather than a percent).

In the example, if the sample size (i.e., number of orders) in each month had varied by less than 20%, the average sample size can be used as the fixed sample size for the Np chart. Since the sample size varies by approximately 30% in this example, a random sample of 100 orders is selected each month for the Np chart.

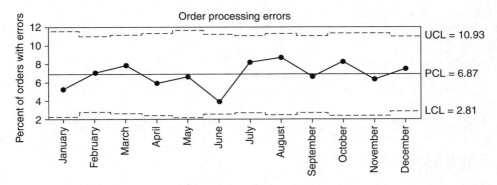

FIGURE 4.1 • p chart of percent of orders with errors from data in Table 4.1.

The number of orders in each month's 100-order sample that contained one or more errors is contained in the "Sample Order with Errors" column of Table 4.1.

Plotted statistic

The number of items in the sample meeting a criterion of interest.

Centerline

$$\overline{np} = \frac{\sum_{j=1}^{m}(\text{count})_j}{m}$$

where m is the number of groups included in the analysis.

In the example:

$$\overline{np} = \frac{\sum_{j=1}^{m}(\text{count})_j}{m} = \frac{81}{12} = 6.75$$

UCL, LCL (upper and lower control limits)

$$\text{UCL}_{np} = \overline{np} + 3\sqrt{\overline{np}(1-\overline{p})}$$
$$\text{LCL}_{np} = \max\left[0, \overline{np} - 3\sqrt{\overline{np}(1-\overline{p})}\right]$$

where n is the sample size, $\overline{np}$ is the average count, and $\overline{p}$ is calculated as follows:

$$\overline{p} = \frac{\sum_{j=1}^{m}(\text{count})_j}{m \times n}$$

In the example:

$$\overline{p} = \frac{\sum_{j=1}^{m}(\text{count})_j}{m \times n} = \frac{81}{12 \times 100} = 0.0675$$

$$\text{UCL}_{np} = \overline{np} + 3\sqrt{\overline{np}(1-p)} = 6.75 + 3\sqrt{100 \times 0.0675(0.9325)} = 14.28$$

$$\text{LCL}_{np} = \max\left[0, \overline{np} - 3\sqrt{\overline{np}(1-\overline{p})}\right] = 6.75 - 3\sqrt{100 \times 0.0675(0.9325)} = 0$$

Figure 4.2 displays the completed control chart based on Table 4.1 data.

The u Chart

The u chart monitors the number of times a condition occurs per sample unit, relative to either a fixed or varying sample size. In this case, a given sample can

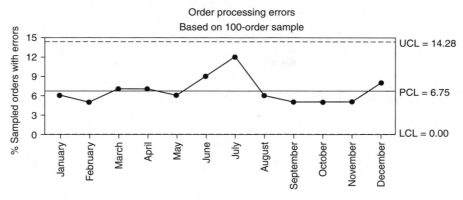

FIGURE 4.2 · Np chart of number of orders with errors in 100-order sample from data in Table 4.1.

have more than one instance of the condition, in which case we count all the times it occurs in the sample.

Using the example data in Table 4.1, the "Total Errors" column contains the count of all errors detected on the "Orders with Errors" samples. In this case, each order may have several instances of the error in question.

Plotted statistic

The average count of occurrences per unit of a criterion of interest in a sample of items.

$$u_j = \frac{(\text{count})_j}{n_j}$$

where n_j is the sample size (number of units) of group j.

For example, the plotted percent for the first subgroup (January) is calculated as 48/268 or 17.9%. The column labeled u_j in Table 4.1 contains the calculated percent for each subgroup. This is provided only for reference, as most SPC software will calculate this value using the input counts and sample sizes. Note below that the sample size is required for calculating the control limits. While most SPC software will allow entry of the errors per sample unit rather than the count, the sample size is needed in either case to allow calculation of the control limits.

Centerline

$$\bar{u} = \frac{\sum_{j=1}^{m} (\text{count})_j}{\sum_{j=1}^{m} n_j}$$

where n_j is the sample size (number of units) of group j, and m is the number of groups included in the analysis.

In the example:

$$\bar{u} = \frac{\sum_{j=1}^{m}(\text{count})_{j}}{\sum_{j=1}^{m} n_{j}} = \frac{573}{3669} = 0.156$$

UCL, LCL (upper and lower control limits)

$$\text{UCL} = \bar{u} + 3\sqrt{\frac{\bar{u}}{n_{j}}}$$

$$\text{LCL} = \max\left(0, \bar{u} - 3\sqrt{\frac{\bar{u}}{n_{j}}}\right)$$

where n_{j} is the sample size (number of units) of group j, and $\bar{u}$ is the average percent.

When the sample size varies from subgroup to subgroup, as in this example, the control limits will vary as well: The control limits are narrower for larger sample sizes, reflecting the improved ability to estimate the true errors per sample for larger samples. In the example, the control limits for the *last* subgroup (i.e., December) are calculated as follows:

$$\text{UCL} = \bar{u} + 3\sqrt{\frac{\bar{u}}{n_{j}}} = .156 + 3\sqrt{\frac{.156}{349}} = 0.219$$

$$\text{LCL} = \max\left(0, \bar{u} - 3\sqrt{\frac{\bar{u}}{n_{j}}}\right) = .156 - 3\sqrt{\frac{.156}{349}} = 0.093$$

Figure 4.3 displays the completed control chart based on Table 4.1 data.

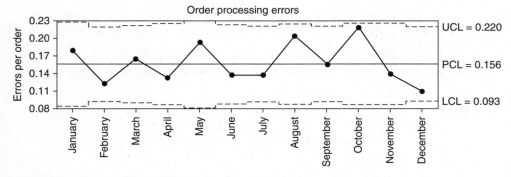

FIGURE 4.3 · u chart of errors per order from data in Table 4.1.

The c Chart

The c chart monitors the number of times a condition occurs per sample, relative to a constant sample size. In this case, a given sample can have more than one instance of the condition, in which case we count all the times it occurs in the sample. In the example, if the sample size (i.e., number of orders) in each month had varied by less than 20%, the average sample size can be used as the fixed sample size for the c chart. Since the sample size varies by approximately 30% in this example, a random sample of 100 orders is selected each month for the c chart. The number of total errors detected in each month's 100-order sample is contained in the "Sample Errors" column of Table 4.1.

Plotted statistic

The count of occurrences of a criterion of interest in a sample of items.

Centerline

$$\bar{c} = \frac{\sum_{j=1}^{m}(\text{count})_j}{m}$$

where m is the number of groups included in the analysis. UCL and LCL are the upper and lower control limits:

In the example:

$$\bar{c} = \frac{\sum_{j=1}^{m}(\text{count})_j}{m} = \frac{191}{12} = 15.92$$

UCL, LCL (upper and lower control limits)

$$UCL = \bar{c} + 3\sqrt{\bar{c}}$$
$$LCL = \max\left(0, \bar{c} - 3\sqrt{\bar{c}}\right)$$

where n is the sample size and $\bar{c}$ is the average count.

In the example:

$$UCL = \bar{c} + 3\sqrt{\bar{c}} = 15.92 + 3\sqrt{15.92} = 27.89$$
$$LCL = \max\left(0, \bar{c} - 3\sqrt{\bar{c}}\right) = \max\left(0, 15.92 - 3\sqrt{15.92}\right) = 3.95$$

Figure 4.4 displays the completed control chart based on Table 4.1 data.

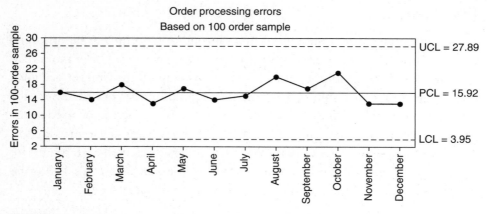

FIGURE 4.4 · c chart of errors per order in the 100-order sample from data in Table 4.1.

Still Struggling?

If you are unsure of which chart to use, you need to consider the type of data you are collecting. Suppose we are interested in understanding a loan processing operation. We sample a number of files each month and record the errors found in the sample files. In so doing, we realize there are two ways we could record the data.

One way to record the data is to record the number of files that have one or more errors in them. In this case, each sample unit is a given file, and the given file either has errors or does not have errors. Note that the count of items (i.e., the number of defective files) could never exceed the number of files we sampled. This data is Binomial data, so we can use either a p chart or an Np chart. We would use an Np chart if we always sampled the same number of files each month, or could use an p chart if we sampled the same number of files or varied the sample size each month.

For this same process, we might decide instead to record the total number of errors found in each file. In this case, the number of errors could exceed the number of files sampled. Since each sample file could have an unlimited opportunity for error, the data is best modeled by the Poisson distribution. We could use a c chart if we always sample the same number of files each month, or could use a u chart if we sampled the same number of files or varied the sample size each month.

Interpretation

Each chart includes statistically determined upper and lower control limits, indicating the bounds of expected process behavior. The fluctuation of the points between the control limits is due to the common cause variation that is intrinsic (built-in) to the process. Any plotted groups outside the control limits can be attributed to a "special cause," implying a shift in the process. When a process is influenced by only common causes, then it is stable, and can be predicted. Thus, a key value of the control chart is to identify the occurrence of special causes, so that they can be removed, with a reduction in overall process variation. Then, the process can be further improved by either relocating the process to an optimal average level, or decreasing the variation due to common causes.

Attribute charts are fairly simple to interpret: merely look for out of control points. If there are any, then the special causes must be eliminated. Brainstorm and conduct designed experiments to find those process elements that contribute to sporadic changes in process location. (See Chapter 7 for further information on process improvement.) When subgroups are detected as out of control, their data should be excluded from the calculations of the average and control limits to remove the statistical bias.

Remember that the variation within control limits is due to the inherent variation in sampling from the process. (Think of Deming's red bead experiment: The proportion of red beads never changed in the bucket, yet each sample had a varying count of red beads.) The bottom line is: React first to special cause variation. Once the process is in statistical control, then work to reduce variation and improve the location of the process through fundamental changes to the system.

The first four Western Electric run test rules may also be applied to each of the attribute control charts. Run tests 2 and 3 increase the sensitivity of the chart by detecting trends within the control limits. Run test 4 identifies a likely multistream condition, where alternate samples are drawn from one of two process streams.

Still Struggling?

Still unsure of why to use control charts for attribute data? It's common for improvement teams to use Pareto diagrams to determine priorities. The Pareto analysis uses categorized attribute data, with the largest categories assumed to offer the best payback for process improvement. Yet, Pareto diagrams do not tell the complete picture: A category that has a large occurrence or cost may result from either common cause or special cause variation. Since removing special causes is generally much easier than redesigning a stable system, improving a process that is out of control may provide a better payback. On the other hand, if the special causes are unlikely to reappear, then their elimination would represent a poor investment of process improvement resources. In this way, an understanding of the nature of the process and its causes for instability, where they exist, are necessary to accurately prioritize the process improvements.

Sampling Considerations

The average count (plotted on the c and Np charts or used in calculating percents in the p and u charts) must be 5 or larger for meaningful control charts. Just as control charts for measurement data requires adequate resolution to properly calculate the statistics of the process, so do the attribute control charts. When the condition of interest occurs infrequently, the sample size must be increased (where possible), or different metrics should be used.

Yet, samples should be taken over a suitably short time frame to ensure that special causes of variation do not systematically occur within samples. A rational subgroup, as described in Chapter 2, will ensure that common cause variation is accurately estimated and special cause variation promptly detected. Counts should be limited to a specific criterion of interest, rather than a set of criteria that may reflect separate systems or subprocesses.

Consider the data in Table 4.2, collected for a sales process. For each sales quarter, the percent of sales inquiries (i.e., each inquiry is a sales prospect or lead) that are converted to a sale is plotted in Figure 4.5.

The p chart shown in Figure 4.5 indicates a well-controlled sales process, which was nonetheless not well-received by management. There were no indications that either of their two marketing campaigns had contributed any success to the conversion rate. A c chart of the number of prospects (Figure 4.6) also provides no hint of increased traffic from the marketing campaigns.

TABLE 4.2	Quarterly sales conversion rate.	
Sales Quarter	Number Prospects	Number Buy
1Q09	2949	353
2Q09	2960	317
3Q09	2936	335
4Q09	2993	345
1Q10	2906	333
2Q10	2995	349
3Q10	3029	351
4Q10	3003	365

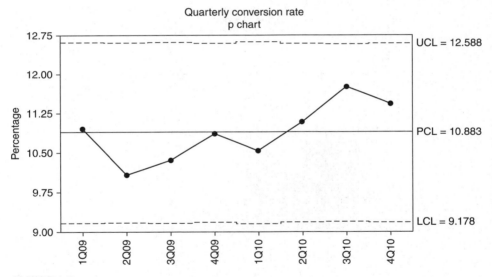

FIGURE 4.5 · Quarterly conversion rate for sales process on p chart.

A more thorough analysis of the process reveals some potential errors in the analysis. There are four products sold, and the sales volumes are quite different between the products, as shown in Figure 4.7. Just over 50% of the sales are associated with Product A, so its sales are likely to dominate the prior analysis. Both of the marketing events were specifically targeted to products C and D. A c chart of the sales for Product C is provided in Figure 4.8.

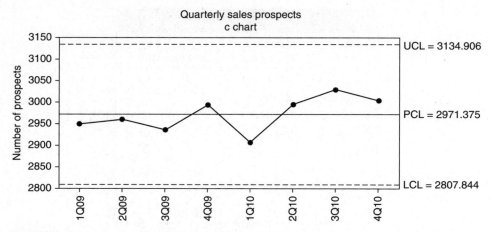

FIGURE 4.6 · Number of sales prospects per quarter on c chart.

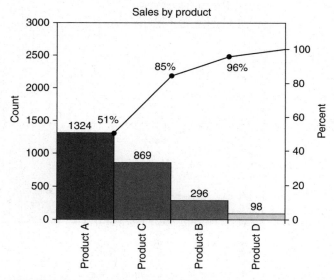

FIGURE 4.7 · Pareto diagram of sales by product.

A review of Product Cs sales provides no indication of special causes that might be traceable to marketing efforts. Seeking clarification, the data is plotted on a monthly basis as shown in Figure 4.9. Special causes are evident here for September and October 2010 (it's likely that August 2010 is also influenced by this same special cause), which coincide with the timing of the second marketing event. There is no evidence of influence from the first marketing event, which occurred the same time in the prior year.

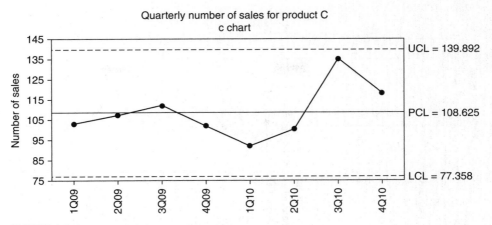

FIGURE 4.8 · Number of sales per quarter for Product C.

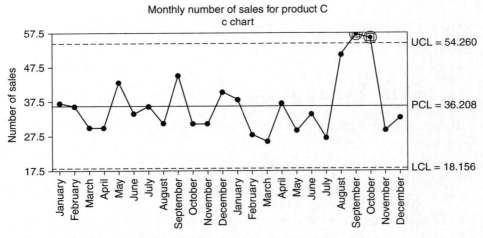

FIGURE 4.9 · Number of sales per month for Product C.

The monthly number of sales for Product D is shown in Figure 4.10. There is no evidence of a special cause of variation; however, note the average count is less than 5, meaning that the chart is poorly suited for detecting special causes of variation. Increasing the sample size by expanding the group to include the 3 months in a quarter increases the average count to an acceptable level, but reduces the likelihood a special cause within a quarter would be detected (as shown for Product C). In this case, a more acceptable metric might be the dollar value of the sales plotted on an x chart (discussed in Chapter 6).

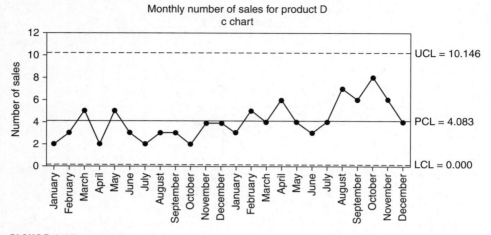

FIGURE 4.10 • Number of sales per month for Product D.

 Still Struggling?

The examples in this last section demonstrate a number of issues that can occur with attribute data:

1. Including multiple categories of items in each sample count desensitizes the chart to fluctuations in each item. Use separate charts for each item category for highest sensitivity.

2. Limit the time period for each sample to reduce the likelihood of special causes occurring within the samples. If special causes are likely within a month's period, include only a week's worth of data within each plotted sample.

3. Each sample must have a sufficient occurrence of the issue (an average of 5 or more in each sample). This requirement conflicts with the two preceding requirements: As we reduce the types of items or the time period for the sample, the count of items are reduced.

4. Use variables data to monitor the process whenever possible. For example, measure the time between occurrences on a chart for individuals data (discussed in Chapter 6) in place of an attributes chart for the number of occurrences within an arbitrary time period.

Summary

As with all control charts, the attribute control charts are useful to prevent reacting to common cause variation as special causes. Through the use of these control charts, process personnel can easily differentiate between the random variation of a stable process and the unexpected shifts due to assignable causes.

Unfortunately, unlike variables control charts which can detect trends toward an undesirable state, most attribute data deal with errors and defects after they occur. When process errors occur only occasionally, then very large sample sizes are often needed.

QUIZ

1. If process errors are counted each month, and most of the months have no errors, with the remaining months having one error, then the process:
   A. is in control.
   B. is out of control.
   C. consistently meets the customer requirements.
   D. sample size is too small to determine statistical control of the error rate.

2. Data collection for attribute control charting require:
   A. the process only influenced by common cause variation during the subgroup sample period.
   B. the average count of items meeting the criteria (i.e., the average count over all the samples) should be 5 or more.
   C. the sample frequency based on the causes of process instability.
   D. All of the above.

3. A hospital is interested in control charting its mortality (death) rate for a surgical procedure. If the number of surgeries varies each month, the best control chart to use is the:
   A. p chart.
   B. Np chart.
   C. u chart.
   D. c chart.

4. A hospital is interested in control charting the number of "pain incidents" following a surgical procedure, where a "pain incident" occurs if a patient complains of excessive pain within 10 days of the procedure, and a given patient may experience multiple pain incidents. The best control chart to use to plot the number of pain incidents per surgical procedure each month is the:
   A. p chart.
   B. Np chart.
   C. u chart.
   D. Pareto chart.

5. The percent of live births from c-sections is in control with an average c-section rate p bar of 0.14. A sample of 125 live births is obtained with 25 c-sections performed in the sample. When plotted on the p chart:
   A. this new sample is out of control on the p chart.
   B. this new sample is in control on the p chart.
   C. this new sample's position on the p chart cannot be determined with the information provided.

6. **A sales process is in control with an average percent of orders paid with credit card p bar of 0.14. A sample of 88 orders is obtained with 25 orders paid using credit card. When plotted on the p chart:**
   A. this new sample is out of control on the p chart.
   B. this new sample is in control on the p chart.
   C. this new sample's position on the p chart cannot be determined with the information provided.

7. **A traffic intersection is monitored over time using a sample of 100 cars for each time interval. The process is in control on an Np chart with an average number of cars illegally passing through a red light of 7 cars. A sample of 88 cars is observed with 15 cars illegally passing through the intersection. When plotted on the Np chart:**
   A. this new sample is out of control on the Np chart.
   B. this new sample is in control on the Np chart.
   C. this new sample's position on the Np chart cannot be determined with the information provided.

8. **An invoicing process is in control with an average error rate u bar = 1.14 errors per invoice. A sample of 88 invoices is obtained with 125 errors detected in the sample. When plotted on the u chart:**
   A. this new sample is out of control on the u chart.
   B. this new sample is in control on the u chart.
   C. this new sample's position on the u chart cannot be determined with the information provided.

9. **A process is in control with an average error rate u bar = 1.14 errors per sample. A sample of 80 units is obtained with 125 errors detected in the sample. When plotted on the u chart:**
   A. this new sample is out of control on the u chart.
   B. this new sample is in control on the u chart.
   C. this new sample's position on the u chart cannot be determined with the information provided.

10. **The number of sales orders each month is in control on a c chart, with lower and upper control limits at 0 and 27, respectively. A month with 19 orders:**
    A. is out of control on the c chart.
    B. is in control on the c chart.
    C. cannot be plotted on the c chart with the information provided.

5

$\overline{X}$ Charts

An $\overline{X}$ (pronounced X-bar) *chart* is a control chart that is useful for variables data. The $\overline{X}$ chart monitors the process location over time based on the average of a collection of observations called a *subgroup*. $\overline{X}$ charts are used for subgroup size of 2 and larger.

$\overline{X}$ charts are used with an accompanying chart for monitoring variation between observations in the subgroup over time—either the range chart or the sigma chart.

CHAPTER OBJECTIVES

After completing this chapter, you will be able to

- Differentiate between the use of the range and sigma charts for monitoring variation
- Understand the construction and use of the $\overline{X}$ chart with emphasis on the rational subgroup formation
- Apply and interpret the $\overline{X}$ chart for typical applications as well as for multi-stream and autocorrelated processes

Chart Construction

Table 5.1 shows data collected from a manufacturing process. Five samples were taken over a 10-minute period of production. Each set of 5 samples (i.e., each row in the table) represents a subgroup. The subgroup provides information on the short-term properties of the process: the conditions present over that approximately 10-minute period. Table 5.1 also provides the average of each subgroup, also known as the $\bar{X}$ for the subgroup, calculated as follows:

$$\bar{x} = \frac{1}{n} \sum_{i=1}^{n} x_i$$

TABLE 5.1　Example data.

Subgroup\Item	1	2	3	4	5	Average	Range	Sigma
1	65.9	65	48.1	45.6	56.3	56.18	20.3	9.35
2	61.4	55.6	70.8	53.9	41.5	56.64	29.3	10.74
3	49.6	51.8	57.4	46.6	56.6	52.4	10.8	4.60
4	47.4	55.5	50.8	51.4	42.1	49.44	13.4	5.01
5	63.1	58.1	64.6	54.3	65.7	61.16	11.4	4.81
6	45.7	64.7	31.8	64.3	48.9	51.08	32.9	13.84
7	46	49.3	48.4	58.1	52.1	50.78	12.1	4.64
8	45.8	39.4	54.7	41	59.2	48.02	19.8	8.63
9	50.1	37.1	54.4	50.9	54.9	49.48	17.8	7.23
10	31.3	31.3	40	42.2	55.8	40.12	24.5	10.07
11	53	61.1	45.8	54.5	57.2	54.32	15.3	5.67
12	53.8	53.7	59.9	60	42	53.88	18	7.33
13	34.5	61.5	37.6	51.8	53.1	47.7	27	11.32
14	62.6	36.7	34.3	38.6	52.8	45	28.3	12.20
15	57.7	59.6	42.3	43.9	48.4	50.38	17.3	7.90
16	52.2	61.1	44.9	44.3	53.1	51.12	16.8	6.89
17	58.9	36.2	60.7	61.4	33	50.04	28.4	14.17
18	54.9	45.1	40.3	56.8	38.1	47.04	18.7	8.46
19	48.9	42.1	61.4	58.3	58.1	53.76	19.3	8.02
20	53.6	55.2	61.1	45.6	52.5	53.6	15.5	5.57
21	53.3	35.2	50.7	40.9	51.3	46.28	18.1	7.84

(Continued)

Subgroup\Item	1	2	3	4	5	Average	Range	Sigma
22	55.9	28.4	44.1	64.1	52.7	49.04	35.7	13.58
23	50.2	29.4	31.1	43.6	52.7	41.4	23.3	10.72
24	49.5	51.4	50.3	58.5	57.4	53.42	9	4.21
25	60.2	54.8	49.2	42.7	33.4	48.06	26.8	10.46
26	47.5	37.1	58.9	51	46.3	48.16	21.8	7.90
27	52.3	45.8	56.9	76.2	60.7	58.38	30.4	11.41
28	59	63	49.6	51.2	48.2	54.2	14.8	6.45
29	53	61.7	38	46.9	34.7	46.86	27	11.00
30	64.2	37.8	41.7	51.2	46	48.18	26.4	10.25
31	61.4	58.6	39.9	37	49.2	49.22	24.4	10.87
32	56.3	48.4	47.4	39.4	75.6	53.42	36.2	13.77
33	54.2	33.6	34.8	65.4	57.2	49.04	31.8	14.16
34	60.7	52.9	49.1	45.7	53.2	52.32	15	5.60
35	35.8	39.8	61.8	52.6	64.1	50.82	28.3	12.72
36	49.8	57.1	57.3	50.5	60.5	55.04	10.7	4.67
37	61	64.4	51.6	47.1	51.9	55.2	17.3	7.21
38	65.1	67.2	49.2	31.6	32	49.02	35.6	17.19
39	48.8	61.6	43.3	54.3	60.7	53.74	18.3	7.81
40	46	35.5	54.1	32.8	53.7	44.42	21.3	9.96
					Average	50.71	21.73	9.11

TABLE 5.1 Example data. (*Continued*)

The subgroup average is simply the sum of each observation, x_i, divided by the number of observations n. The bar notation indicates the average of the parameter, so $\overline{X}$ is the average of the observations (the x's) in the subgroup. For example, the average of the first subgroup is calculated as:

$$\overline{X}_1 = (65.9 + 65 + 48.1 + 45.6 + 56.3)/5 = 56.18$$

The range of each subgroup is also provided in the table, calculated as follows:

$$R_j = \max(x_1, x_2, \ldots, x_n) - \min(x_1, x_2, \ldots, x_n)$$

For example, the range of the first subgroup is calculated as:

$$R_1 = \max(65.9, 65, 48.1, 45.6, 56.3) - \min(65.9, 65, 48.1, 45.6, 56.3) = 20.3$$

The last line of the table provides the overall average $(\overline{\overline{X}}$, pronounced X double bar) and the average range $(\overline{R}$, pronounced R bar), calculated as:

$$\overline{\overline{x}} = \frac{1}{m} \sum_{j=1}^{m} \overline{x}_j \qquad \overline{R} = \frac{1}{m} \sum_{j=1}^{m} R_j$$

where n is the subgroup size and m is the total number of subgroups included in the analysis.

The subgroup data is plotted on the $\overline{X}$ and range charts as shown in Figure 5.1. The top chart in Figure 5.1 is the $\overline{X}$ chart, which plots each of the subgroup averages shown in Table 5.1. The bottom chart is the range chart, which plots each of the subgroup ranges from Table 5.1.

The control limits for both the $\overline{X}$ and range charts are based on the short-term variation. The range statistic $\overline{R}$ (calculation shown above) estimates the average short-term variation.

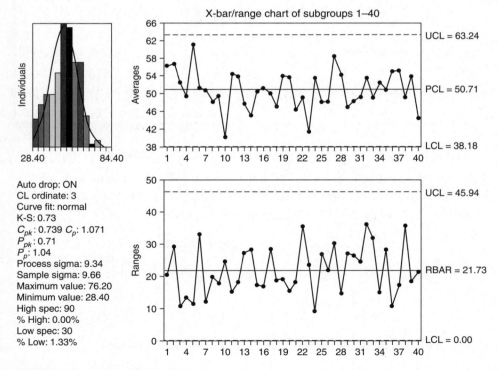

FIGURE 5.1 · Example $\overline{X}$/range chart based on Table 5.1 data.

The upper control limit (UCL) and lower control limit (LCL) are shown for both the $\bar{X}$ and range charts in Figure 5.1. The control limits for the $\bar{X}$ chart are calculated as:

$$UCL_{\bar{x}} = \bar{\bar{x}} + 3\left(\frac{\sigma_x}{\sqrt{n}}\right)$$

$$LCL_{\bar{x}} = \bar{\bar{x}} - 3\left(\frac{\sigma_x}{\sqrt{n}}\right)$$

where $\bar{\bar{x}}$ is the grand average and σ_x is process sigma, which is calculated using the average range as $\bar{R}/d_2$. Some authors prefer to write the $\bar{X}$ chart control limits in the form:

$$UCL_{\bar{x}} = \bar{\bar{x}} + A_2\bar{R}$$

$$LCL_{\bar{x}} = \bar{\bar{x}} - A_2\bar{R}$$

where A_2 is a tabulated value (see Appendix) based on subgroup size n, and is mathematically identical to the value $3/(d_2 \times \sqrt{n})$. Although both sets of formulas necessarily achieve identical results, the first method clearly shows:

1. The use of three sigma control limits, evidenced by the factor 3. Recall from Chapter 1 that three sigma limits are used to decrease the false alarm rate because false alarms lead to tampering and a resulting increase in process variation.

2. The use of process sigma to calculate the control limits, where process sigma is based on the average short-term variation ($\bar{R}$ in this case). In other words: *The expected variation in the subgroup averages is calculated using the average variation within the subgroups.* In this way, statistical control is synonymous with process stability: when short-term variation predicts longer-term variation, then the process is in control. Recall that this differs from the enumerative methods discussed in Chapter 1, where the variation is calculated using a pooled estimate of standard deviation (sometimes referred to as a sample standard deviation).

3. The control limits are based on the average value of the plotted statistic, plus or minus three standard deviations of the plotted statistic. This becomes evident in the equations above because process sigma divided by the square root of n equals the standard deviation of the $\bar{X}$ values.

For example, to calculate the $\bar{X}$ control limits the process sigma value is first calculated using a d_2 value of 2.326, which is obtained from Appendix for a subgroup size n of 5.

$$\sigma_x = \bar{R}/d_2 = 21.73/2.326 = 9.34$$

$$UCL_{\bar{x}} = \bar{\bar{x}} + 3\left(\frac{\sigma_x}{\sqrt{n}}\right) = 50.71 + (3 \times 9.34/\sqrt{5}) = 63.24$$

$$LCL_{\bar{x}} = \bar{\bar{x}} - 3\left(\frac{\sigma_x}{\sqrt{n}}\right) = 50.71 - (3 \times 9.34/\sqrt{5}) = 38.18$$

The control limits for the range chart are calculated as:

$$UCL_R = \bar{R} + 3d_3\sigma_x$$

$$LCL_R = \max(0, \bar{R} - 3d_3\sigma_x)$$

where d_3 is a function of n (tabulated in Appendix), which may also be identically written as:

$$UCL_R = \bar{R}D_4$$

$$LCL_R = \bar{R}D_3$$

where D_3 and D_4 are a function of n (tabulated in Appendix).

For example, to calculate the range chart control limits the d_3 value of 0.864 is obtained from Appendix for a subgroup size n of 5.

$$UCL_R = 21.73 + 3 \times 0.864 \times 9.34 = 45.94$$

$$LCL_R = \max(0, 21.73 - 3 \times 0.864 \times 9.34) = 0$$

The calculations themselves are only shown here for reference and for understanding of their origins. In most cases, you'll use software that automatically calculates these values.

Sigma Chart

Similarly, the sigma chart could be used in place of the range chart. Table 5.1 shows the sample standard deviation for each subgroup, calculated as:

$$S_j = \sqrt{\frac{\sum_{i=1}^{n}(x_i - \bar{x}_j)^2}{n-1}}$$

where x_i's are the observations in subgroup j, $\bar{x}_j$ is the subgroup average for subgroup j, and n is the subgroup size. For example, the standard deviation for subgroup 1 may be calculated as:

$$S_j = \sqrt{\frac{(65.9-56.18)^2+(65-56.18)^2+(48.1-56.18)^2+(45.6-56.18)^2+(56.3-56.18)^2}{5-1}} = 9.35$$

The centerline for the sigma chart is the average of the subgroup sigma values. The upper and lower control limits for the sigma chart are calculated as:

$$\text{UCL}_s = \bar{S} + 3\left(\frac{\bar{S}}{c_4}\right)\sqrt{1-c_4^2}$$

$$\text{LCL}_s = \min\left[0, \bar{S} - 3(\bar{S}/c_4)\sqrt{1-c_4^2}\right]$$

where $\bar{S}$ is the average sigma, and c_4 is a function of n (tabulated in Appendix). As above, a mathematically identical formula for calculating the control limits may also be shown as:

$$\text{UCL}_s = \bar{S}B_4$$

$$\text{LCL}_s = \bar{S}B_3$$

where B_3 and B_4 are a function of n (tabulated in Appendix).

An $\bar{X}$/sigma chart for the Table 5.1 data is shown in Figure 5.2. Note that the control limits on the $\bar{X}$ chart vary slightly from Figure 5.1, indicative of the differences between the two methods (subgroup range and subgroup standard deviation) for estimating process sigma.

The control limits on the $\bar{X}$ chart are calculated using process sigma based on the sigma chart:

$$\text{UCL}_{\bar{x}} = \bar{\bar{x}} + 3\left(\frac{\sigma_x}{\sqrt{n}}\right)$$

$$\text{LCL}_{\bar{x}} = \bar{\bar{x}} - 3\left(\frac{\sigma_x}{\sqrt{n}}\right)$$

where $\bar{\bar{x}}$ is the grand average and σ_x is process sigma, which is calculated using the average sigma as $\bar{S}/c_4$ (c_4 is a function of n tabulated in Appendix).

For larger subgroup sizes, the sigma chart is preferred over the range chart for its ability to more accurately estimate short-term variation. The range statistic effectively uses only two of the observations in the subgroup (the smallest and

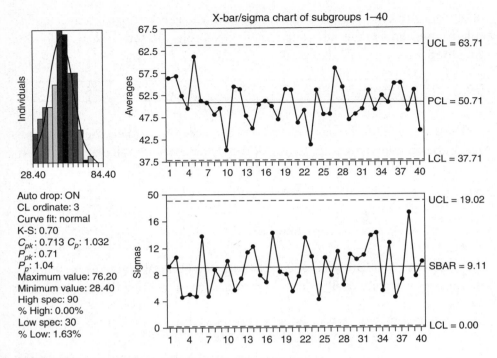

FIGURE 5.2 · Example $\bar{X}$/sigma chart based on Table 5.1 data.

largest) to determine the standard deviation, while the sigma statistic uses all the observations in the subgroup. Referring to Table 5.2 (Montgomery, 1991), the ability of the range statistic to accurately estimate the subgroup standard deviation decays dramatically with larger subgroup sizes, and it should not be used for subgroups larger than 10 observations. (Most credible SPC software will not allow use of the range chart for subgroup sizes larger than 10.)

TABLE 5.2 Efficiency of range statistic relative to sigma statistic.	
Subgroup Size (*n*)	**Relative Efficiency**
2	1.000
3	0.992
4	0.975
5	0.955
6	0.930
10	0.850

The popularity of the range chart is somewhat a reflection of the age in which it was developed: In the 1920s shop floor personnel and their engineers did not have computers to generate their SPC charts. Instead, they manually calculated the control limits. The range statistic is more easily calculated than a subgroup standard deviation, so the range chart became the default chart of choice. In today's world, computer software removes the burden of calculations. Nonetheless, the range chart is often simpler to explain and teach, so retains some appeal for smaller subgroup sizes, which are usually preferred. Recall from Chapter 2 the relative performance in detecting process shifts is not greatly improved for subgroups larger than 4 or 5 observations. The risks of forming irrational subgroups increases with subgroup size, so the moderately sized groups of 4 or 5 are most often recommended. The efficiency of the range chart relative to the sigma chart is quite good for these smaller subgroups.

Interpretation

When using the $\bar{X}$ chart, always review the range (or sigma) chart first. If the range/sigma chart is out of control, the estimate of process sigma is biased by the special cause variation. Since the average range/sigma value is used to calculate the control limits on the $\bar{X}$ chart, these control limits are similarly biased. The special cause in the range/sigma chart must be removed before the $\bar{X}$ chart can be analyzed.

Review the range/sigma chart to ensure there are five or more distinct values plotted, and no one value appears more than 25% of the time (This pattern is more evident on range charts than on sigma charts.). If values are repeated too often, then there is inadequate resolution in the measurements, which will adversely affect control limit calculations. In this case, consider the method by which the variable is measured and look for more precise instrumentation or methods (see also Chapter 2 discussion of resolution and Chapter 8 discussion of measurement systems; see the range chart of Figure 5.9 for an example of the distinct levels typically observed with this issue).

An increase in process variation may be detected as an out of control condition on the range/sigma chart. If there are out of control groups on the range/sigma chart, then the special causes must be eliminated, as discussed in Chapter 1. Brainstorm and conduct designed experiments to find the process elements that contribute to sporadic changes in variation. (See also Chapter 7). To predict the capability of the process after special causes have been eliminated, remove the out of control points from the analysis. This removes the statistical bias of the out of control points from the calculations of the average range/sigma, the range/sigma control limits, and the $\bar{X}$ control limits.

Once the effects of the out of control groups are removed from the range/sigma chart, the $\bar{X}$ chart can be analyzed. If the process is stable, the subgroup averages, the $\bar{X}$s, will vary between the $\bar{X}$ control limits. Interpret the points on the $\bar{X}$ chart relative to the control limits and run test rules, and try to ignore the inherent point to point variation that exists within the control limits.

Look for obviously nonrandom behavior using the run test rules, which apply statistical tests for trends to the plotted points. If there are any run test violations or out of control points on the $\bar{X}$ chart, then the special causes must be eliminated. Brainstorm and conduct designed experiments to find the process elements that contribute to sporadic changes in process location. (See also Chapter 7). To predict the capability of the process after special causes have been eliminated, remove the out of control points from the analysis, which will remove the statistical bias of the out of control points from the calculations of $\bar{\bar{X}}$ and the $\bar{X}$ control limits.

The plotted subgroups on the $\bar{X}$ chart should *never* be compared directly to specifications. Customer specifications refer to the individual observations, and not the subgroup averages. Most credible SPC software will not allow the specification lines to be shown on the $\bar{X}$ chart, to avoid confusion by the lay person.

Still Struggling

If you are confused as to why specifications should not be shown on the $\bar{X}$ chart, consider a process that has an upper specification limit (USL) set to 12, and the lower specification limit (LSL) set to 8. A plotted subgroup average of 10 would fall right between the two specifications, implying a perfectly targeted process. Yet, if that subgroup average was composed of the values 7, 6, 13, and 14, although the average value is dead center in the middle of the specifications not one of the observations is within the specification!

Recall from Figure 2.7 that the distribution of the plotted averages is much narrower than the distribution of observations. Specifications refer to observations: Customers want *each* instance of product or service within their specifications, not *on average*. Thus, the averages and the specifications are apples and oranges that cannot be directly compared because the observations from the process vary much more than the subgroup averages.

As discussed in Chapters 1 and 3, the proper way to verify process conformance with requirements is through the use of process capability estimates. Figure 5.1 provides the capability estimates for the original Table 5.1 data with an upper specification limit (USL) of 90 and a lower specification limit (LSL) of 30 in the statistics pane beneath the histogram:

- A C_p value of 1.07 and a C_{pk} of 0.74 are obtained. The C_{pk} value less than 1 is unacceptable by most standards (see Chapter 3 for a more complete discussion of capability estimates). The larger C_p value (considered marginal at 1) indicates the best process capability that could be attained by centering the process at the midpoint of the specifications (a value of 60 in this example).

- The capability index C_{pk} predicts that 0% of the process will exceed the upper specification and 1.33% will exceed the lower specification. These are longer-term projections based on the stability of the process at these current levels.

- The capability indices were estimated using a normal distribution. The K-S value of 0.73 (much larger than 0.05) confirms the suitability of the normal distribution to the data (See Chapter 3 for discussion of the K-S statistic).

Process Shift Example

Continuing the example from Table 5.1, additional data is collected as shown in Table 5.3. Assuming first that the data is collected and analyzed in real time, one subgroup at a time, the effects of plotting the first subgroup (subgroup 41) of Table 5.3 is shown in Figure 5.3. Note how the subgroup is plotted out of control (i.e., a special cause is detected) beyond the upper control limit. In this case, the software's auto drop feature automatically removed the biasing effect of the subgroup from the calculation of $\bar{\bar{X}}$ because it was detected as a special cause on the $\bar{X}$ chart (exceeding the UCL). The value was retained in the calculation of $\bar{R}$, as indicated by the slight difference in $\bar{R}$ and the control limits as compared to Figure 5.1. (See description of the automatic dropping function near the end of Chapter 1.)

Figure 5.4 shows the effect of adding all the data in Table 5.3 to the analysis. Note now that two of the new subgroups (subgroups 42 and 45) exceed the $\bar{X}$ UCL, and there are a number of run test violations (indicated by circled points on the chart). In addition, there are a number of out of control and run

TABLE 5.3 Additional data for process data of Table 5.1.

Subgroup\Item	1	2	3	4	5	Average	Range	Sigma
41	75.9	75	58.1	55.6	66.3	66.18	20.3	9.35
42	71.4	65.6	80.8	63.9	51.5	66.64	29.3	10.74
43	59.6	61.8	67.4	56.6	66.6	62.4	10.8	4.60
44	57.4	65.5	60.8	61.4	52.1	59.44	13.4	5.01
45	73.1	68.1	74.6	64.3	75.7	71.16	11.4	4.81
46	55.7	74.7	41.8	74.3	58.9	61.08	32.9	13.84
47	56	59.3	58.4	68.1	62.1	60.78	12.1	4.64
48	55.8	49.4	64.7	51	69.2	58.02	19.8	8.63
49	60.1	47.1	64.4	60.9	64.9	59.48	17.8	7.23
50	41.3	41.3	50	52.2	65.8	50.12	24.5	10.07
51	63	71.1	55.8	64.5	67.2	64.32	15.3	5.67
52	63.8	63.7	69.9	70	52	63.88	18	7.33
53	44.5	71.5	47.6	61.8	63.1	57.7	27	11.32
54	72.6	46.7	44.3	48.6	62.8	55	28.3	12.20
55	67.7	69.6	52.3	53.9	58.4	60.38	17.3	7.90
56	62.2	71.1	54.9	54.3	63.1	61.12	16.8	6.89
57	68.9	46.2	70.7	71.4	43	60.04	28.4	14.17
58	64.9	55.1	50.3	66.8	48.1	57.04	18.7	8.46
59	58.9	52.1	71.4	68.3	68.1	63.76	19.3	8.02
60	63.6	65.2	71.1	55.6	62.5	63.6	15.5	5.57
					Average	61.11	19.85	8.32

test violations in the earlier region (subgroups 1–40) that were previously shown to be in control.

The complication here is that, even with the automatic dropping of out of control groups, the sum total of the new groups from the Table 5.3 data biased the estimate of the average so that the original data is now considerably below the process centerline. This results in violations of several run test rules (run test 2 in particular: 9 points in a row on same side of the centerline).

Situations like this happen frequently when data is analyzed retrospectively (i.e., after the fact). When the data is analyzed in real time, as it is collected, subgroup 41 is properly identified as an out of control subgroup, indicating the presence of a special cause. The persistence of the special cause is evident as

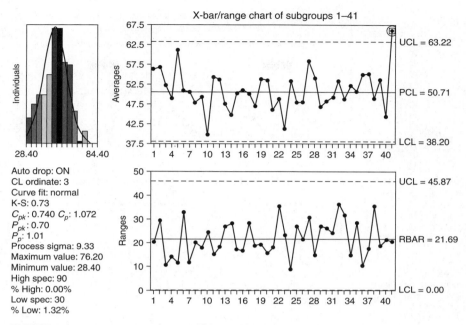

FIGURE 5.3 • Effect of adding subgroup 41 to Figure 5.1 analysis.

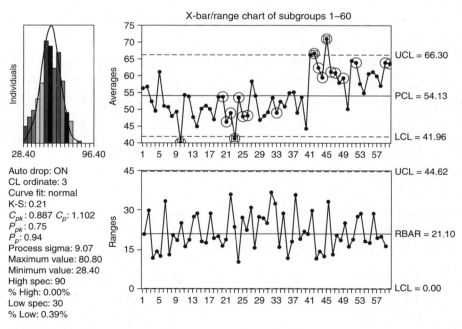

FIGURE 5.4 • Effect of adding subgroups 41–60 to Figure 5.1 analysis.

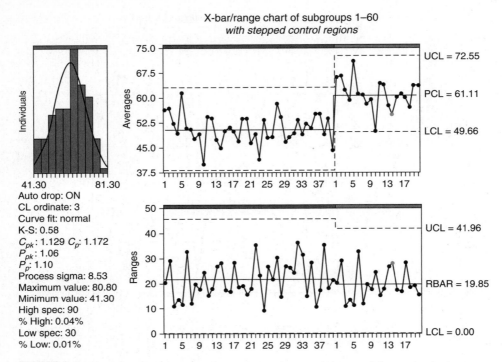

X-bar/range chart of subgroups 1–60
with stepped control regions

UCL = 72.55
PCL = 61.11
LCL = 49.66

UCL = 41.96
RBAR = 19.85
LCL = 0.00

41.30   81.30
Auto drop: ON
CL ordinate: 3
Curve fit: normal
K-S: 0.58
C_{pk}: 1.129 C_p: 1.172
P_{pk}: 1.06
P_p: 1.10
Process sigma: 8.53
Maximum value: 80.80
Minimum value: 41.30
High spec: 90
% High: 0.04%
Low spec: 30
% Low: 0.01%

FIGURE 5.5 • New control region created to accommodate persistent special cause beginning at group 41.

new data is added one group at a time, which would prompt revision of the control limits to the new process level, as shown in Figure 5.5. Note that the histogram in Figure 5.5 is based on the new process distribution associated with groups 41 through 60. If you were to click within the initial control region corresponding to groups 1 through 40, the software would provide the histogram for the initial distribution, which is identical to that shown in Figure 5.1.

In a retrospective analysis, software allows for easy "what-if" analysis to test assumptions. It appeared that a persistent special cause at group 41 was biasing the results, and a quick right mouse option to create a new control region provided statistical justification for that assertion.

The process capability of the new region is analyzed as follows:

- A C_p value of 1.17 and a C_{pk} of 1.13 are obtained. The C_{pk} value is now much closer to the C_p value, indicating better centering of the process. Since C_{pk} is still less than 1.33, the process is considered marginal and not yet capable.

- The capability index C_{pk} predicts a 0.04% beyond the upper specification and 0.01% below the lower specification. These are longer-term projections based on the stability of the process at these current levels.

- The capability indices were estimated using a normal distribution. The K-S value of 0.58 (much larger than 0.05) confirms the suitability of the normal distribution to the data.

- The common cause variation of the process is still too large, as indicated by the marginal C_{pk} and C_p values and the corresponding longer-term error-rate predictions.

Subgroup Formation Concerns

Multistream Processes

Figure 5.6 shows a process that at first glance might suggest a reduction in process variation as the cause of the subgroups hugging the $\bar{X}$ chart's centerline. Yet, the range chart shows no evidence of variation reduction.

This data, provided by a major cosmetic manufacturer, represents the fill weight for bottles of nail polish. The filling machine has three heads, so

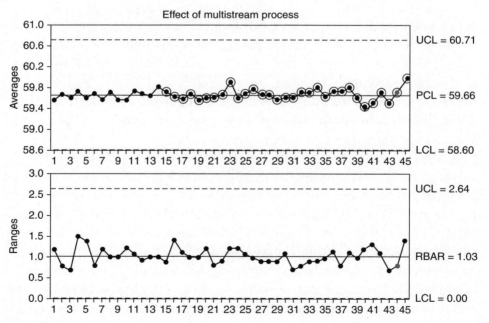

FIGURE 5.6 • Centerline hugging indicative of multistream effects within subgroup.

subgroups were conveniently formed by taking a sample from each fill head at a given point in time. The problem (that this control chart helped identify) is that the fill heads have statistically significant differences in their average values, in this case due to pressurization issues. This variation between fill heads is reflected in the within subgroup variation (as plotted on the range chart), which is much larger than the variation over time between the average weight of the three fill heads (represented graphically by the pattern of the plotted points on the $\bar{X}$ chart). Since the $\bar{X}$ chart control limits are calculated based on the range chart, they are much wider than the variation in plotted subgroup averages.

The underlying problem is that the premise of a rational subgroup (defined in Chapter 2) has been violated: Each subgroup contains output of multiple process streams rather than output of a single, stable process. Yet, the chart excelled as a learning tool: The fill heads are different, and overall variation could be reduced by making them more similar. Note the circles that highlight subgroups 15 and on. The software has indicated a violation of run test 7 (15 points in a row within one sigma of centerline), which was developed to search for this type of irrational subgroup. The implication of the run test first occurring with group 15 is that all data beginning with group 1 are impacted by this rational subgroup issue.

Multistream behavior is not limited to cosmetic filling operations. Multiple head filling stations for beverages, food products, and chemicals; multiple cavity molding operations; and multiple piece fixtures for machining are similar examples. Transactional processes can also experience irrational subgroup formation due to multiple stream processes. Consider a call center supervisor who constructs subgroups based on a selection of 5 employee's response times. If the response times consistently differ for one or more of the employees, such as due to their experience level, the subgroup is irrational.

In cases where the multiple stream effects cannot be eliminated, a modification of the $\bar{X}$ chart is recommended. A *batch means chart*, available in some advanced SPC software, accommodate the multiple stream process by converting the $\bar{X}$ chart into a simple x chart (discussed in Chapter 6), where the plotted value is the subgroup average. The range chart is maintained to provide estimate of the within subgroup variation: in this case the between stream variation. Special causes disrupting the stream to stream differences would be noted as out of control on the range chart. The x chart monitors the overall average of the multiple streams, providing indication of the process

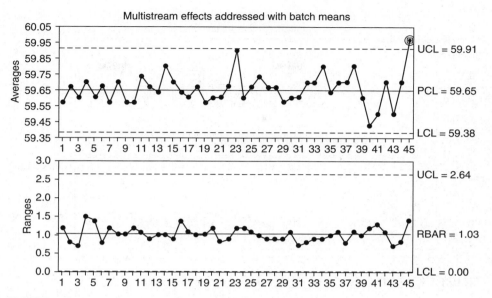

FIGURE 5.7 · Batch means chart of multistream process shown in Figure 5.6.

location. The only difference between the batch mean and the standard $\bar{X}$ chart is the control limits, which are calculated based on the moving range between the subgroup (multiple stream) averages. This follows the general approach for $n = 1$ individuals data for the standard x chart (discussed in detail in Chapter 6).

Figure 5.7 shows the batch means chart for the data previously presented in Figure 5.6. Note the range chart is unchanged from Figure 5.6. The plotted groups on the $\bar{X}$ chart are also unchanged. The control limits on the $\bar{X}$ chart are calculated based on the short-term variation between subgroups, as is done on a standard x chart for individuals data. A change in the average output of the multiple streams is now evident on the batch means x chart, indicated by an out of control condition at group 45.

Figure 5.8 provides a revised batch means chart with a new control region beginning at group 45 to accommodate the process shift.

The process capability of the multistream process is more complicated, since a single distribution cannot be fit to the multiple streams. By definition, the multiple streams each require unique distributions, and unique estimates of process capability. The process capability for a multistream process would generally be expressed using the worst case stream.

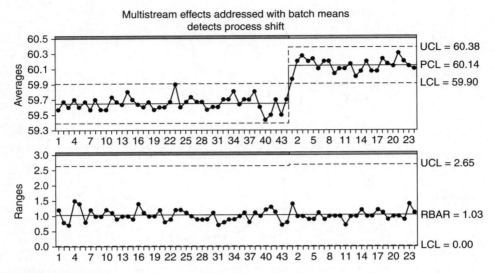

FIGURE 5.8 · Batch means chart of multistream process showing process shift.

Autocorrelated Processes

Consider the $\bar{X}$ chart shown in Figure 5.9, representing the amount of time in queue for a service process. The subgroup is formed by clocking the time five consecutive customers waited in line. Is the process out of control, or is something else going on?

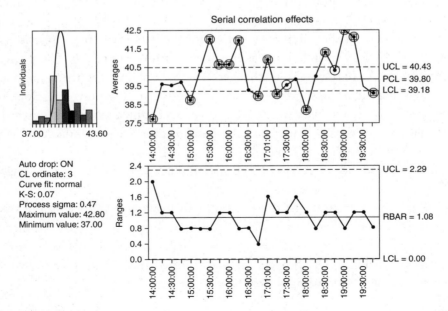

FIGURE 5.9 · Effect of autocorrelation within subgroup on $\bar{X}$ chart.

The range chart is in control, but the rabid out of control behavior on both sides of the X̄ chart is a clue to a potential problem. The within subgroup variation (estimated by the R̄ statistic and evidenced by the X̄ control limits) is much smaller than the variation from group to group on the X̄ chart. This is further substantiated by violation of run test rule 8 (eight successive groups not within one sigma of the center line) for groups 12 through 15.

An analysis for autocorrelation in the data (see Figure 5.10) shows autocorrelation out to lag 4 to be statistically significant, violating the requirement that data within the subgroup be independent of one another. Recall from Chapter 2 that autocorrelation occurs when a given observation is dependent on more or more prior observations.

Since the autocorrelation function suggests that data within subgroups are dependent, but data between subgroups (lag 5 and higher) are independent, a reasonable remedy would be to use either a single data value from each subgroup, or the average data value from each subgroup, as an indication of the short-term queue time. Since the subgroups were taken at 15-minute intervals, either of those approaches seems reasonably valid for maintaining estimates of the short-term variation. A review of the autocorrelation for the first data value in each subgroup (discarding the remaining four values in the subgroup) shows no significant autocorrelation exists, supporting the notion of independence

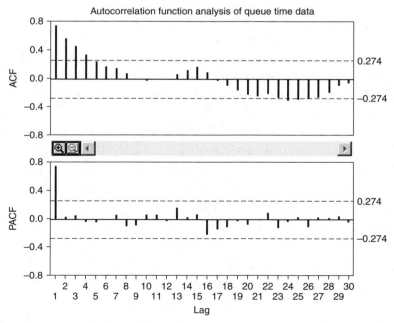

FIGURE 5.10 · Autocorrelation and partial autocorrelation analysis of queue data from Figure 5.9.

between subgroups. The single observation from each subgroup can be evaluated as individuals data using the methods shown in Chapter 6. A batch means approach to this data is shown in Figure 9.20.

Autocorrelation exists in many industries, including:

- *Chemical processes:* Autocorrelation occurs due to the inertia of large batches, the continuous flow of material, and/or feedback and feedforward process control systems.
- *Service processes:* Queuing theory predicts autocorrelation for situations where the processing time associated with a given sample is dependent on the time associated with earlier samples when the earlier samples must be completed before the current sample can begin.
- *Manufacturing processes:* Computer control of production equipment, especially using feedback/feed-forward controls, as well as downstream pooling of multiple stream processes create autocorrelation within the samples.

The autocorrelation function is used to estimate the strength of dependence between samples at various *lags*. Lag 1 autocorrelation, for example, estimates the correlation between adjacent observations (i.e., correlation between observations 1 and 2, 2 and 3, 3 and 4, and so on). Similarly, it will test at other lags. For instance, the autocorrelation at lag 4 tests whether observations 1 and 5, 2 and 6, . . . , 19 and 23, and so on are correlated.

In some cases, the effect of autocorrelation at smaller lags influences the estimate of autocorrelation at longer lags. For instance, a strong lag 1 autocorrelation causes observation 5 to influence observation 6 and observation 6 to influence 7; in some cases there may appear to be correlation between observations 5 and 7, even though no direct correlation exists. The partial autocorrelation function (PACF) removes the effect of shorter lag autocorrelation from the correlation estimate for longer lags. This estimate is valid only to one decimal place.

ACFs and PACFs each vary between ± 1. Values closer to ± 1 indicate strong correlation. Lags exceeding the confidence limits imply autocorrelation significantly different from zero.

In general, test for autocorrelation at lag 1 to lag $n/4$, where n is the total number of observations in the analysis. Estimates at longer lags have been shown to be statistically unreliable (Box & Jenkins, 1970).

When autocorrelation is significant only at low lags, the time between samples should be increased to lessen its effect, as recommended in the earlier example. If data is collected at a rate of one sample per minute (such as in automated data collection in chemical processes), and there is significant autocorrelation out to lag 10, then the interval between samples must be greater than 10 minutes to ensure independent samples.

The autocorrelation function can also detect the effects of multiple stream processes. For example, when monitoring order processing times, if each data point is the time taken by each of three employees operating at a different average level, then significant autocorrelation may appear at lag 3.

Still Struggling

The techniques described thus far as subgroup formation concerns highlight the application of the SPC chart as a problem-solving tool. In both cases (multi-stream and autocorrelated processes), the initial control chart analysis identified special causes that were not indicative of process instability but rather of errors in assumption: The formation of a rational subgroup is a fundamental assumption of the control chart.

In both cases, the run test rule violations provided insight into the root cause of the problem. An understanding of the fundamental interpretation of a control chart, notably the use of short-term estimates to predict longer-term performance, provided the means to understand how the errors in subgroup formation influenced the resulting control chart.

Fortunately, these two issues constitute the vast majority of subgroup formation errors seen in practice. If you understand the rationale behind identifying the issue, and can apply this to your own processes, you are close to mastering the $\bar{X}$ chart.

Short Run Applications

As discussed in Chapter 2, when the process nominal value changes as different products or services are delivered, short run techniques can be employed to plot the varied products or services on the same chart. Since each product has a unique operating level, a standardization technique is used to provide consistent numerical values.

The simplest method of data standardization for short run applications is sometimes referred to as nominal standardization. In this case, the nominal value for each run is subtracted from each of the data (x_i) in that run:

$$z_i = x_i - \text{nominal}$$

where x_i is the raw observation and z_t is the standardized observation. The nominal value is typically the desired or target value for each run, or preferably the historical process average when available. Once standardized, the data can be plotted on any variables control chart, including the charts for individuals data presented in Chapter 6.

The columns 1 through 5 in Table 5.4 present each of the 5 observations of 25 subgroups for three different part numbers in a machining process. The "Part Number" column provides the start and stop for each *run* in this short run analysis. Table 5.5 shows the calculated nominal standardization for each run's data using the values provided in Table 5.4's "Historical Mean" column for each run.

TABLE 5.4	Raw data from several different part numbers, shown with historical values of average and standard deviation for each part.							
Subgroup	**Part Number**	**1**	**2**	**3**	**4**	**5**	**Historic Mean**	**Historic Process Sigma**
1	PN 13672	9	9.3	10.2	9.4	10.1	9.73	0.344
2	PN 13672	9.6	9.9	10.1	9.8	9.9	9.73	0.344
3	PN 32643	19.8	19.8	20.1	19.8	19.9	19.83	0.215
4	PN 32643	19.8	19.9	20	19.6	20.2	19.83	0.215
5	PN 32643	19.7	19.4	19.6	20	19.8	19.83	0.215
6	PN 46735	29.9	30.1	30.4	29	30.5	29.9	0.516
7	PN 46735	30.2	30.6	29.8	29.5	29.4	29.9	0.516
8	PN 46735	30	29.5	30.1	30.3	29.4	29.9	0.516
9	PN 13672	9.5	10.6	9.9	10.1	10.3	9.73	0.344
10	PN 13672	9.7	10.4	9.6	9.8	10.4	9.73	0.344
11	PN 13672	9.7	9.3	9.9	9.9	9.3	9.73	0.344
12	PN 13672	9.7	9.8	9.7	9.7	9.8	9.73	0.344
13	PN 32643	19.8	20.1	19.8	19.9	19.8	19.83	0.215
14	PN 32643	19.8	20	19.8	19.8	19.6	19.83	0.215
15	PN 32643	19.7	19.6	19.7	19.9	20	19.83	0.215
16	PN 32643	19.8	19.8	19.9	19.4	20	19.83	0.215
17	PN 32643	19.9	19.6	19.9	20	19.6	19.83	0.215
18	PN 32643	19.4	20	19.4	19.6	20	19.83	0.215
19	PN 13672	9.4	9.2	10.1	9.6	9.7	9.73	0.344
20	PN 13672	9.8	9.5	10.1	9.9	9.5	9.73	0.344
21	PN 13672	10.1	9.7	9.9	10.6	9.5	9.73	0.344
22	PN 13672	9.9	9.4	10.3	9.2	9.6	9.73	0.344
23	PN 46735	30	28.1	29.4	29.5	30.4	29.9	0.516
24	PN 46735	29.9	30.5	29.4	30.3	31.1	29.9	0.516
25	PN 46735	30.2	29.5	30.5	29.7	30.1	29.9	0.516

TABLE 5.5 Nominal standardization for the data of Table 5.4.

Subgroup	Part Number	1	2	3	4	5	SG Avg	SG Range
1	PN 13672	−0.73	−0.43	0.47	−0.33	0.37	−0.130	1.200
2	PN 13672	−0.13	0.17	0.37	0.07	0.17	0.130	0.500
3	PN 32643	−0.03	−0.03	0.27	−0.03	0.07	0.050	0.300
4	PN 32643	−0.03	0.07	0.17	−0.23	0.37	0.070	0.600
5	PN 32643	−0.13	−0.43	−0.23	0.17	−0.03	−0.130	0.600
6	PN 46735	0.00	0.20	0.50	−0.90	0.60	0.080	1.500
7	PN 46735	0.30	0.70	−0.10	−0.40	−0.50	0.000	1.200
8	PN 46735	0.10	−0.40	0.20	0.40	−0.50	−0.040	0.900
9	PN 13672	−0.23	0.87	0.17	0.37	0.57	0.350	1.100
10	PN 13672	−0.03	0.67	−0.13	0.07	0.67	0.250	0.800
11	PN 13672	−0.03	−0.43	0.17	0.17	−0.43	−0.110	0.600
12	PN 13672	−0.03	0.07	−0.03	−0.03	0.07	0.010	0.100
13	PN 32643	−0.03	0.27	−0.03	0.07	−0.03	0.050	0.300
14	PN 32643	−0.03	0.17	−0.03	−0.03	−0.23	−0.030	0.400
15	PN 32643	−0.13	−0.23	−0.13	0.07	0.17	−0.050	0.400
16	PN 32643	−0.03	−0.03	0.07	−0.43	0.17	−0.050	0.600
17	PN 32643	0.07	−0.23	0.07	0.17	−0.23	−0.030	0.400
18	PN 32643	−0.43	0.17	−0.43	−0.23	0.17	−0.150	0.600
19	PN 13672	−0.33	−0.53	0.37	−0.13	−0.03	−0.130	0.900
20	PN 13672	0.07	−0.23	0.37	0.17	−0.23	0.030	0.600
21	PN 13672	0.37	−0.03	0.17	0.87	−0.23	0.230	1.100
22	PN 13672	0.17	−0.33	0.57	−0.53	−0.13	−0.050	1.100
23	PN 46735	0.10	−1.80	−0.50	−0.40	0.50	−0.420	2.300
24	PN 46735	0.00	0.60	−0.50	0.40	1.20	0.340	1.700
25	PN 46735	0.30	−0.40	0.60	−0.20	0.20	0.100	1.000

The standardized data is plotted on an $\bar{X}$ chart in Figure 5.11. The chart indicates a relatively controlled process relative to the historical average for each part; however, note that the subgroup range values for the runs corresponding to PN 32643 are consistently below the average range $\bar{R}$ while those for PN 46735 are consistently above the average range. This demonstrates a violation of a fundamental assumption that the variation within runs is consistent. Although this simple standardization will work in some applications, it is

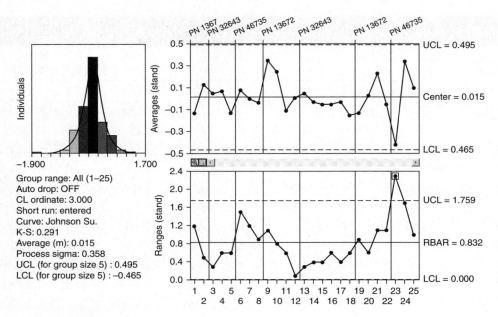

FIGURE 5.11 · Standardized $\bar{X}$ chart using Table 5.5 data.

a poor assumption for many processes and a more rigorous stabilized standardization is thus recommended for all cases.

When the level of variation is not similar for all runs, then data is standardized relative to both the nominal value and some estimate of the run variance. The standard stabilization technique for an $\bar{X}$/range chart is expressed as:

$$z_i = \frac{x_i - \text{nominal}}{\text{range}}$$

where x_i is the observation, and nominal and range are constants based on prior data or a desired values. This typical approach to standardization is based on the prevalence of the range chart in historical applications. When software is used for analysis and calculated values of process sigma are readily available, it is often more convenient to use those estimates. The stabilization may be rewritten using values of process standard deviation as:

$$z_i = \frac{x_i - \text{nominal}}{\sigma_x d_2}$$

	Part							SG
Subgroup	Number	1	2	3	4	5	SG Avg	Range
1	PN 13672	−0.91	−0.54	0.59	−0.41	0.46	−0.162	1.500
2	PN 13672	−0.16	0.21	0.46	0.09	0.21	0.162	0.625
3	PN 32643	−0.06	−0.06	0.54	−0.06	0.14	0.100	0.600
4	PN 32643	−0.06	0.14	0.34	−0.46	0.74	0.140	1.200
5	PN 32643	−0.26	−0.86	−0.46	0.34	−0.06	−0.260	1.200
6	PN 46735	0.00	0.17	0.42	−0.75	0.50	0.067	1.250
7	PN 46735	0.25	0.58	−0.08	−0.33	−0.42	0.000	1.000
8	PN 46735	0.08	−0.33	0.17	0.33	−0.42	−0.033	0.750
9	PN 13672	−0.29	1.09	0.21	0.46	0.71	0.437	1.375
10	PN 13672	−0.04	0.84	−0.16	0.09	0.84	0.312	1.000
11	PN 13672	−0.04	−0.54	0.21	0.21	−0.54	−0.137	0.750
12	PN 13672	−0.04	0.09	−0.04	−0.04	0.09	0.012	0.125
13	PN 32643	−0.06	0.54	−0.06	0.14	−0.06	0.100	0.600
14	PN 32643	−0.06	0.34	−0.06	−0.06	−0.46	−0.060	0.800
15	PN 32643	−0.26	−0.46	−0.26	0.14	0.34	−0.100	0.800
16	PN 32643	−0.06	−0.06	0.14	−0.86	0.34	−0.100	1.200
17	PN 32643	0.14	−0.46	0.14	0.34	−0.46	−0.060	0.800
18	PN 32643	−0.86	0.34	−0.86	−0.46	0.34	−0.300	1.200
19	PN 13672	−0.41	−0.66	0.46	−0.16	−0.04	−0.162	1.125
20	PN 13672	0.09	−0.29	0.46	0.21	−0.29	0.037	0.750
21	PN 13672	0.46	−0.04	0.21	1.09	−0.29	0.287	1.375
22	PN 13672	0.21	−0.41	0.71	−0.66	−0.16	−0.062	1.375
23	PN 46735	0.08	−1.50	−0.42	−0.33	0.42	−0.350	1.916
24	PN 46735	0.00	0.50	−0.42	0.33	1.00	0.283	1.416
25	PN 46735	0.25	−0.33	0.50	−0.17	0.17	0.083	0.833

TABLE 5.6 Stabilized data from Table 5.4.

where d_2 is obtained as above from Appendix based on the subgroup size. Stabilized values are shown in Table 5.6 and plotted in Figure 5.12. Note that the subgroup average and range estimates now more randomly straddle the average lines on each chart.

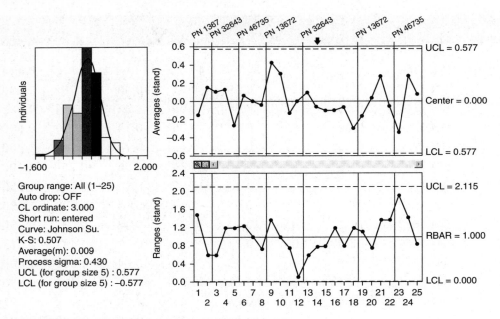

FIGURE 5.12 · Stabilized $\bar{X}$ chart based on Table 5.6 data.

Summary

$\bar{X}$ charts are versatile tools for process monitoring and improvement. They rely upon the formation of rational subgroups. When rational subgroups cannot be formed, charts for individuals data should be used, as discussed in Chapter 6.

QUIZ

1. If a process is in a state of statistical control on an $\bar{X}$ range chart, then:

    A. each individual observation from the process will be within the $\bar{X}$ control limits.

    B. any estimate of the process mean may vary by as much as plus or minus $3 \times \bar{R}/d_2$.

    C. All of the above.

    D. None of the above.

2. An $\bar{X}$ and range chart is used to monitor a process using a subgroup size of 4. The upper and lower control limits on the $\bar{X}$ chart are calculated to be 53.5 and 47.5, respectively. The upper and lower control limits for the range chart are 9.4 and 0, respectively. A new subgroup is sampled from the process with these values: 45, 41, 46, 49. This new sample indicates:

    A. the process mean has increased.

    B. the process mean has decreased.

    C. the process variation has decreased.

    D. Both B and C.

3. An $\bar{X}$ and range chart is used to monitor a process using a subgroup size of 4. The upper and lower control limits on the $\bar{X}$ chart are calculated to be 53.5 and 47.5, respectively. The upper and lower control limits for the range chart are 9.4 and 0, respectively. The upper and lower specifications for the process, as specified by the customer, are 55 and 45, respectively. A new sample is taken from the process with these values: 57, 52, 48, 50. This new sample indicates:

    A. the process mean has increased.

    B. one or more process observations exceed the customer requirements.

    C. the process is out of control.

    D. All of the above.

4. An $\bar{X}$ and range chart is used to monitor a process using a subgroup size of 4. The upper and lower control limits on the $\bar{X}$ chart are calculated to be 53.5 and 47.5, respectively. The upper and lower control limits for the range chart are 9.4 and 0, respectively. A new subgroup is sampled from the process with these values: 55, 51, 46, 50. This new sample indicates:

    A. the process mean has shifted.

    B. the process variation is excessive.

    C. Both of the above.

    D. None of the above.

5. Using an $\bar{X}$ chart with a subgroup size of 5, the overall process mean is calculated as 100, and the average within subgroup standard deviation is 5. The upper control limit for the $\bar{X}$ chart is approximately

    A. It cannot be calculated using this information.

    B. 106.7.

    C. 102.9.

    D. 107.1.

6. Using an $\bar{X}$ chart with a subgroup size of 5, the overall process mean is calculated as 100, and the average within subgroup range is 5. The upper control limit for the $\bar{X}$ chart is approximately

   A. 101
   B. 97.9
   C. 102.9
   D. 106.4

7. Using an $\bar{X}$ chart with a subgroup size of 5, the overall process mean is calculated as 100, and the average within subgroup range is 5. The lower control limit for the range chart is approximately

   A. 0
   B. −0.6
   C. 0.6
   D. A range chart is not applicable in this situation

8. If the statistical control limits based on three standard deviations of the process statistic are replaced with those based on two standard deviations:

   A. the control chart is more sensitive to the real demands of the process.
   B. the amount of variation in the process is reduced.
   C. adjustments to the process based on the two sigma limits may increase process variation.
   D. we ensure that customer requirements for consistent product or service is maintained.

9. When an $\bar{X}$ chart is used to control a process using a sample size of 12:

   A. the sigma chart should be used to estimate the process variation.
   B. the range chart should be used to estimate the process variation.
   C. either the range or sigma chart may be used to estimate the process variation.
   D. None of the above.

10. An invoicing process generates only 10–15 orders per month. In establishing the statistical control of the invoice process:

   A. use a subgroup size of 1.
   B. use a subgroup size of 5, which is generally the best size.
   C. use a subgroup size of 10.
   D. use a subgroup size of 15.

chapter 6

Charts for Individuals Data

Individuals data refers to variables data with a rational subgroup size of 1. There are several charts useful for individuals data, including the individual x chart, the moving average chart and the exponentially weighted moving average (EWMA) chart.

CHAPTER OBJECTIVES

After completing this chapter, you will be able to

- Differentiate between the various charts useful for individuals ($n = 1$) data
- Apply and interpret the moving average and EWMA charts
- Apply and interpret the individual x chart when the process distribution can be established

Description and Use

These charts are used when measurements cannot be grouped into rational subgroups larger than one observation or when it's more convenient to monitor actual observations rather than subgroup averages. Each subgroup, consisting of a single observation, represents a "snapshot" of the process at a given point in time. The charts' x-axes are time-based, so the charts show a history of the process. The data must be time-ordered (entered in the sequence from which the process generated the data). If this is not the case, then trends or shifts in the process may not be detected instead attributed to random (common cause) variation.

Moving Average Charts

The moving average chart monitors the process location over time, based on the average of the current subgroup and one or more prior subgroups. It is used in conjunction with a moving range chart to monitor the process variation over time.

The plotted points for a moving average chart, called a cell, include the current subgroup and one or more prior subgroups. Table 6.1 provides data collected from an accounting process, as well as the moving average based on a cell size of 3, calculated as follows:

The moving average of each cell is calculated as the average of the current subgroup and the $w - 1$ prior subgroups, where w is the cell size (the number of subgroups included in each plotted moving average):

$$\bar{x} = \frac{1}{w} \sum_{k=1}^{w} x_k$$

For example, the moving average for the third subgroup is calculated as:

$$x \text{ bar}_1 = (6.7 + 13.9 + 7.6)/3 = 9.4$$

The moving average for the first subgroup is simply the first observation; the moving average for the second subgroup is the average of the first two subgroups.

The moving range of cells $j > 1$ is also provided in the table, calculated as follows:

$$R_j = x_j - x_{j-1}$$

TABLE 6.1 Data observations and calculated values for plotting.

Subgroup	Cycle Time	Moving Range	Moving Average ($w = 3$)	EWMA ($\lambda = 0.4$)
1	6.7	—	6.7	7.41
2	13.9	7.2	10.3	10.01
3	7.6	6.3	9.4	9.05
4	2.2	5.4	7.9	6.31
5	10.2	8	6.67	7.87
6	5.8	4.4	6.07	7.04
7	19	13.2	11.67	11.82
8	3.7	15.3	9.50	8.57
9	11.2	7.5	11.30	9.62
10	17.7	6.5	10.87	12.85
11	13.4	4.3	14.10	13.07
12	15.2	1.8	15.43	13.92
13	17.6	2.4	15.40	15.39
14	7.4	10.2	13.40	12.19
15	6.7	0.7	10.57	9.99
16	8	1.3	7.37	9.19
17	10.3	2.3	8.33	9.63
18	12.4	2.1	10.23	10.74
19	8.3	4.1	10.33	9.76
20	8.8	0.5	9.83	9.38
21	4.3	4.5	7.13	7.35
22	4.1	0.2	5.73	6.05
23	9.7	5.6	6.03	7.51
24	4.8	4.9	6.20	6.43
25	13.8	9	9.43	9.38
26	6.6	7.2	8.40	8.27
27	1	5.6	7.13	5.36
28	6.1	5.1	4.57	5.66
29	19.2	13.1	8.77	11.08
30	3	16.2	9.43	7.85
31	14.3	11.3	12.17	10.43
32	10.3	4	9.20	10.38

(Continued)

Subgroup	Cycle Time	Moving Range	Moving Average ($w = 3$)	EWMA ($\lambda = 0.4$)
33	4.4	5.9	9.67	7.99
34	0.5	3.9	5.07	4.99
35	10.2	9.7	5.03	7.07
36	4.8	5.4	5.17	6.16
37	5.1	0.3	6.70	5.74
38	12.8	7.7	7.57	8.56
39	8.4	4.4	8.77	8.5
40	12	3.6	11.07	9.9
41	14.9	2.9	11.77	11.9
42	11.9	3	12.93	11.9
43	7.3	4.6	11.37	10.06
44	3.8	3.5	7.67	7.56
45	6.5	2.7	5.87	7.14
46	7.1	0.6	5.80	7.12
47	3.3	3.8	5.63	5.59
48	17.1	13.8	9.17	10.19
49	19.4	2.3	13.27	13.87
50	1.5	17.9	12.67	8.92
51	10	8.5	10.30	9.35
52	7	3	6.17	8.41
53	7.2	0.2	8.07	7.93
54	3.5	3.7	5.90	6.16
55	5.8	2.3	5.50	6.02
56	2.2	3.6	3.83	4.49
57	10.1	7.9	6.03	6.73
58	10.2	0.1	7.50	8.12
59	2.2	8	7.50	5.75
60	3.3	1.1	5.23	4.77
61	13.4	10.1	6.30	8.22
62	6.2	7.2	7.63	7.41
63	15.6	9.4	11.73	10.69
64	3.1	12.5	8.30	7.65

TABLE 6.1 Data observations and calculated values for plotting. (*Continued*)

(*Continued*)

TABLE 6.1 Data observations and calculated values for plotting. (*Continued*)

Subgroup	Cycle Time	Moving Range	Moving Average ($w = 3$)	EWMA ($\lambda = 0.4$)
65	5.1	2	7.93	6.63
66	15.2	10.1	7.80	10.06
67	0.4	14.8	6.90	6.2
68	2.8	2.4	6.13	4.84
69	12.2	9.4	5.13	7.78
70	13	0.8	9.33	9.87
71	2.9	10.1	9.37	7.08
72	8.2	5.3	8.03	7.53
73	13.4	5.2	8.17	9.88
74	2.9	10.5	8.17	7.09
75	10.4	7.5	8.90	8.41
76	10.2	0.2	7.83	9.13
77	1.3	8.9	7.30	6
78	1.7	0.4	4.40	4.28
79	3	1.3	2.00	3.77
80	2.7	0.3	2.47	3.34
81	7.3	4.6	4.33	4.92
82	3	4.3	4.33	4.15
83	4.5	1.5	4.93	4.29
84	2.9	1.6	3.47	3.73
85	9.8	6.9	5.73	6.16
86	17.9	8.1	10.20	10.86
87	6	11.9	11.23	8.92
88	5.4	0.6	9.77	7.51
89	3.2	2.2	4.87	5.79
90	7.7	4.5	5.43	6.55
91	7.9	0.2	6.27	7.09
92	0.7	7.2	5.43	4.53
93	4	3.3	4.20	4.32
94	15.1	11.1	6.60	8.63
95	8.1	7	9.07	8.42
96	10.5	2.4	11.23	9.25

(*Continued*)

TABLE 6.1 Data observations and calculated values for plotting. (*Continued*)

Subgroup	Cycle Time	Moving Range	Moving Average ($w = 3$)	EWMA ($\lambda = 0.4$)
97	6.7	3.8	8.43	8.23
98	11.6	4.9	9.60	9.58
99	5.9	5.7	8.07	8.11
100	6	0.1	7.83	7.27
101	8.4	2.4	6.77	7.72
102	2.9	5.5	5.77	5.79
103	18.8	15.9	10.03	10.99
104	3.3	15.5	8.33	7.91
105	4.7	1.4	8.93	6.63
106	11.3	6.6	6.43	8.5
107	8.8	2.5	8.27	8.62
108	13.9	5.1	11.33	10.73
109	8.2	5.7	10.30	9.72
110	1.2	7	7.77	6.31
111	3.3	2.1	4.23	5.11
112	2.9	0.4	2.47	4.23
113	16.6	13.7	7.60	9.18
114	6.3	10.3	8.60	8.03
115	1.1	5.2	8.00	5.26
116	8.6	7.5	5.33	6.6
117	2.2	6.4	3.97	4.84
118	16.3	14.1	9.03	9.42
119	0.9	15.4	6.47	6.01
120	5.7	4.8	7.63	5.89
121	9	3.3	5.20	7.13
122	2.6	6.4	5.77	5.32
123	12.4	9.8	8.00	8.15
124	2.3	10.1	5.77	5.81
125	2.2	0.1	5.63	4.37
126	3.9	1.7	2.80	4.18
127	16.9	13	7.67	9.27

(*Continued*)

	TABLE 6.1	Data observations and calculated values for plotting. (*Continued*)		
Subgroup	Cycle Time	Moving Range	Moving Average ($w = 3$)	EWMA ($\lambda = 0.4$)
128	16.3	0.6	12.37	12.08
129	1.5	14.8	11.57	7.85
130	11.7	10.2	9.83	9.39
131	14.5	2.8	9.23	11.43
132	11	3.5	12.40	11.26
133	1.3	9.7	8.93	7.28
134	0.7	0.6	4.33	4.65
135	5.7	5	2.57	5.07
136	9.6	3.9	5.33	6.88
137	2.5	7.1	5.93	5.13
138	11.3	8.8	7.80	7.6
139	10	1.3	7.93	8.56
140	9.3	0.7	10.20	8.86
141	4.7	4.6	8.00	7.2
142	10.7	6	8.23	8.6
143	10.4	0.3	8.60	9.32
144	10.5	0.1	10.53	9.79
145	2.7	7.8	7.87	6.95
146	9	6.3	7.40	7.77
Average	**7.89**	**5.73**		

For example, the first plotted moving range is the moving range for the second subgroup, calculated as the range between the second group and the first group:

$$R_1 = 13.9 - 6.7 = 7.2$$

The last line of the table provides the overall average $(\overline{\overline{X}})$ and the average range $(\overline{R})$, calculated as:

$$\overline{\overline{x}} = \frac{1}{m} \sum_{j=1}^{m} x_j \qquad \overline{R} = \frac{1}{m} \sum_{j=1}^{m} R_j$$

where m is the total number of subgroups included in the analysis.

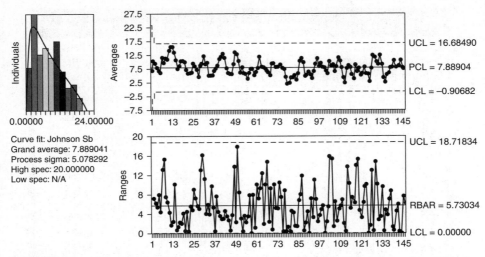

FIGURE 6.1 · Example moving average/moving range chart based on cycle time data from Table 6.1.

The cell data is plotted on the moving average and moving range charts as shown in Figure 6.1. The top chart in Figure 6.1 is the moving average chart, which plots each of the cell averages shown in the column labeled "Moving Average ($w = 3$)" in Table 6.1. The bottom chart is the moving range chart, which plots each of the cell ranges from the "Moving Range" column in Table 6.1.

The control limits for both the moving average and moving range charts are based on the short-term variation. The moving range statistic $\overline{R}$ (calculation shown above) estimates this short-term variation.

The upper control limit (UCL) and lower control limit (LCL) are shown for both the moving average and moving range charts in Figure 6.1. The control limits for the moving average chart are calculated as:

Control limits:

$$\text{UCL}_{MA} = \overline{\overline{x}} + 3\left(\frac{\sigma_x}{\sqrt{w}}\right)$$

$$\text{LCL}_{MA} = \overline{\overline{x}} - 3\left(\frac{\sigma_x}{\sqrt{w}}\right)$$

$\overline{\overline{X}}$ is the grand average and σ_x is process sigma, which is calculated using the average moving range as $\overline{R}/d_2$, where the d_2 value of 1.128 is obtained from Appendix for a range calculated based on two observations ($n = 2$).

For example, to calculate the moving average control limits:

$$\sigma_x = \overline{R}/d_2 = 5.73/1.128 = 5.078$$

$$UCL_{MA} = \overline{\overline{x}} + 3\left(\frac{\sigma_x}{\sqrt{w}}\right) = 7.889 + 3\left(\frac{5.078}{\sqrt{3}}\right) = 16.68$$

$$LCL_{MA} = \overline{\overline{x}} - 3\left(\frac{\sigma_x}{\sqrt{w}}\right) = 7.889 + 3\left(\frac{5.078}{\sqrt{3}}\right) = -0.91$$

The control limits for the first $w - 1$ cells are adjusted to reflect the incomplete cell.

The control limits for the range chart are calculated as:

$$UCL_R = \overline{R} + 3d_3\sigma_x$$

$$LCL_R = \max(0, \overline{R} - 3d_3\sigma_x)$$

where d_3 is based on $n = 2$ as 0.853 (tabulated in Appendix). For example, to calculate the range chart control limits in Figure 6.1:

$$UCL_R = 5.73 + (3 \times 0.853 \times 5.078) = 18.72$$

$$LCL_R = \max[0, 5.73 + (3 \times 0.853 \times 5.08)] = 0$$

The calculations themselves are only shown here for reference and for understanding of their origins. It is strongly recommended to use software to automatically calculate these values.

The interpretation of the moving average and range charts are nearly the same as the $\overline{X}$ chart previously discussed in Chapter 5. Moving average charts detect small shifts in the process mean (shifts of 0.5 sigma to 2 sigma) much faster than individual x or $\overline{X}$ charts with the same sample size. They can, however, be slower in detecting large shifts in the process mean. In addition, typical run test rules cannot be used because of the inherent dependence of data points. This dependence is based on the simple fact that each subgroup contains data that is also plotted in the $w - 1$ previous subgroups, where w is the cell width. For example, when $w = 3$, any given plotted moving average includes the current group and the two prior observations. The prior plotted group includes those two same observations (as well as an earlier observation).

Moving average charts are preferred when the subgroups are of size $n = 1$. Since each plotted point includes several observations, the central limit theorem is used to assert that the average of the observations (or the moving average, in this case) is normally distributed. This allows use of the normal distribution to conveniently define the moving average control limits. This works well for a vast majority of cases; however, when a process is extremely non-normal, the moving range statistic can improperly indicate special causes of variation that do not exist. When extreme non-normality is suspected, use an $\overline{X}$ chart (a subgroup size of 5 usually works well) to group the data for the purpose of analysis.

Consider the moving average chart shown in Figure 6.2. Note the histogram which suggests an extremely skewed process distribution. The moving average chart (using a cell size of 5) is in control, yet the moving range chart is out of control. An $\overline{X}$ chart using a subgroup size of 5 is shown in Figure 6.3. Note both the $\overline{X}$ and range charts are in statistical control, suggesting that a distribution can now be fit to the data, such as using the individual x chart discussed below.

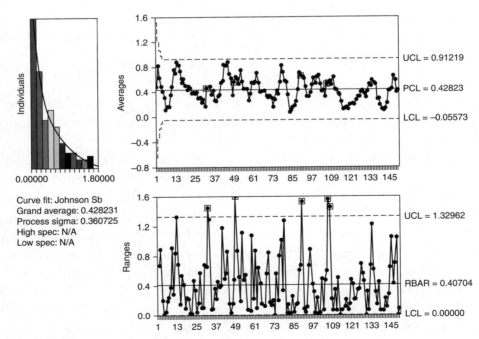

Curve fit: Johnson Sb
Grand average: 0.428231
Process sigma: 0.360725
High spec: N/A
Low spec: N/A

FIGURE 6.2 • Moving average chart of extremely non-normal process data.

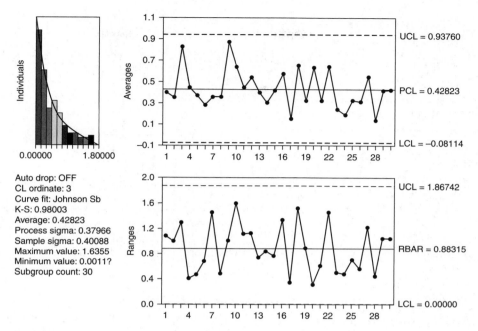

Auto drop: OFF
CL ordinate: 3
Curve fit: Johnson Sb
K-S: 0.98003
Average: 0.42823
Process sigma: 0.37966
Sample sigma: 0.40088
Maximum value: 1.6355
Minimum value: 0.0011?
Subgroup count: 30

FIGURE 6.3 · $\bar{X}$ chart of extremely non-normal process data plotted in Figure 6.2.

Exponentially Weighted Moving Average Charts

An *exponentially weighted moving average* (EWMA) *chart* is a control chart for variables data which plots weighted moving average values. Initially developed for use in financial applications, a weighting factor is chosen which determines the relative impact of older data to more recent data. The moving range chart is used to monitor process variation.

The EWMA chart shares most of the benefits and risks of the moving average chart previously discussed: able to detect small process shifts; slower in detecting large shifts in the process mean; run tests cannot be used; normal distribution can be assumed for calculating the control limits.

EWMA charts are also used to smooth the effect of known, uncontrollable noise in the data such as found in accounting, service, and chemical processes. While day-to-day fluctuations in these processes may be large, they are not indicative of process instability. The choice of the EWMA weighting factor λ can be used to make the chart more or less sensitive to these daily fluctuations.

When choosing the value of λ used for weighting, it is recommended to use small values (such as 0.2) to detect small shifts and larger values (between

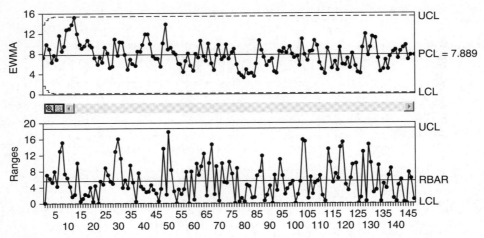

FIGURE 6.4 · Example EWMA/moving range chart based on cycle time data from Table 6.1.

0.2 and 0.4) for larger shifts. An EWMA chart with $\lambda = 1.0$ is an $\overline{X}$ chart (for subgroups larger than 1) or an individual x chart (when subgroup size equals 1).

The cycle time observations of Table 6.1 are plotted on the EWMA and moving range charts as shown in Figure 6.4. The top chart in Figure 6.4 is the EWMA chart, which plots each of the values shown in the column labeled "EWMA ($\lambda = 0.4$)" in Table 6.1. The bottom chart is the moving range chart, which plots each of the cell ranges from the "Moving Range" column in Table 6.1.

Each plotted value of the EWMA is calculated as:

$$z_t = \lambda x_t + (1 - \lambda)z_{t-1}$$

where λ is the value of the weighting factor, x_t is the observation for the current subgroup at time t, and the value of z at time zero (z_0) is either a target value or the overall average of the selected subgroups. The typical choice of z_0 as the overall average is most representative of the control chart use for establishing process stability, as discussed in Chapter 2.

For example, the EWMA statistic for the first two subgroups using a weighting factor $\lambda = 0.4$ is calculated as:

$$Z_1 = (0.4 \times 6.7) + (0.6 \times 7.889) = 7.41$$

$$Z_2 = (0.4 \times 13.9) + (0.6 \times 7.41) = 10.01$$

The control limits at time, t, for subgroups of size $n = 1$ are calculated as:

$$UCL_t = z_0 + (3\sigma_x)\sqrt{\frac{\lambda[1 - (1 - \lambda)^{2t}]}{(2 - \lambda)}}$$

$$LCL_t = z_0 - (3\sigma_x)\sqrt{\frac{\lambda[1 - (1 - \lambda)^{2t}]}{(2 - \lambda)}}$$

where z_0 is the starting value (either the target value or process mean value), t is the subgroups number ($t = 1$ for first subgroup; $t = 2$ for second subgroup,…) and σ_x is process sigma. Process sigma is calculated using the average moving range $(\overline{R}/d_2)$, where the d_2 value of 1.128 is obtained from Appendix for a range calculated based on two observations ($n = 2$).

For example the upper control limits for the first two subgroups using a weighting factor $\lambda = 0.4$ are calculated using the process sigma value of 5.078 obtained from the moving range chart in the previously discussed moving average example:

$$UCL_{t=1} = 7.889 + (3 \times 5.078)\sqrt{\frac{0.4 \times [1 - (1 - 0.4)^2]}{(2 - 0.4)}} = 13.98$$

$$UCL_{t=2} = 7.889 + (3 \times 5.078)\sqrt{\frac{0.4 \times [1 - (1 - 0.4)^4]}{(2 - 0.4)}} = 15.00$$

As t becomes larger, the term $[1 - (1 - \lambda)^{2t}]$ diminishes and the control limits stabilize to the level defined by:

$$UCL = 7.889 + (3 \times 5.078)\sqrt{\frac{0.4}{(2 - 0.4)}} = 15.51$$

$$LCL = 7.889 - (3 \times 5.078)\sqrt{\frac{0.4}{(2 - 0.4)}} = 0.27$$

The EWMA chart in this example produces similar results to the moving average chart previously discussed. In both cases, process control is evident, permitting capability analysis. The first step in capability analysis (after the prerequisite process control is established) is to determine an appropriate statistical distribution for the process data.

Process Capability and Distributional Assessment

The observational cycle time data of Table 6.1 is shown in the histogram of Figure 6.5 and the normal probability plot of Figure 6.6. Note that all of the data in Figure 6.5 are greater than zero, so there is a sharp demarcation at the zero point representing a bound.

The statistics provided with the histogram of Figure 6.5 indicate a K-S value of approximately 0.95 for a non-normal curve fit based on the Johnson transformation (see Chapter 3 for further discussion of the curve-fitting technique). In this case, the curve fit was improved in the SPC software by specifying a lower bound of zero, reflective of the physical bound of the cycle time metric. Note the normal probability plot of Figure 6.6 provides a K-S value of approximately 0.33. While the normal distribution K-S value is well above the critical p-value of 0.05, it is much less than the K-S associated with the non-normal fitted curve. Furthermore, note the dipping of the data below the fitted normal distribution line on the left side (small probabilities) and above the line on the

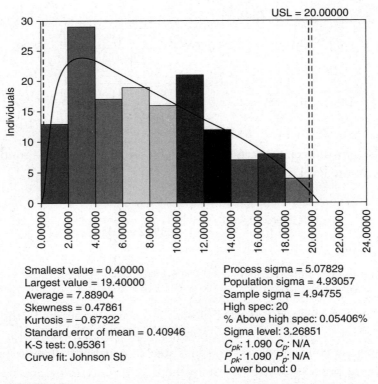

Smallest value = 0.40000
Largest value = 19.40000
Average = 7.88904
Skewness = 0.47861
Kurtosis = −0.67322
Standard error of mean = 0.40946
K-S test: 0.95361
Curve fit: Johnson Sb

Process sigma = 5.07829
Population sigma = 4.93057
Sample sigma = 4.94755
High spec: 20
% Above high spec: 0.05406%
Sigma level: 3.26851
C_{pk}: 1.090 C_p: N/A
P_{pk}: 1.090 P_p: N/A
Lower bound: 0

FIGURE 6.5 · Example histogram based on cycle time data from Table 6.1.

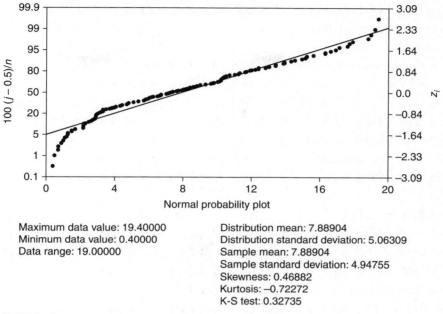

Maximum data value: 19.40000   Distribution mean: 7.88904
Minimum data value: 0.40000   Distribution standard deviation: 5.06309
Data range: 19.00000   Sample mean: 7.88904
                                      Sample standard deviation: 4.94755
                                      Skewness: 0.46882
                                      Kurtosis: −0.72272
                                      K-S test: 0.32735

FIGURE 6.6 · Example probability plot based on cycle time data from Table 6.1.

right side (high probabilities), indicative of a lack of fit to the data in the tails. Finally, an individual x plot of the data assuming normality (shown in the next section) provides a lower control limit of −7.35, far away from the smallest possible value of 0 for the cycle time process.

Individual x Charts

The individual x chart monitors the process location over time based on a subgroup containing a single observation. The moving range chart is used to monitor the variation between consecutive subgroups over time.

If rational subgroups can be formed, $\overline{X}$ charts are preferred because the control limits are easily calculated using the normal distribution. When rational subgroups of size $n > 1$ cannot be formed, then assumptions about the distribution of the process are needed to calculate the statistical control limits on an individual x chart, particularly when the process distribution is very skewed or bounded.

Individual x charts are efficient at detecting relatively moderate to large shifts in the process average, typically shifts of 2.5σ to 3σ or larger, as shown previously in Table 2.2. If $\overline{X}$ charts can be used, their larger subgroups will detect smaller shifts much quicker. Moving average and EWMA charts also can be used at any subgroup size to increase the sensitivity to smaller process shifts.

An important consideration for the individual x chart is the choice of curve fit used for determining the control limits. There is a fundamental dilemma, in that a distribution should not be fit to the data unless the data is from a controlled process, yet the process distribution must be assumed to determine the control limits. Because of this limitation, use of the $\overline{X}$ chart, moving average, or EWMA chart is needed to first establish process control, after which a distribution can be fit to the data and applied to the individual x chart.

Chart Construction

One of the most attractive features of the individuals chart is that the plotted statistic is the data observation: no calculation required! This makes the chart fundamentally appealing for use by data entry personnel that may not be well-versed in statistics, or may be uncomfortable with calculations. In these cases, the data entry persons are told to simply plot the data, and react when the plotted value exceeds a control limit. This is entirely appropriate only after process control has been verified, and the process distribution and corresponding control limits established.

The centerline of the individual x chart is the median of the fitted distribution, which corresponds to the calculated average for normal distributions. The control limits when normality is assumed are calculated as:

$$UCL_x = \overline{X} + 3\sigma_x$$
$$LCL_x = \overline{X} - 3\sigma_x$$

where $\overline{X}$ is the calculated average and σ_x is the process sigma. Process sigma is calculated as shown above in the moving average section. Note that some authors prefer to write this as:

$$UCL_x = \overline{X} + E_2\,\overline{R}$$
$$LCL_x = \overline{X} - E_2\,\overline{R}$$

The factor E_2 is tabulated in Appendix; $\overline{R}$ is the average moving range.

Research has shown that for processes following the normal distribution, when a special cause is detected on the moving range chart, it also will appear on the individual x chart, thus making the moving range chart redundant.

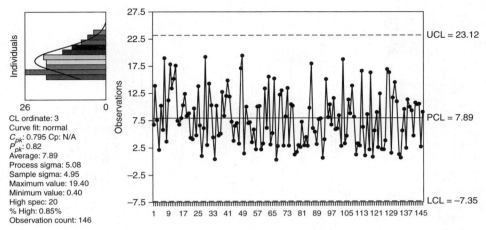

FIGURE 6.7 • Example individual x chart assuming normality of cycle time data in Table 6.1.

For non-normal distributions, the UCL is defined at the 99.865 percentile of the fitted curve, and the LCL is defined at the 0.135 percentile of the fitted curve. These percentiles correspond to the plus and minus three sigma values used in the normal distribution assumption.

An individual x chart with normal distribution limits based on the cycle time data of Table 6.1 is shown in Figure 6.7. As mentioned previously, the lower control limit is predicted as −7.35, which is physically impossible for the metric. As a result, the control chart would never detect improvements to the process as an out of control condition below its LCL. Likewise, the lack of data in the upper tail predicted by the normal distribution (as discussed above for the normal probability plot of the data) would also decrease sensitivity to process shifts in the upward direction.

An individual x chart with non-normal distribution limits based on the cycle time data of Table 6.1 is shown in Figure 6.8. Process control is evident, as shown earlier with the moving average and EWMA charts of the data. The individual x chart conveniently shows the expected range of the process between 0.23 and 19.78. If the process has an upper specification limit of 20, with no lower specification limit (as is often the case with bounded process metrics such as cycle time), its capability is estimated by the C_{pk} index as 1.09, corresponding to approximately 0.05% out of specification. Although there are no observations in the sample beyond the specifications, the capability index predicts, based on the assumed distribution, the longer-term potential of the process for meeting the requirements.

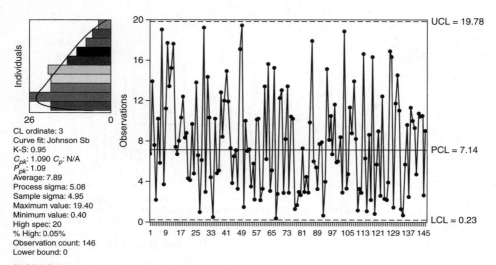

CL ordinate: 3
Curve fit: Johnson Sb
K-S: 0.95
C_{pk}: 1.090 C_p: N/A
P_{pk}: 1.09
Average: 7.89
Process sigma: 5.08
Sample sigma: 4.95
Maximum value: 19.40
Minimum value: 0.40
High spec: 20
% High: 0.05%
Observation count: 146
Lower bound: 0

FIGURE 6.8 • Example individual x chart of cycle time data from Table 6.1 based on fitted non-normal distribution.

Note that while specification limits do not apply to the plotted values on the X-bar chart, they are directly pertinent to the plotted values on the individuals chart. Nonetheless, their use on an individuals chart is generally discouraged to avoid reaction to plotted values approaching or exceeding a specification limit. Recall the hazards associated with responding to out of specification by adjustment: This *tampering* will increase the overall variation in the process. This is certainly a difficult concept for some to accept, but as Yoda might say: "Accepted it must be." If the analyst is concerned that customers not receive out of specification product or service, the process must be improved to reduce its variation. Until that improvement is achieved, only 100% sampling of the process will ensure product is acceptable. Process adjustments based on violations of specs will only increase variation (see Chapters 1 and 3 for further discussion).

Run test rules can also be applied to non-normal distribution. When non-normal distributions are used for individual x charts, the *average* is replaced with the *median*, and zones are defined to provide the same probabilities as the normal curve at the stated sigma level. For example, run test 1 is interpreted as any point in the 0.135% tails on either side of the median. This ensures that 99.73% of the fitted distribution is maintained within the control limits, just as in a normal distribution, even though this would probably not be plus minus three sigma for a non-normal distribution.

Still Struggling

When a process distribution is highly skewed, the classic control limits defined at ±3 standard deviations will not provide a reasonable model for the individuals data. While the individual x chart can be constructed using control limits defined at either the ±3 standard deviations or at levels specific to a fitted non-normal distribution, only a process that is stable (i.e., in a state of statistical control) can be modeled by a single distribution. Therefore, the use of the individual x chart is limited to those processes that are either reasonably assumed to be adequately modeled by a normal distribution, or shown to be in control using a different control chart. The EWMA and moving average charts discussed earlier are useful for evaluating the process for statistical control, as is the classic Shewhart $\bar{X}$/range chart discussed in Chapter 5. When using these charts, the plotted values (averages, moving averages, or exponentially weighted moving averages) are well-modeled by the normal distribution, regardless of the actual distribution of the process observations, based on the central limit theorem. Once the process is determined to be in control, the process observations can then be modeled by a non-normal distribution, and control limits established to provide the comparable protection associated with the normal distribution's ±3 standard deviations.

Example x Chart Application in Asthma Care

An interesting application of an individual x chart is provided by Dr. Peter Boggs, MD (Boggs, 1999, 1998, 1996). Dr. Boggs became familiar with control charts some years ago, and wondered if they would provide usefulness beyond detection of the condition, to prevent its occurrence.

An example is shown in Figure 6.9, which plots a given patient's morning measurement of forced expiratory volume (FEV: the volume of air exhaled within a given time span) on an individual x chart. The patient's data was previously determined to be approximated well by a normal distribution. Prior data, also analyzed on a control chart for individuals, established so-called *personal best* for the parameter, which removes some of the subjectivity of the analysis and improves sensitivity to departures from the patient's past behavior.

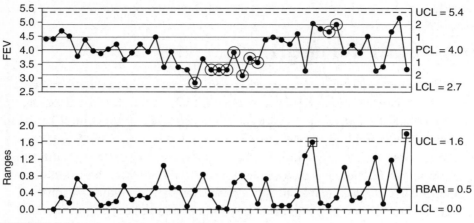

FIGURE 6.9 · Morning FEV measurements for an asthma patient.

The control chart in Figure 6.9 shows a special cause detected as a violation of run test 6 (4 out of 5 groups beyond one sigma), indicating a decrease in lung capacity for the patient. The FEV chart is monitored in conjunction with an individual x plot of the peak expiratory flow rate (PEFR: a measure of the maximum airflow rate during exhalation) from the same date and time. Referring to Figure 6.10, a relative increase in range is suggested toward the middle of the range chart, finally culminating in a *near miss* (i.e., critical care) experience for the patient evidenced by the out of control group.

The charts demonstrate the power of the control chart in analyzing critical parameters for the process of living. Dr. Boggs has similarly applied control charts showing the impact of medication changes on a patient's asthma function,

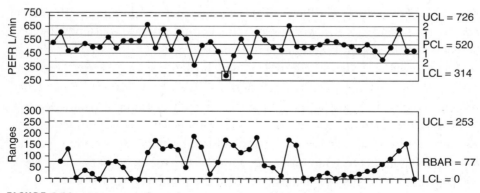

FIGURE 6.10 · PEFR control chart for asthma patient monitored in Figure 6.9.

as well as charts that fail to show any real impact from a change in medicine in spite of manufacturer's claims to the contrary.

The analysis provides compelling real world application of SPC to patient care. The time-basis of patient response to special cause behavior cannot be ignored: The biological process is not a population, and should not be treated as such.

In these days of rising health care costs, the risk and expense associated with managing increasingly prevalent diseases such as diabetes, obesity, high blood pressure, arthritis, and so on, can simply not be ignored. In the right hands, SPC could provide that critical view to predict and manage care and its subsequent cost in a timely and efficient manner.

Summary

Individuals data is perhaps the most prevalent data available to the process analyst. Since the central limit theorem cannot be used to assume a normal distribution of plotted individual values, plotted statistics such as the moving average and EWMA provide a valuable means of assessing the statistical control of the process. Once control is established, a statistical distribution may be fit to the data for use in capability assessments or for ease of plotting on an individual x chart.

QUIZ

1. **When an observation is observed beyond the three sigma limits on the individual x chart:**
   A. wait to see if more observations go beyond the limits, since there is a chance that subgroups will be out of control when the process has not shifted.
   B. respond immediately, since the chance of an out of control point is very small unless the process has shifted.
   C. verify if the point also fails run test rules before responding.
   D. only respond if the characteristic is critical to the customer.

2. **When a process is extremely non-normal:**
   A. an individual x chart with three sigma limits may predict control limits that don't match the process.
   B. an EWMA or moving average chart may be useful, since the plotted points assume normality.
   C. understand why the process is so distributed.
   D. All of the above.

3. **An individual x chart with limits at plus and minus 3 standard deviations:**
   A. uses the moving range statistic to estimate short-term process variation.
   B. is useful unless the process distribution is very non-normal.
   C. plots the individual values instead of subgroup averages.
   D. All of the above.

4. **An advantage of using control charts for individuals data is:**
   A. there is less data to collect.
   B. the control limits can be directly compared to the specifications.
   C. it costs less than larger subgroup sizes.
   D. All of the above.

5. **A process shows statistical control using an individual x chart. Assuming the implementation cost of a different chart is negligible, but the cost of sampling is significant, the most economical method for increasing the sensitivity of the chart to small process shifts is:**
   A. increase the subgroup size.
   B. use an EWMA or moving average chart.
   C. use the X-bar/range chart.
   D. All of the above.

6. **The EWMA statistic:**
   A. has historical use in financial applications.
   B. is useful in chemical processes where the data is dependent.
   C. is used for autocorrelated processes.
   D. All of the above.

7. **To analyze data for statistical control on an individual x chart:**
   A. use the normal distribution in all cases.
   B. use a non-normal distribution in all cases.
   C. analyze the data first on a moving average or EWMA chart, verify the process is in control, then fit a distribution to the data for use on the individual x chart.
   D. each of the above strategies works equally well.

8. **The Western Electric run test rules:**
   A. do not apply to individual x charts.
   B. do not apply to moving average charts.
   C. apply to short run processes only.
   D. must be modified for specific processes to ensure they are relevant.

9. **Rational subgroups of size $n = 1$ are often necessary because of:**
   A. autocorrelation in the process data.
   B. processes that don't generate data very often.
   C. multiple stream processes.
   D. All of the above.

10. **A set of individuals data is obtained from a process. The data is plotted on the histogram with a K-S value of .75 calculated for a normal distribution. An individual x chart of this data should:**
    A. confirm the normal distribution provides a good curve fit.
    B. provide good ability to detect shifts in the process.
    C. not be used until the process is first verified in control by a moving average, EWMA, or X-bar chart.
    D. use a non-normal curve fit since they tend to be more robust.

chapter 7

Process Improvement

While control charts provide a critical role in differentiating between common and special causes of variation, additional tools are often required to determine sources of common and special causes so that process improvement is achieved.

CHAPTER OBJECTIVES

After completing this chapter, you will be able to

- Apply various tools for stratifying data to look for process factors contributing to variation

- Use scatter diagrams, ANOVA, and residuals analysis to quantify the significance of process factors on a process metric

- Understand the need for designed experiments to collect and analyze meaningful data for process improvement

Overview

The control charts discussed thus far are the necessary first step toward process improvement: They provide differentiation between common cause variation built into the process and special cause variation associated with internal or external changes to the process. A failure to distinguish between these types of variation leads to tampering (reacting to common cause variation as if it were due to special causes), which increases process variation, as discussed in Chapter 1.

The occurrence of special cause variation, evidenced by out of control or run test violations, provides indication that the process location or variation has changed, depending on the chart. The special cause provides two critical pieces of information: The process location (or variation) has changed, and the time frame the change was detected. As shown in Figure 1.9 and Table 2.2, process shifts are not necessarily detected as soon as they occur, depending on the type of chart, its sample size and frequency, and the size of the shift. Therefore, the control chart's indication of the timing of the process shift may be delayed from when the process shift actually began. This is an important consideration when brainstorming potential causes of the shift.

Sometimes, rigorous brainstorming of the possible root cause of a process shift can lead to identification of the source. The outcome, or effect, is often stated in terms of the problem experienced to aid the brainstorming. It is convenient at times to categorize the potential causes using the 5 Ms and E or 4 Ps to ensure that all areas are considered:

- *5 Ms & E*: Manpower, Machines, Methods, Material, Measurement, and Environment
- *4 Ps*: Policy, Procedures, Plant, and People

The results of the brainstorming can be graphically shown on a cause & effect diagram. While the classic form of a cause & effect diagram is a fishbone, any hierarchal structure that allows for categorizations may be used, such as shown in Figure 7.1. The cause & effect diagram provides the *potential causes*; at this point this is little data to support whether any of the causes actually contributed to the problem. As in all brainstorming activities, judgment of the merits of any particular cause should be reserved until further data can be collected to confirm its relevance.

Brainstorming should include the key process stakeholders, including those that operate the process on a daily basis, process experts or support personnel, and perhaps even those who supply product or operate processes that feed into

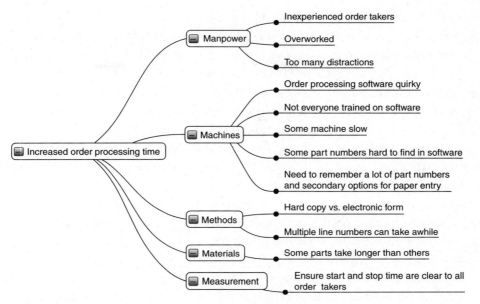

FIGURE 7.1 • Example cause & effect diagram using *Green Belt XL* software.

the process under investigation. Subtle changes to processes or their feeder processes, seemingly benign to those responsible, are sometimes the culprit.

Obviously, most internal or external supplies would not knowingly make changes that would certainly impact their customers. Similarly, process personnel would not engage in manipulating the process unless they felt the change insignificant (or on the contrary significant and beneficial) to the end result. It is thus paramount to engage internal and external suppliers and process personnel in a positive manner, without fear of retribution. Engaging these personnel is a critical first step toward building buy-in, which precedes any meaningful contribution toward process improvement.

In simple cases, the source of the special cause can be quickly identified and addressed: a procedure not followed; a worker untrained in a particular aspect of the process; inconsistent material from a supplier; a sudden change in environmental conditions. Other times, the source of the special cause variation requires further investigation, as is often the case when trying to identify significant sources of common cause variation.

Common cause variation, by its very nature, consists of the combined effect of many factors influencing the process. The combined effect on the process is what is common (as in *common cause variation*) to all affected subgroups, even though the factors that are significant in producing the effect may themselves vary in some predictable fashion. Understanding the relationship between a significant factor's variation and the effect of that variation on the process is necessary to reduce common cause variation. This in itself is not a trivial analysis, yet is further complicated when a factor's effect is influenced by the relative presence of other factors. Some occurrences of special cause variation are also manifested in this way: for example, if a supplier's inconsistency is only a significant issue when the process is run at a higher throughput.

As a result, the process changes necessary to reduce these forms of special cause variation and almost all forms of common cause variation are themselves significant. As such, they demand sufficient management buy-in to allocate necessary resources and encourage cross-functional participation. A proper Six Sigma project, sponsored by management and executed by a cross-functional team of stakeholders led by a Black Belt trained in statistical problem solving, is perfectly suited to address these issues (Keller, 2011).

An overview of the techniques used to understand the sources of variation follows. A detailed discussion of the quantification of error attributable to measurement systems is found in Chapter 8.

Stratification

Once a list of potential sources of variation has been assembled, in some cases they can be used as data classifications to break-down existing data to better understand the process dynamics. Recall how the variation in support satisfaction observed in the u chart of Figure 2.3 was broken down by the type of support. In this case, a Pareto diagram was used to sum the count of inquiries related to each type of call.

This rather simple analysis provided the impetus for separate control charts for each type of support, which in turn revealed special cause variation attributable to just one type of call (new product features). The result of addressing this special cause was a change to the process flow and personnel training, which retargeted the process at an improved level of performance, and decreased the overall common cause variation.

Similarly, the plotted points on an individuals chart might be stratified by any number of variables to look for patterns. Figure 7.2 shows the control chart of order processing time (previously analyzed using a moving averages chart in Figure 6.1) stratified by product. In this case, a Pareto diagram would quantify the number of observations associated with each product, as shown in Figure 7.3. The Pareto diagram might be useful for determining the impact of a process

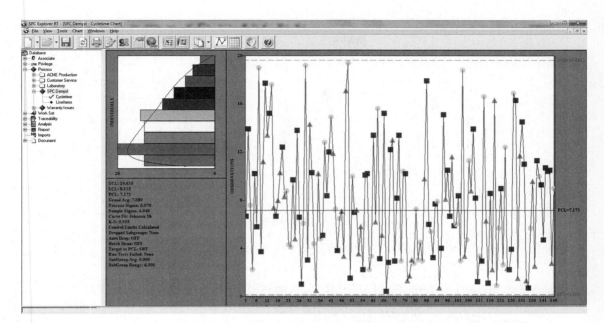

FIGURE 7.2 · Individual x control chart stratified by product (using Quality America's *SPC-PC IV Explorer* software).

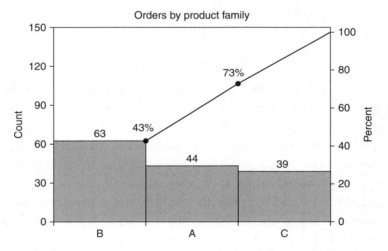

FIGURE 7.3 · Pareto chart of number of observations for each product.

change on the various products, such as for estimating the financial impact of the change.

A box-whisker chart, such as shown in Figure 7.4, can be used to show the relative amount of variation associated with each product. A box-whisker chart is a simple tool for comparing data sets, where each data set may be associated

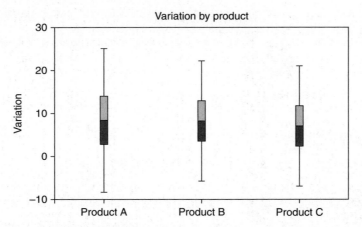

FIGURE 7.4 · Box-whisker chart of data by product.

with a unique characteristic, condition, or other useful category. Each box (for each product in Figure 7.4) contains the first through third quartile of the data (i.e., the 25th through 75th percentile of the data). The *whiskers* protrude from each box, representing the expected variation of each category based on its first (Q1) and third (Q3) quartile:

$$\text{Lower limit} = Q1 - 1.5 \times (Q3 - Q1)$$
$$\text{Upper limit} = Q3 + 1.5 \times (Q3 - Q1)$$

Quartiles are often used in the box-whisker chart because they are nonparametric (not dependent on the distribution of the data). If normality can be assumed, the box-whisker plot may use the mean and standard deviation of the data to define the box and whisker lengths: the edges of the box defined at ±1 sample standard deviations with the whiskers extending to ±3 sample standard deviations. Extreme values also may be shown, usually as dots beyond the whiskers.

In Figure 7.4, Product C has slightly less variation than Product A or B, but the general properties of the three products are similar. There doesn't seem to be too much difference between each product's order processing time, as indicated by this analysis. A similar result was obtained when analyzing the order processing time by person in a box-whisker chart.

While stratification offers a simple graphical means of identifying potential categorizations of data that may lead to identification of underlying sources of variation, they are by no means conclusive. The regression techniques discussed in the next section provide a start toward quantifying the variation in a process metric associated with various sources.

Regression Analysis

Regression analysis is used to model how a response (termed a dependent variable) will change as one or more process factors (termed independent variables) are manipulated. When a factor is correlated with a response, then the response changes as the factor's level or setting is changed. For example, the cooking time (a response) is affected as the dial on the burner (a process factor) is manipulated: The cooking time is correlated with the burner's dial setting.

Although the presence of correlation may indicate a cause and effect relationship, this is not always the case. Consider the correlation of shoe size and scores on a math quiz. As shoe size increases from toddler through children then adult sizes, math scores are likely to increase, demonstrating correlation between the shoe size and math score. Yet, this does not mean that an increased shoe size causes the math score to increase, nor that purchasing a larger shoe would improve one's score on the math quiz.

For example, the time required to process an order has been plotted on a control chart. The chart indicates statistical control, and a team of stakeholders is assembled to reduce the time taken to process orders. An initial discussion focuses on the number of items processed on a given order, and it is suspected that orders with more line items take longer than orders with less line items.

Order processing time data is collected for orders containing specified number of items, as shown in Table 7.1. A scatter diagram of the data is shown in Figure 7.5.

The scatter diagram provides a graphical means of determining if there is a linear correlation between the independent variable plotted on the x-axis and the dependent variable plotted on the y-axis. Technically, both variables should be continuous in nature (see Chapter 2). In this example, while the order processing time would certainly satisfy the requirement of continuity, the number of line items (plotted on the x-axis) is a discrete variable, as evidenced by the clustering of the data at each level of line items, and the lack of data along the continuum. When analyzing discrete data, a more rigorous analysis using logistical regression can be performed; however, given the moderate number of levels (14) in the line item data, it is not unreasonable to assume continuity for this relatively crude analysis.

If a linear relationship exists, the plotted data on the scatter diagram should be approximately normally distributed about the fitted line: The closer the data

TABLE 7.1 Order processing time data based on number of line items per order.

Subgroup	Cycle Time	Line Items	Predicted Cycle Time	Residual	Standardized Residual
1	6.7	5	7.301	−0.601	−0.1602
2	13.9	5	7.301	6.599	1.7588
3	7.6	8	10.778	−3.178	−0.8470
4	2.2	5	7.301	−5.101	−1.3596
5	10.2	5	7.301	2.899	0.7727
6	5.8	3	4.983	0.817	0.2178
7	19	14	17.732	1.268	0.3380
8	3.7	2	3.824	−0.124	−0.0330
9	11.2	6	8.46	2.74	0.7303
10	17.7	7	9.619	8.081	2.1538
11	13.4	6	8.46	4.94	1.3166
12	15.2	7	9.619	5.581	1.4875
13	17.6	13	16.573	1.027	0.2737
14	7.4	4	6.142	1.258	0.3353
15	6.7	2	3.824	2.876	0.7665
16	8	5	7.301	0.699	0.1863
17	10.3	5	7.301	2.999	0.7993
18	12.4	7	9.619	2.781	0.7412
19	8.3	5	7.301	0.999	0.2663
20	8.8	9	11.937	−3.137	−0.8361
21	4.3	7	9.619	−5.319	−1.4177
22	4.1	6	8.46	−4.36	−1.1621
23	9.7	3	4.983	4.717	1.2572
24	4.8	5	7.301	−2.501	−0.6666
25	13.8	6	8.46	5.34	1.4233
26	6.6	3	4.983	1.617	0.4310
27	1	2	3.824	−2.824	−0.7527
28	6.1	7	9.619	−3.519	−0.9379
29	19.2	14	17.732	1.468	0.3913
30	3	3	4.983	−1.983	−0.5285
31	14.3	6	8.46	5.84	1.5565
32	10.3	5	7.301	2.999	0.7993
33	4.4	7	9.619	−5.219	−1.3910

(Continued)

TABLE 7.1 Order processing time data based on number of line items per order. (*Continued*)

Subgroup	Cycle Time	Line Items	Predicted Cycle Time	Residual	Standardized Residual
34	0.5	3	4.983	−4.483	−1.1948
35	10.2	5	7.301	2.899	0.7727
36	4.8	7	9.619	−4.819	−1.2844
37	5.1	4	6.142	−1.042	−0.2777
38	12.8	10	13.096	−0.296	−0.0789
39	8.4	4	6.142	2.258	0.6018
40	12	4	6.142	5.858	1.5613
41	14.9	11	14.255	0.645	0.1719
42	11.9	6	8.46	3.44	0.9169
43	7.3	8	10.778	−3.478	−0.9270
44	3.8	3	4.983	−1.183	−0.3153
45	6.5	8	10.778	−4.278	−1.1402
46	7.1	5	7.301	−0.201	−0.0536
47	3.3	3	4.983	−1.683	−0.4486
48	17.1	7	9.619	7.481	1.9939
49	19.4	13	16.573	2.827	0.7535
50	1.5	2	3.824	−2.324	−0.6194
51	10	9	11.937	−1.937	−0.5163
52	7	3	4.983	2.017	0.5376
53	7.2	5	7.301	−0.101	−0.0269
54	3.5	4	6.142	−2.642	−0.7042
55	5.8	4	6.142	−0.342	−0.0912
56	2.2	2	3.824	−1.624	−0.4328
57	10.1	5	7.301	2.799	0.7460
58	10.2	4	6.142	4.058	1.0816
59	2.2	6	8.46	−6.26	−1.6685
60	3.3	6	8.46	−5.16	−1.3753
61	13.4	4	6.142	7.258	1.9345
62	6.2	5	7.301	−1.101	−0.2934
63	15.6	12	15.414	0.186	0.0496
64	3.1	2	3.824	−0.724	−0.1930
65	5.1	5	7.301	−2.201	−0.5866

(*Continued*)

TABLE 7.1 Order processing time data based on number of line items per order. *(Continued)*

Subgroup	Cycle Time	Line Items	Predicted Cycle Time	Residual	Standardized Residual
66	15.2	5	7.301	7.899	2.1053
67	0.4	2	3.824	−3.424	−0.9126
68	2.8	3	4.983	−2.183	−0.5818
69	12.2	6	8.46	3.74	0.9968
70	13	6	8.46	4.54	1.2100
71	2.9	2	3.824	−0.924	−0.2463
72	8.2	4	6.142	2.058	0.5485
73	13.4	6	8.46	4.94	1.3166
74	2.9	6	8.46	−5.56	−1.4819
75	10.4	10	13.096	−2.696	−0.7186
76	10.2	4	6.142	4.058	1.0816
77	1.3	3	4.983	−3.683	−0.9816
78	1.7	4	6.142	−4.442	−1.1839
79	3	4	6.142	−3.142	−0.8374
80	2.7	6	8.46	−5.76	−1.5352
81	7.3	9	11.937	−4.637	−1.2359
82	3	6	8.46	−5.46	−1.4552
83	4.5	7	9.619	−5.119	−1.3644
84	2.9	5	7.301	−4.401	−1.1730
85	9.8	6	8.46	1.34	0.3571
86	17.9	8	10.778	7.122	1.8982
87	6	4	6.142	−0.142	−0.0378
88	5.4	7	9.619	−4.219	−1.1245
89	3.2	3	4.983	−1.783	−0.4752
90	7.7	4	6.142	1.558	0.4152
91	7.9	9	11.937	−4.037	−1.0760
92	0.7	3	4.983	−4.283	−1.1415
93	4	2	3.824	0.176	0.0469
94	15.1	5	7.301	7.799	2.0786
95	8.1	5	7.301	0.799	0.2130
96	10.5	4	6.142	4.358	1.1615
97	6.7	2	3.824	2.876	0.7665

(Continued)

TABLE 7.1   Order processing time data based on number of line items per order. *(Continued)*

Subgroup	Cycle Time	Line Items	Predicted Cycle Time	Residual	Standardized Residual
98	11.6	6	8.46	3.14	0.8369
99	5.9	3	4.983	0.917	0.2444
100	6	8	10.778	−4.778	−1.2735
101	8.4	4	6.142	2.258	0.6018
102	2.9	6	8.46	−5.56	−1.4819
103	18.8	14	17.732	1.068	0.2847
104	3.3	3	4.983	−1.683	−0.4486
105	4.7	7	9.619	−4.919	−1.3110
106	11.3	10	13.096	−1.796	−0.4787
107	8.8	5	7.301	1.499	0.3995
108	13.9	6	8.46	5.44	1.4499
109	8.2	3	4.983	3.217	0.8574
110	1.2	2	3.824	−2.624	−0.6994
111	3.3	6	8.46	−5.16	−1.3753
112	2.9	3	4.983	−2.083	−0.5552
113	16.6	12	15.414	1.186	0.3161
114	6.3	4	6.142	0.158	0.0421
115	1.1	1	2.665	−1.565	−0.4171
116	8.6	4	6.142	2.458	0.6551
117	2.2	4	6.142	−3.942	−1.0507
118	16.3	7	9.619	6.681	1.7807
119	0.9	5	7.301	−6.401	−1.7060
120	5.7	7	9.619	−3.919	−1.0445
121	9	5	7.301	1.699	0.4528
122	2.6	6	8.46	−5.86	−1.5619
123	12.4	11	14.255	−1.855	−0.4944
124	2.3	3	4.983	−2.683	−0.7151
125	2.2	2	3.824	−1.624	−0.4328
126	3.9	2	3.824	0.076	0.0203
127	16.9	13	16.573	0.327	0.0872
128	16.3	7	9.619	6.681	1.7807
129	1.5	3	4.983	−3.483	−0.9283

(Continued)

TABLE 7.1 Order processing time data based on number of line items per order. (*Continued*)

Subgroup	Cycle Time	Line Items	Predicted Cycle Time	Residual	Standardized Residual
130	11.7	6	8.46	3.24	0.8635
131	14.5	5	7.301	7.199	1.9187
132	11	5	7.301	3.699	0.9859
133	1.3	3	4.983	−3.683	−0.9816
134	0.7	1	2.665	−1.965	−0.5237
135	5.7	8	10.778	−5.078	−1.3534
136	9.6	5	7.301	2.299	0.6127
137	2.5	4	6.142	−3.642	−0.9707
138	11.3	6	8.46	2.84	0.7569
139	10	9	11.937	−1.937	−0.5163
140	9.3	5	7.301	1.999	0.5328
141	4.7	4	6.142	−1.442	−0.3843
142	10.7	4	6.142	4.558	1.2148
143	10.4	5	7.301	3.099	0.8260
144	10.5	4	6.142	4.358	1.1615
145	2.7	3	4.983	−2.283	−0.6085
146	9	9	11.937	−2.937	−0.7828

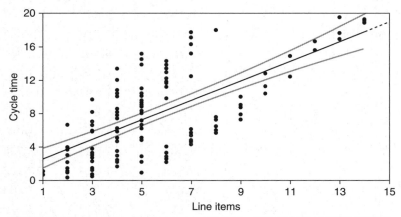

Regression function: $y = 1.506 + 1.159 \times x$
Correlation coefficient: 0.652
Function explains 42.491% of variation

Regression: 1 (df) 1508.151 (SS) 1508.151 (MS)
Residual: 144 (df) 2041.191 (SS) 14.175 (MS)
F: 106.396
Prob F: 0.000

FIGURE 7.5 · Scatter diagram of Table 7.1 data.

pattern approaches a line in appearance, the stronger the linear correlation between the two variables. Strong linear correlation implies that the line predicts the relationship well; weak correlation usually means there are one or more other variables responsible for the change in y. Weak correlation is evident by a near horizontal line (a given change in x produces little change in y).

A positive slope on the line, as evidenced in Figure 7.5, is referred to as *positive correlation*: As the independent x variable increases, so does the dependent y variable. Negative correlation, implied by a slope less than zero, occurs when the y-values decrease for increasing x-values.

The scatter diagram is limited by the data it includes. It is bounded by the smallest and largest observed x-values. Since there is no data beyond these values in either direction, the scatter diagram cannot reliably predict (or *extrapolate*) to these regions, regardless of the strength of correlation within the region of data. It is thus important to collect data over the full range of interest.

The objective of the regression analysis is to determine if the dependent variable can be adequately predicted by the independent (x-axis) variable. A sample of possible x-values is obtained over the range of interest and a model is generated. When only one independent variable is considered, such as in the scatter diagram of Figure 7.5, the model is that of a straight line and the analysis is referred to as *simple linear regression*. The equation of the straight line may be written in a number of equivalent forms, including:

$$Y = mx + b \text{ where } m \text{ is the slope and } b \text{ is the y-intercept; or}$$

$$Y = \beta_0 + \beta_1 x \text{ where } \beta_1 \text{ is the slope and } \beta_0 \text{ is the y-intercept.}$$

The y-intercept is simply the value of y when x equals 0. Most statistical textbooks use the Greek letter notation provided by the second equation, since it is easily expanded with additional terms for multiple regression analysis (discussed below).

Two parameters are estimated for the simple linear regression model: slope and intercept. The method often used is known as the *method of least squares*, which determines values for slope and intercept such that the fitted line has a minimum squared distance from each of the experimental data values.

The equations noted above are sometimes shown with an additional term for the error, an acknowledgement that even if all possible values were sampled there would still be unpredictability in the outcome. This unpredictability is due to many possibilities, including measurement error in either the dependent or independent variable, the effects of other unknown variables, or nonlinear effects.

The scatter diagram of Figure 7.5 provides the regression model for the data as:

$$\text{Cycle time} = 1.506 + 1.159 \times (\text{line items})$$

The slope of this line is 1.159; the y-intercept is 1.506. The coefficient of the x term is positive, so the correlation is positive: As the number of line items increases, so does the cycle time. The regression model represents the best estimate of y for given values of x within the region of data. For example, for ten line items (i.e., x equals 10), the best guess for cycle time is $1.506 + 1.159 \times 10$, which equals 13.096 minutes. Similarly, predicted values of y can be calculated for any value of x using the regression model; extrapolation beyond the data region (1 to 14 line items) should be done with caution.

Figure 7.5 also includes an ANOVA table. ANOVA is an acronym for ANalysis Of VAriation, which is a statistical tool for partitioning variation, in this case amongst the terms of a regression model. The ANOVA table also provides an indication of the statistical significance of the regression, indicating the amount of variation predicted by the regression model.

Statistical significance should not be confused with physical significance. If a given factor is statistically significant in determining a response for a given set of data, it may still lack any real (i.e., physical) significance in influencing the response in the real (i.e., physical) world. Recall the example above with shoe size and scores on a math quiz. Factors may be coincident with other factors, some of which may be significant; factors may be significant for a given set of data, which may not be relevant to the larger world.

The ANOVA table uses the F-statistic (named for its developer, Sir Ronald Fisher) to compare the variability accounted for by the regression model with the remaining variation observed (due to error in the model). The F-statistic is applied to the (null) hypothesis that the slope of the regression line is zero, implying no statistical correlation between the two variables. The null hypothesis is rejected for p-values of the F-statistic less than 0.05 (in some cases 0.10 is used, particularly in initial stages of investigation). When rejected, the alternative hypothesis that the slope is non-zero is accepted, implying some level of correlation between the two variables. The regression results shown in Figure 7.5 provide a p-value of 0.00 associated with the F-test, so the null hypothesis of zero slope should be rejected. As such, it is reasonable to suggest a statistical relationship between the number of line items and the cycle time.

Another useful statistic provided by the ANOVA table is the coefficient of determination, sometimes called R^2. R^2 varies between zero and one, and represents the amount of variation in the data accounted for by the regression model. For example, the regression results shown in Figure 7.5 provide an R-value (the correlation coefficient) of 0.652; R^2 is thus 0.425, meaning that approximately 42.5% of the variation in cycle time is explained by the regression function (in this case, the linear equation).

In other words, approximately 43% of the common cause variation observed for the order processing time metric is apparently due to processing time differences associated with the number of line items in the order. This provides food for thought, in terms of how the process might be redesigned to more seamlessly address variation in the number of line items without an increase in the order processing time. It also begs the question: What are the sources of the remaining 57% of the processing time variation?

A large R^2 value does not imply that the slope of the regression line is steep, that the correct model was used, or that the model will accurately predict future observations. It simply means that the model happens to account for a large percent of the variation observed in this particular set of data.

Confidence lines, such as shown in Figure 7.5, may be used to indicate the bounds of variation that can be expected for the fitted regression function. While the confidence limits do not indicate where future values might lie, or whether the current data "fits the model," they provide the range of possible regression models based on the variability of the data. The divergence of the confidence lines at the ends, and convergence in the middle, may be explained either of two ways:

1. The regression function, in this case a line, requires estimation of two parameters: slope and y-intercept. The error in estimating intercept provides a gap in the vertical direction, parallel to the y-axis. The error in estimating slope can be visualized by imagining the fitted line rotating about its middle. This results in the hourglass-shaped region shown by the confidence intervals.
2. The confidence of the regression model is best at the center of the data, so the confidence limits is narrower at the middle. There is less data near the end points, so the confidence is less and the confidence interval is wider at each end.

Prediction intervals may also be defined for new data, based on the assumption that the new data is independent of the data used to fit the regression model. The best estimate for the y-value based on a given x-value is determined using the regression equation at the x-value. Yet, there will be variation in the actual y-values observed due to error in our model. The prediction interval for these future observations is dependent on the error in the regression model as well as sampling error associated with future data. The prediction interval is similar in shape to the confidence interval, but wider.

Residuals Analysis

Once a model has been developed, the model *residuals* may be analyzed for abnormal patterns indicative of a poor model. A residual is the error (i.e., the mathematical difference) between a given observation's value and the predicted value based on the regression model.

Table 7.1 includes the predicted value of cycle time (based on the regression model shown in Figure 7.5) and the residual, calculated as the difference between the observed data value and the predicted value. For example, the predicted cycle time and its residual for the first row, where the number of line items equals 5 and the observed cycle time is 6.7 minutes, is calculated as:

$$\text{Predicted cycle time} = 1.506 + 1.159 \times (5) = 7.301$$

$$\text{Residual} = \text{observed value} - \text{predicted value} = 6.7 - 7.301 = -0.601$$

Statisticians rarely use the raw residual calculation. More typically, a standardized residual (also shown in Table 7.1) is calculated by dividing the calculated residual by the standard deviation of the residuals:

$$e_i = \frac{y_i - \hat{y}_i}{s_e}$$

In the example, the standard deviation of the residuals is calculated as 3.752. The standardized residual for the first row is calculated as $-0.601/3.752 = -0.160$.

The effect of standardizing the residuals is to scale the error to achieve a variance of one, which helps make outliers more prominent. An absolute value of two or larger is generally considered an indication of an unusual data value, as indicated by three of the standardized residuals in Table 7.1 (subgroups 10, 66, and 94).

There are a number of tools useful for finding patterns in residuals.

- *Normality test for standardized residuals*: If the error between the model & the data is random, then the residuals are normally distributed with a mean of 0. A normal probability plot is used with the K-S goodness of fit test to

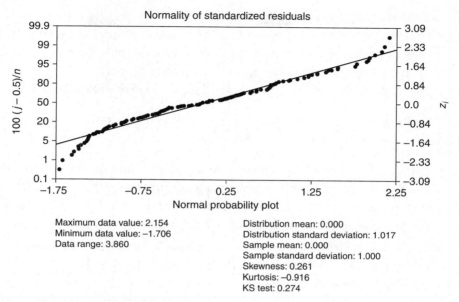

FIGURE 7.6 · Normal probability plot of standardized residuals from Table 7.1.

detect departures from normality, indicating a poor fit of the model to the data. These methods were discussed in Chapter 3. A normal probability plot for the standardized residuals from Table 7.1 is shown in Figure 7.6. A lack of data in the tails of the distribution is evident by the plotted values beneath the fitted line on the left side and above the fitted line on the right side. The K-S value of 0.274 is not small enough to reject the normality assumption, yet is sufficiently small to confirm the suspected lack of data in the tails.

- *Scatter plot of independent variable (x) versus standardized residual*: There should be no pattern, or any significant correlation, when plotting residuals (y-axis) & an independent variable (x-axis) on a scatter diagram. Patterns imply the model changes as a function of the x variable, meaning that a separate model is needed for particular values of x (such as if a hidden factor is present which interacts with the plotted independent variable). A scatter plot of the line items versus the standardized residuals in Table 7.1 shows no correlation (a p-value of 0.999).

- *Scatter plot of standardized residuals versus fitted model*: There should be no pattern, or any significant correlation, when plotting residuals (y-axis) and the fitted model (x-axis) on a scatter diagram. A pattern suggests the model does not fit well over the range of the response. If there are repeated runs at each experimental condition, then a Bartlett's equality of variance test can be performed to check for non-constant variance of the response. Non-constant variance, when present, can be indicative of a number of conditions such as nonlinearity of measurement error (see Chapter 8) or the need for additional terms in the model. A scatter plot of the standardized residuals versus the predicted cycle time from Table 7.1 shows weak correlation.

If the time at which each data value was observed is available, then additional analysis of the model residuals can include:

- *Individual x chart of standardized residuals*: An individual x chart of the residuals (assuming normality) can detect if the residual error is stable, or if it changes over time. If special causes are present, look for a hidden factor that changes over time, coincident with the special causes observed.
- *Test for autocorrelation of standardized residuals*: Significant autocorrelation of the residuals (detected using the autocorrelation function discussed in Chapter 5) implies that the error at any point in time is influenced by earlier error. In this case, look for a hidden factor that changes over time.

Multiple Regression

Multiple regression refers to regression models that include more than one independent variable to influence the dependent response. For example, the order processing time in the earlier example may be impacted by the number of line items purchased and the time of day. In this case, there are two independent variables: number of line items purchased and time of day.

Multiple regression requires one or more additional terms to the simple linear regression model shown earlier. An additional term is added for each additional factor; however, if there is sufficient data of the right type a term can also be added to estimate the interaction between each pair of factors. For example, perhaps the effect of time of day varies depending on the number of items purchased. It may be that when only a few items are purchased, the time of day makes a big difference, yet when many items are purchased, time of day makes little difference.

The general model for multiple regression is of the form:

$$Y = \beta_0 + \beta_1 x_1 + \beta_2 x_2 + \cdots + \beta_i x_i$$

where β_0 is the slope and β_i is the coefficient of factor x_i for i factors in the model.

The analysis method is similar to the simple linear regression model discussed earlier: An F-statistic is calculated for each factor (or interaction between factors), with a corresponding p-value to determine the term's significance; an (adjusted) R^2 value indicates the amount of variation in the data accounted for by the model; and residuals may be analyzed to verify there are no abnormal patterns to the model's fit.

MS Excel includes a convenient regression option within its *data analysis* tool pack. The data from Table 7.1, with additional columns included for product family (A, B, or C) and person processing the order (Andrew, Bob, or Charlie), provided the results shown in Table 7.2.

The adjusted R^2 value indicates 73% of the total variation in order processing time is predicted by the regression model:

$$\text{cycle time} = -4.13 + 2.09 \times (\text{line items}) + 1.71 \times (\text{product}) + 3.04 \times (\text{person})$$

TABLE 7.2 MS Excel regression output.

Summary Output

Regression Statistics	
Multiple R	0.858023
R Square	0.736203
Adjusted R square	0.73063
Standard error	2.567819
Observations	146

ANOVA

	df	SS	MS	F	Significance F
Regression	3	2613.038	871.0127	132.0978	0.0000
Residual	142	936.3045	6.593693		
Total	145	3549.342			

	Coefficients	Standard Error	t Stat	p-Value
Intercept	−4.12524	0.642738	−6.41822	0.0000
Line items	2.094202	0.10595	19.7659	0.0000
Product	1.714908	0.34498	4.971031	0.0000
Person	3.035409	0.284313	10.6763	0.0000

where the product family classifications (A, B, C) and persons (Andrew, Bob, or Charlie) are coded as $(-1, 0, 1)$, respectively, for purpose of calculation. The p-value (significance) of the F-statistics is less than 0.05, indicating significance of the regression function. The coefficients of each term allows easy quantification of its effect: A unit change in the number of line items is coincident with an increase in cycle time of 2.09 minutes; a change from Product A to B or B to C is coincident with an increase of 1.71 minutes in cycle time; a change from Andrew to Bob or Bob to Charlie is coincident with an increase of 3.04 minutes in cycle time.

It is not uncommon to use this type of data mining to look for patterns or significance of process factors. While it has some usefulness, historical (sometimes called *happenstance*) data of this sort is usually incapable of detecting interactions. The effects of interactions can only be estimated when the data includes the necessary combinations of factors, randomized to remove bias from main effects.

Happenstance data may also lack sufficient variation in each factor or interaction to estimate significance of the main factors x_i. The uncontrolled nature of the data collection may allow other factors (often unrecorded) to contribute to noise in the data that may cloud the effects of each factor. Any patterns to the data collection, such as if one factor was held constant for a period, can increase the likelihood that unrecognized factors that vary over time will bias the results.

A correlation analysis of the above data (using the MS Excel data analysis tool pack) is shown in Table 7.3. Note the correlation term $R = 0.652$ agrees with the simple linear regression analysis of Figure 7.5, accounting for nearly 43% of the variation. While the line items term is reasonably well correlated with cycle time, the product and person terms are not, with each accounting for less than 1% of the variation.

Yet, the regression analysis indicated the regression function accounted for a much larger portion (73%) of the variation in processing time. Why the difference?

TABLE 7.3 Correlation table for extended Table 7.1 data.

	Cycle Time	Line Items	Product	Person
Cycle time	1			
Line items	0.651851	1		
Product	−0.09435	−0.54922	1	
Person	−0.01117	−0.63054	0.479533	1

Note in Table 7.3 how the product and person terms are correlated with line items (−0.55 and −0.63, respectively), as well as with each other (0.48). In other words, at least in the data set available for analysis, a change in the number of line items was (at least sometimes) coincident with a change in the product and/or person processing the order. In fact, some products were more likely to have a higher number of line items (products or services sold in conjunction with the main product); likewise, each person tended to specialize in a given product, where Andrew sold more of Product A, Bob sold more of Product B, and so on. This correlation built into the data prevented an independent calculation of whether product or person really had an influence on the order processing time.

Designed experiments are the preferred alternative to happenstance data, allowing estimation of parameter effects with a small number of well-chosen (i.e., orthogonal) data values. A given design is quickly constructed to detect specific factors and their interactions. The data is collected over relatively small period of time, allowing the experimenters to control the conditions under which the data is collected. Casual factors such as environmental conditions, personnel, and so on are observed or controlled, with anomalies recorded.

Designed Experiments

Designed experiments are a critical part of many successful improvement projects. While statistical process control provides predictive capabilities for a stable process, designed experiments provide prediction of the process potential that is achievable by manipulating the sources of the common and special causes of variation seen on the control chart.

A designed experiment differs from the traditional experiment learned in grade school, sometimes referred to as a *one factor at a time* (or OFAT) experiment. For example, consider the experimental runs shown for targeting a catapult in Table 7.4, which contains one measured response (distance from target) and three factors with two settings (or levels) each:

- Rubber band [thin, wide]
- Drawback distance [short, long]
- Boulder weight [light, heavy]

An initial baseline condition is obtained in row 1 of Table 7.4 by measuring the response when each of the factors is set at its low level. The second trial is

TABLE 7.4   Example traditional one factor at a time experiment.

Trial	Rubber Band	Drawback Distance	Boulder Weight	Distance from Target
1	Thin	Short	Light	35
2	Wide	Short	Light	27
3	Thin	Long	Light	29
4	Thin	Short	Heavy	55

run to estimate the effect of the first factor (rubber band), which is calculated as the difference in the response between the baseline (Trial 1) and Trial 2. In this case, the effect of the wide rubber band is estimated as a decreased distance from target of 8 units (calculated as 35 − 27).

Likewise, the effect of the longer drawback distance is estimated as a decrease of 6 units by comparing Trials 3 and 1; the effect of boulder weight estimated as an increase of 20 units by comparing Trials 4 and 1. Based on these observations, distance from target is minimized by setting the factors as follows: rubber band: wide; drawback distance: short; boulder weight: light.

One problem with the traditional one-factor-at-a-time experiment is that it ignores the effect of interactions. Figure 7.7, developed using data from a simple eight-run experimental design of the process, indicates an interaction between drawback distance and rubber band size. This is evidenced by the nonparallel lines in the figure: For the thin rubber band, the drawback distance has less effect than for the wide rubber band. Stated differently, the estimated effect due to the drawback distance changes depending on whether it is measured for a thin or wide rubber band.

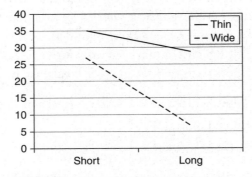

FIGURE 7.7 · Interaction plot of drawback distance and rubber band size.

When interactions are ignored, improvement efforts are hampered in one or more of the following ways (Keller, 2011):

- A significant factor seems unimportant if other factors are not varied at the same time, as shown in the example.

- The process improvement is only maintained if other factors remain constant. The process improvement "goes away" when a factor that was not considered (or considered insignificant) changes.

- A given factor's effect may be larger than necessary, increasing the process variation. When factors interact, it's possible to reduce the effect of one factor by minimizing the variation of another. This is an example of the Taguchi approach to *robust design*. In the previous example, since the effect of drawback distance was small for the thin rubber band, use of the thin rubber band reduces the influence of fluctuations in drawback distance.

Defining the Experiment

Once a team has brainstormed a list of potential factors influencing a process response (i.e., the outcome of the experiment; the dependent variable), an initial experiment may be conducted. In the initial experiment, called a *screening experiment*, each of the factors (i.e., independent variables) is set to one of two levels (a maximum and minimum condition) and the response is (or responses are) measured. Manipulating the factors over a wide range (i.e., a high maximum and low minimum condition) provides the best chance of detecting a change in the process that may be otherwise too subtle to detect. If a factor that truly influences the process is excluded from the experiment, the effect of this *hidden factor* will contribute to the error calculated in the ANOVA. The error thus provides indication of how well the model predicts the response

In running the experiment at various conditions of each of the factors, the effect of each factor on the response can be calculated. In an injection molding process, a team may consider the effect of furnace temperature, fill pressure, and the raw material moisture on the resulting part density. The raw material moisture cannot be "set" by the process; however, material can be sampled and segregated into a low level and high level to obtain samples useful for experimentation. Likewise in a service process, to test the effect of two different designs for order processing, sample orders can be run through each process design as if they were real orders.

The factors that are not generally controlled in your operations are casual, or subsidiary, factors. Taguchi referred to these as noise factors, or the outer array. Examples include ambient temperature, humidity, and vibration. If these factors are considered important, they should be experimental factors and set to specific levels for the experiment. If not, they should at least be measured to see if they are correlated with the response, which suggests the need for additional experimental runs to analyze their effect (by treating them as experimental factors).

The order of data collection is randomized in a designed experiment to prevent any bias in the estimates. In some case, however, the experimental trials cannot be completely randomized, and must be run in portions or *blocks*. In this case, a blocking factor is defined to estimate its effect. For example, cookies are baked in batches. A number of parameters might be varied within each batch, such as the ingredients and the method of mixing, for example. While these factors may be varied within each batch, the cooking time and cooking temperature are applied for a given batch. In this case, time and temperature are coincident with the batch. If they appear to be significant, the analysis must consider whether it is truly one of the factors that is significant or if there is some hidden effect that is also coincident with the batch.

More than one response can often be measured in an experiment. In some cases, the responses are converted or transformed during analysis to simplify the model, or uncover factors that contribute to variation in the response. The most useful responses are quantitative variables, rather than qualitative attributes. When responses are qualitative, we can sometimes convert them to quantitative scores (such as Likert scales). When conversion is not convenient or helpful, logistic regression techniques should be used for analysis. Sufficient resolution of the measured variable is needed for the regression techniques. Before conducting the experiment, the measurement system should be analyzed as discussed in Chapter 8.

When planning resources for experimental design, don't commit more than 20% of your total resources on any one experiment. Each successive experiment will provide information that will be confirmed or expanded on in subsequent experiments. The results of each experiment will provide information on what went wrong, and what to do next. If a critical factor was not included, or not varied sufficiently, subsequent experimental runs will be needed.

The best, and most common, approach is to begin with an effective screening design, which will provide information on key factors and the two-factor interactions between these factors.

Helpful guidelines to implement the experimental design include:

- Be an active participant in observing the data collection, a critical part of the learning experience. It's not uncommon for observations during the course of the experiment to lead to better understanding of the process dynamics. Let the normal process personnel operate the process; in some cases issues not discussed in brainstorming will become evident.
- Randomize trials to limit potential bias introduced during the experiment.
- Ensure the independence of runs. When each condition is run, the process should not be influenced by the prior conditions. Some processes will require their setup conditions to be torn down and reset.

Analyzing Experimental Results

Table 7.5 contains a randomized sixteen-run experimental design useful for analyzing the four factors identified during team brainstorming as potentially most important for reducing the cycle time for the order processing improvement

TABLE 7.5	Experimental design template with example data.			
A	B	C	D	Response
1	1	−1	1	19.2
−1	−1	1	−1	6.5
−1	1	−1	−1	5.7
−1	1	1	1	9.3
1	1	1	−1	11.8
−1	−1	−1	1	8.2
1	−1	1	1	17.6
1	−1	−1	−1	10.8
−1	1	−1	1	10.3
1	1	1	1	17.8
−1	−1	−1	−1	6.2
1	−1	1	−1	10.8
−1	−1	1	1	9.3
−1	1	1	−1	6.4
1	1	−1	−1	10.8
1	−1	−1	1	17

data presented in tables 7.1 through 7.3. The four factors, listed with their low and high experimental levels, are

- Factor A: Number of line items in order (2, 14)
- Factor B: Product family (A, B)
- Factor C: Person processing order (Charlie, Andrew)
- Factor D: Method of order processing (computer, paper)

The choice of product and person were made with some consideration toward best and worst case. Of the multiple operators working the process, Andrew is the most experienced; Charlie the least experienced. Referring to Figure 7.4, Product A has the lowest median but highest variation, while product B has a similar level of variation as Product C, but a higher median. Since it is a rare case when there is only a single line item on an order, the low level for line items was chosen as two; the upper level of 14 was chosen based on a review of the available data. Factor D, the method of order processing, was added even though some team members felt it largely irrelevant; its levels D were based on the two methods available.

A value of minus one (−1) in Table 7.5 specifies the low level of the factor; a value of plus one (1) refers to the high level for the factor. For example, in this case the first row response was obtained by collecting a measurement of cycle time when the number of line items (A) is 14 (high level); the product family (B) is Product B (high level); the person processing the order (C) is Charlie (low level); the method (D) is via paper (high level).

The experimental design in Table 7.5 can actually be applied as a template to *any process* to estimate the effect of three or four potentially critical factors. The Response column data will be replaced by the actual experimental results for your process, and the factors A, B, C and D are replaced by your actual factors and each of their two levels. If there are only three factors of interest, either the top eight rows or the lower eight rows are sufficient to fully estimate the three factors (A, B, C), their three two-factor interactions (AB, AC, BC), the intercept and the error. For three factors, the full sixteen runs will be a *replicated* design in that the lower eight rows are a (randomized) repetition of the upper eight rows. The replication is useful to better estimate error.

Generally speaking, a design needs at least one unique run (of the proper factor-level setting combination) to estimate each term. There are algorithms to assist in developing the runs, but in consideration of brevity (and the reality of business) it will be assumed that experimental design software such as

Minitab (www.minitab.com) or *Black Belt XL* (www.qualityamerica.com) is used to generate and analyze the design.

When there are four factors, eight runs are insufficient to estimate the four main factors (A, B, C, D), their six two-factor interactions (AB, AC, AD, BC, BD, CD), the intercept and the error; however the sixteen runs are sufficient.

This sixteen-run design template could also estimate five factors (A, B, C, D, E), their ten two-factor interactions (AB, AC, AD, AE, BC, BD, BE, CD, CE, DE), and the intercept, but would not have any additional runs to estimate error. Estimating error is important, as shown in the example below, since the significance of the model and its terms are based on their contribution to variation relative to the variation associated with residual error. If just one of the ten two-factor interaction terms was excluded from the analysis (such as based on a general consensus that it were unlikely to occur) an estimate of error could be obtained. This would allow use of the sixteen-run design template for cases of five factors. The fifth factor's level for each run is obtained by multiplying the coded values for factors A, B, C, and D for that run. For example, in the first run the factor level for E is calculated using the first row's values as $1 \times 1 \times (-1) \times 1 = -1$; in the second row the E level is obtained as $(-1) \times (-1) \times 1 \times (-1) = -1$; and so on. (This is known as *aliasing* factor E with the interaction ABCD.)

Initial analysis results for Table 7.5's example data is shown in Figure 7.8. The important statistics are highlighted:

- The adjusted R^2 value of 0.979 indicates that nearly 98% of the variation in the data is accommodated by the model. That is generally high for a regression, although for limited data sets such as in a designed experiment it is not especially unusual.
- The significance of the F-statistic for the regression is reported as much less than 0.05, indicating the model fits the data well.
- The p-values for the A (number of line items), D (processing method), and the AD interaction terms are significant (less than 0.05).

When there are a sufficient number of runs to estimate the residual error, the F-test can be used to evaluate the significance of the overall regression model; the t-test is used for each term in the model. In most cases, a p-value of 0.05 or less is suitable to assert statistical significance. (In initial models with limited data, a value of 0.10 is sometimes used so that terms with borderline significance are not prematurely discarded.)

Regression statistics						
Multiple R	0.996508493					
R square	0.993029176					
Adjusted R square	0.979087528					
Standard error	0.647012365					
Observations	16					
ANOVA						
	df	SS	MS	F	Significance F	
Regression	10	298.17625	29.817625	71.2275306	0.0001	
Residual	5	2.093125	0.418625			
Total	15	300.269375				
	Coefficients	Standard Error	t Stat	p-Value	Lower 95%	Upper 95%
Intercept	11.10625	0.161753091	68.6617481	0.00000	10.69045044	11.52204956
A	3.36875	0.161753091	20.82649534	0.00000	2.952950442	3.784549558
B	0.30625	0.161753091	1.893317759	0.11686	-0.109549558	0.722049558
C	0.08125	0.161753091	0.502308793	0.63679	-0.334549558	0.497049558
D	2.48125	0.161753091	15.33973776	0.00002	2.065450442	2.897049558
AB	0.11875	0.161753091	0.734143621	0.49582	-0.297049558	0.534549558
AC	-0.05625	0.161753091	-0.347752241	0.74219	-0.472049558	0.359549558
AD	0.94375	0.161753091	5.834509827	0.00209	0.527950442	1.359549558
BC	-0.16875	0.161753091	-1.043256724	0.34462	-0.584549558	0.247049558
BD	0.25625	0.161753091	1.584204655	0.17400	-0.159549558	0.672049558
CD	-0.16875	0.161753091	-1.043256724	0.34462	-0.584549558	0.247049558

FIGURE 7.8 • Initial analysis results of Table 7.5 experimental results (using Quality America's *Black Belt XL* software).

Terms should generally be removed one at a time from the model, so that the error may be partially reapportioned among the remaining parameters. Remove the interaction terms first, based on the term with the highest p-value. Terms with borderline significance, such as a p-value between 0.05 and 0.10, are best left in the model, particularly at the early stages.

If a main factor is removed from the model because it is nonsignificant, then all its interactions should also be removed from the model. Likewise, if the interaction is significant, then all its main factors should be retained. When interaction terms are significant, and one or more of their main factors are insignificant, then consider whether the interaction may be confounded with another interaction or main factor, or perhaps even a factor not included in the model. Confounding means that the factors move together, often because of the way in which the data was collected. Randomizing the data collection helps to reduce the instances of confounding.

In the initial analysis results of Figure 7.8, the AC interaction term has the largest p-value (0.742), so it should be removed from the model. When the analysis is repeated without that term, the p-values of the remaining terms will

Regression statistics						
Multiple R	0.990063679					
R square	0.980226089					
Adjusted R square	0.975282611					
Standard error	0.703414292					
Observations	16					
ANOVA						
	df	SS	MS	F	Significance F	
Regression	3	294.331875	98.11063	198.2867368	0.0000	
Residual	12	5.9375	0.494792			
Total	15	300.269375				
	Coefficients	Standard Error	t Stat	p-Value	Lower 95%	Upper 95%
Intercept	11.10625	0.175853573	63.15624	0.00000	10.72309798	11.48940202
A	3.36875	0.175853573	19.15656	0.00000	2.985597979	3.751902021
D	2.48125	0.175853573	14.10975	0.00000	2.098097979	2.864402021
AD	0.94375	0.175853573	5.366681	0.00017	0.560597979	1.326902021

FIGURE 7.9 • Resulting analysis of Table 7.5 data (after removing insignificant terms).

be slightly adjusted to reapportion the error. After removing all insignificant terms, the analysis and resulting model is shown in Figure 7.9. Note that only terms A (number of line items), D (processing method), and their interaction AD are significant.

The regression model (using the terms displayed in the "coefficients" column) is

$$\text{cycle time} = 11.11 + 3.37 \times (\text{line items}) + 2.48 \times (\text{method}) + 0.94$$
$$\times (\text{line items}) \times (\text{method})$$

where in this case the line items and method are both expressed in coded $(-1,1)$ terms.

A correlation analysis indicates the approximate percent of total variation in the order processing time associated with each term in the model:

- Number of line items: 60%
- Processing method: 33%
- Line items × method interaction: 5%

The results indicate that the majority of the variation in order processing time is associated with the differences in the number of items ordered. This in itself is not surprising; however, it is clear that the relative impact of the person processing the order as well as the product family had no significance, contrary to the results of the data stratification. As suggested by the earlier correlation analysis, the analysis of the happenstance data was unduly influenced by the nature of the data itself: Orders for certain product families had higher propensity for more line items, so the influence of the number of line items on processing time appeared to be an influence due to product family. Similarly, specific persons tended to process orders depending on the product family, so this also appeared significant. Product family and person were both correlated with the number of line items, so it was impossible to distinguish their effects individually with the happenstance data.

The experimental data was also pivotal in identifying the processing method as a significant factor. This factor was not noted in the happenstance data.

With the experimental results in hand, the team then sets out to identify potential changes to the process flow related to these significant factors. They consider ways to reduce the impact of more line items in the order, such as methods that would allow line items to be quickly added to the order. They consider the impact of standardizing on the computer method for order processing, since the paper method was shown to account for over 30% of the increased processing time. The effects of these proposed changes are then analyzed using simulation and additional experimental runs. Once the proposed changes are validated by additional experimental runs, they can be implemented to reduce both the median processing time as well as the variation in processing time.

 ## Still Struggling?

This chapter discusses a number of common problem-solving tools, including cause & effect diagrams, stratification and statistical analysis of historical data. It concludes with an example demonstrating how these tools, used exclusively, can lead to erroneous results. This may well be troubling to many readers, given the prevalence of these practices. Yet, it should be clear that these tools provide useful, yet inconclusive, information about the process. In practice, any of these tools may indeed find significant process factors that will lead to meaningful improvement; the error is in assuming they necessarily will find those factors. Once a factor has been proposed as being significant to the process variation, the question becomes: Is it significant, and if so, how much variation does it contribute to the process?

Operationally, those questions are answered using a properly designed statistical control chart. If any process change leads to improvement, it should be evident as either a special cause on the control chart (i.e., a process shift) or as an elimination of an existing special cause on a control chart.

The use of the experimental design approach is advocated because it is the quickest means of eliminating factors that are statistically insignificant. In the absence of a proper experimental design, the analyst would change process factors and wait to see if their impact could be detected on the control chart. In the order processing example shown in this chapter, consider the wasted effort that would have been expended trying to improve the process with respect to the product family and personnel, when these are in fact insignificant, as shown with the designed experiment!

Summary

Simple stratification and enumerative techniques such as box-whisker and Pareto diagrams can be used to suggest possible process factors contributing to variation. Happenstance data available from process operations often lacks the clarity to reach meaningful conclusions. Multiple regression analysis used with experimental design techniques offer a simple and a quick means to determine the significance of factors in any process. In the example above, the 16 experimental runs provided much more information than was available in the 146 happenstance process observations (which actually provided more misinformation than information). In this way, a seemingly complex process with many variables is reduced in scope to only a few significant factors that contribute most to the process variation.

QUIZ

1. **Stratification is useful for detecting process factors:**
    A. which contribute to special cause variation.
    B. which contribute to common cause variation.
    C. which may be coincident with causes of special or common cause variation.
    D. All of the above.

2. **If the coefficient of determination $R^2 = 0.83$ for a set of data and a predicted model, then:**
    A. the slope of regression line is steep.
    B. the proper model was used.
    C. the model fits the data well.
    D. All of the above.

3. **A value of R-squared of 0.20 indicates:**
    A. for every unit increase in x, there is a 20% increase in y.
    B. there are probably other variables that contribute to the variation in the response.
    C. 20% of the time we will predict y correctly.
    D. All of the above.

4. **The flaring of the confidence intervals about the regression line is evidence of:**
    A. the inability to predict y values at the extremes with as much certainty.
    B. the relative absence of data at the endpoints.
    C. the error in predicting the slope.
    D. All of the above.

5. **If the cycle time of a process is predicted by cycle time = 5.25 × (number of items) + 4.3, with a correlation of 0.8, then the predicted cycle time for six items is:**
    A. 54.1.
    B. 28.64.
    C. 35.8.
    D. 31.05.

6. **Strong correlation implies that:**
    A. the dependent variable improves as the independent variable increases.
    B. there is little error between the predicted response and the actual response of the dependent variable.
    C. the dependent variable increases rapidly as the independent variable increases.
    D. All of the above.

7. **In linear regression analysis, if the slope of the line is low, then:**
   A. the dependent variable is not well-predicted by the model.
   B. there is weak correlation between the variables.
   C. as the independent variable changes, there is a small change in the dependent variable.
   D. All of the above.

8. **An ANOVA analysis provides the following p-values:**

$$\text{Intercept} = 0.03$$
$$\text{Factor A} = 0.73$$
$$\text{Factor B} = 0.02$$
$$\text{Factor C} = 0.10$$

   Given this data, we might assume:
   A. of the three factors investigated, Factor A is most significant.
   B. of the three factors investigated, Factor B is most significant.
   C. of the three factors investigated, Factor C is most significant.
   D. None of the above.

9. **In the expression cycle time (in minutes) = 3 + 1.4 × (number of orders) − 2.1 × (number of clerks) − .034 × (process distance):**
   A. there is an interaction between the number of orders and the number of clerks.
   B. the number of orders goes down as the number of clerks goes up.
   C. the number of orders stays constant as the number of clerks goes up.
   D. None of the above.

10. **In the interaction plot below, it is evident that:**

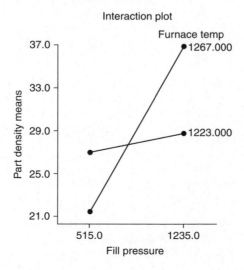

A. there is an interaction between furnace temperature and fill pressure.
B. at higher furnace temperature, an increase in fill pressure has more effect on part density.
C. the effect of fill pressure on part density changes as we change the furnace temperature.
D. All of the above.

chapter **8**

Measurement Systems Analysis

Measurement error contributes to errors in estimates of common causes, special causes, and process capability. In some cases, measurement error is a dominant source of common cause process variation estimated in the process capability study; in other cases measurement error contributes to special cause variation. In cases where measurement error is dominant, process improvement is synonymous with improvement of the measurement system. Measurement systems analysis can also be used to qualify measurement fixtures or methods for suitability of use, or operators' proficiency on these equipment and methods.

CHAPTER OBJECTIVES

After completing this chapter, you will be able to

- Describe the applications of statistical control charts in evaluating the measurement system reliably in estimating process location and variation
- Differentiate between the various types of analyses, including:
  - Stability studies to evaluate the long-term accuracy of the measurement equipment
  - Linearity analysis to evaluate variation in measurement as a function of the size of the measurement
  - R&R analysis to categorize measurement error as either repeatability or reproducibility error

Overview

Estimated process variation is composed of the actual variation in the pieces or units of service that are measured, and error associated with the measurement. Mathematically, the variance of the unit plus the variance of the measurement equals the total variance observed:

$$\sigma^2_{total} = \sigma^2_{unit} + \sigma^2_{measurement}$$

In this way, many measurements are affected by error, including inspection related to product dispositions or service acceptability, as well as the process stability estimates using control charts, and their resulting effect on profitability. The proper evaluation of measurement systems recognizes the importance of not just the measurement equipment or instruments, but also the fixtures used for clamping production pieces, the setup of fixtures, the preparation of samples, the methodology of measurement, and the personnel obtaining and evaluating the measurements.

There are some process metrics that will require only basic analysis of their measurement system. When measuring the process cycle time, for example, each data value may be "measured" using a stopwatch, wall clocks, or even a calendar. The choice of unit of measure (seconds, minutes, hours, or days) should be specific to the process to ensure that there is an adequate number of unique data values, as discussed in Chapter 2. When measurements are made in large units, such as days or perhaps even hours, it may be sufficient to limit measurement systems analysis to the definition of the metric (at what point does the measurement start and end), and the resolution required (hours or days) to sufficiently measure process variation. The analysis of the measurement system for these cases may be limited to verification of proper classification of start and end time, for example.

Stability

The stability of a measurement system is a measure of the extent to which the measurement system is subject to time-based deterioration. For example, does the measurement instrument show signs of wear over time, such that the accuracy of the measurements degrades over time? Are measurements influenced by factors, such as environmental conditions, that cause their accuracy to change during the course of the day?

The stability of the measurement system is evaluated by estimating the statistical *bias*, or *accuracy*, over the course of time. A lack of measurement system stability can be detected using a statistical control chart of the bias statistic.

Bias, also known as accuracy, is the difference between the recorded measurement and the true value. Since there may be variation between multiple measurements of the same piece of product or unit of service taken at any point in time (due to "repeatability error" discussed below), bias is often estimated using the average of several measurements of the same item.

$$\text{Bias} = \text{average of measurements} - \text{reference value}$$
$$\% \text{ Bias} = (\text{bias/PV}) \times 100\%$$
$$\text{PV process variation} = 6 \times \text{process sigma (from control chart)}$$

The reference (or "true") value of the item is obtained using higher accuracy equipment. Equipment used for daily operations are often not of the highest accuracy; they are selected for use because of their convenience or low cost of operation. To estimate the accuracy of the operational equipment, their measurements can be compared against those from higher accuracy equipment, such as may be found in a laboratory rather than in production operations. For example, while the production operation may use micrometers to measure pieces in production, the inspection laboratory may include coordinate measurement machines or rigid indicators that permit higher accuracy of measurement.

For estimation of accuracy, it is often convenient to measure *standards* that have been certified at a particular measured value, using higher accurate equipment. These standards are measured with equipment whose calibration is traceable to NIST (National Institute for Standards and Technology). NIST maintains standards for many types of measurements, including dimensional, time, temperature, and so on.

To understand the severity of the bias, the bias is compared to the process variation, as estimated by a control chart using the methods discussed in Chapters 5 and 6. Process variation is estimated using the plus and minus three sigma levels of process sigma.

Although bias may be measured in a simple study such as described above, it is recommended to estimate bias on a regular basis and plot the bias value on an individual x control chart. (Normality is often assumed for the bias estimates.) This provides a visual aid in seeing the natural variation in the measurement process, a component of the natural variation in the business processes. As for any process, if common cause variation is assumed to be special cause variation, and the process is adjusted accordingly, then the process variation is increased due to this tampering (as discussed in Chapter 1).

Measurement system tampering occurs frequently in production processes, due to inherent ignorance of measurement system variation. It is not uncommon for process operators to begin each day, or perhaps periodically throughout the day, with a calibration check whereby a standard is measured and the measurement equipment adjusted to attain the standard value. Just as process adjustments move the centerline of a process, so calibrations move the centerline of the stability control chart, causing an increase in measurement system bias.

Instead, periodic checks of the measurement bias should be plotted on a control chart, and only adjusted as follows:

- When the stability control chart is in control, adjust only as needed to move the average stability estimate to zero.

- When the stability control chart is out of control, identify and remove the special causes of variation.

An example is shown in Figure 8.1. Daily bias estimates are recorded, with no adjustments made to the process until a sufficient number of estimates have

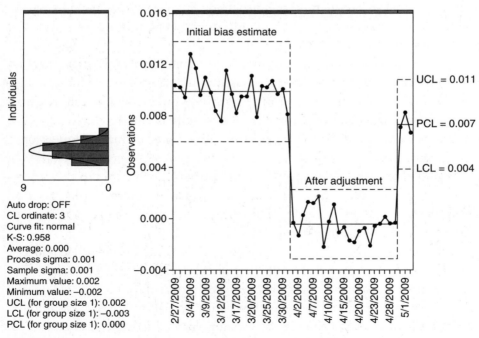

FIGURE 8.1 • Measurement system stability plotted on control chart.

been collected. In this case, 24 estimates of bias (obtained from a sample of 4 measurements each) were considered sufficient to establish the stability of the bias statistic. The measurement equipment was adjusted by the average bias observed (0.010), then additional data obtained which confirmed the measurement process stability closer to the reference value. After a period of time a special cause is observed. The special cause was investigated and determined to be related to an unauthorized adjustment to the equipment. The equipment was adjusted by 0.007 (the average of the last three points attributed to the special cause). Subsequent data was collected (not shown) and over a sufficient period of time the bias centerline was determined to be at 0.002, which was below the threshold for adjustment.

Linearity

Linearity provides an indication of whether the bias error associated with the measurement method is constant throughout its operating range. In other words, does the measurement method have the same accuracy when taking large measurements as when taking small measurements?

The Automotive Industry Action Group (AIAG, 1995) suggests the following methodology for estimating linearity:

- Measure the reference value for two or more sample items using a method with higher accuracy. The items selected should span the operating range of the method to be analyzed.

- Have one or more appraisers measure the same items multiple times using the method being analyzed. Calculate the average of these appraiser measurements.

- Calculate the bias for each sample item as the difference between the average measurements and the reference values, as explained earlier.

- Plot the reference value on the x-axis versus the bias on the y-axis of a scatter diagram.

- The method is acceptable for use only if the coefficient of determination $R^2 > 0.70$. This implies that the true variation in the parts or service items accounts for 70% (or more) of the observed variation.

- Linearity may then be calculated as the absolute value of the slope of the regression line multiplied by the part or item variation.

TABLE 8.1 Example data for linearity analysis.

Part	Observation	Part Avg.	Reference Value	Bias
A	6.10	6.105	6.093	0.012
	6.08			
	6.13			
	6.11			
B	7.65	7.6825	7.682	0.0005
	7.69			
	7.72			
	7.67			
C	10.45	10.39	10.368	0.022
	10.35			
	10.38			
	10.38			

Consider the data shown in Table 8.1. The bias is estimated for three nominal part sizes: 6, 8, and 10 inches. An average is calculated for the four measurements obtained for a single piece at each size. The reference value provides an estimate of the true value, obtained via more accurate measurement equipment.

The bias is plotted with the reference value on the scatter diagram of Figure 8.2 (see Chapter 7 for further discussion of scatter diagrams). The linear regression explains nearly 74% of the variation in bias. The slope of the regression is provided in Figure 8.2 as 0.0021; if the process variation is 0.5, the linearity is calculated as $0.0021 \times 0.5 = 0.0011$.

Repeatability & Reproducibility (R&R)

Repeatability, also known as equipment variation, is the error attributed to the measurement equipment. The repeatability is estimated using the variation between repeat trials using the same measurement instrument on the same unit of product. Each appraiser measures the same production piece several times. The repeatability is the average difference between the measurements on the same piece.

Reproducibility, also known as appraiser variation, is the error attributed to personnel. Reproducibility is estimated using the variation between the

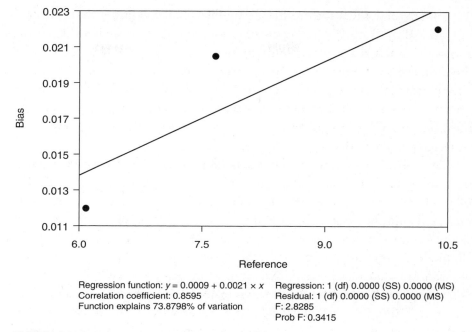

Regression function: $y = 0.0009 + 0.0021 \times x$
Correlation coefficient: 0.8595
Function explains 73.8798% of variation

Regression: 1 (df) 0.0000 (SS) 0.0000 (MS)
Residual: 1 (df) 0.0000 (SS) 0.0000 (MS)
F: 2.8285
Prob F: 0.3415

FIGURE 8.2 · Scatter diagram to analyze linearity.

appraisers' average measurements of the pieces when several appraisers measure the same units.

AIAG recommends a few different formats for conveniently estimating the effects of R&R error.

- The AIAG Long Study uses three appraisers to each measure 10 sample units three times each.

- The AIAG Short Study uses two appraisers to each measure five sample units two times each.

Other combinations of appraisers, trials and pieces are also permitted, so long as they provide enough samples to properly estimate R&R.

R&R studies are conducted offline using real samples from the process (i.e., production units), rather than the reference standards often used for bias and linearity estimates. The use of actual production pieces provides a realistic estimate of the R&R error that will contribute to overall measurement error in daily operations. The variation within a given production unit may be significant, and a proper analysis of this effect in an R&R study will result in changes to measurement methods to address the within item variation.

Similarly, an R&R study must replicate the actual conditions that exist in the operational practices, including fixtures, methods, and procedures. Each measurement in the study (90 measurements in the Long Study or 20 measurements in the Short Study), requires a complete tear-down and setup of fixtures, preparation of samples, and so on, just as if the measurement was taken for operational assessment. Samples presented to an appraiser for measurement must be randomized to prevent systematic sources of error from being masked by item (part) variation.

These techniques are neither limited to mechanical inspections nor to material parts. They also can be applied to optical inspections, chemical analyses, surveys or rating systems, or any other system designed to measure process performance, its output, or its subject matter. In chemical analyses and patient care, sample preparation may be a critical component of the measurement and should be incorporated into the measurement systems analysis.

After obtaining a representative sample, process personnel (i.e., appraisers) will inspect each sample multiple times (each inspection is termed a *trial*). The number of samples, personnel, and trials can vary from case to case; however, multiple trials are needed to estimate repeatability, and multiple persons are needed to estimate reproducibility. Larger sample sizes provide better estimates of repeatability and reproducibility, as well as overall sample variation, but offer diminishing return given the cost of the exercise. The typical studies outlined above are usually sufficient.

Consider the study data shown in Table 8.2. Two appraisers (Joe and Jill) each measure three items three times. The data was collected in a randomized

TABLE 8.2	Example R&R data.				
Item	**Joe**	**Jill**	**Joe Range**	**Jill Range**	**Part Avg.**
1	3.26	3.26	0.02	0.01	3.267
	3.28	3.27			
	3.27	3.26			
2	3.25	3.24	0.01	0.02	3.247
	3.26	3.23			
	3.25	3.25			
3	3.22	3.21	0.01	0.03	3.222
	3.22	3.21			
	3.23	3.24			
Average	**3.2489**	**3.2411**	**0.0133**	**0.0200**	**3.2450**

fashion, where the order of the three items was varied on each trial to prevent bias in the data collection. In addition, the identity of each of the samples was hidden from each appraiser, so as to not influence their measurements. The columns labeled Joe and Jill contain the raw data from each appraiser.

Range Method of R&R Analysis

Historically, the most common method for analysis of R&R study data uses the range statistic.

The repeatability standard deviation σ_e is estimated using the average range between the repeated trials as:

$$\sigma_e = \frac{\bar{R}}{d_2^*}$$

The constant d_2^* is related to the d_2 used to calculate process sigma in Chapters 5 and 6. Whereas d_2 is used when the number of subgroups is assumed to be "large," in a typical R&R analysis we only have five or ten subgroups to calculate variation, so d_2^* is used instead.

Tabulated values for d_2^* are shown in Table 8.3. There are two parameters of d_2^*: the number of items used to calculate each range (the subgroup size, m), and the number of range estimates used in the analysis (g). For the Repeatability chart, the subgroup size m is the number of trials, and the number of subgroups (g) is the number of appraisers times the number of items.

In this example, m equals 3 trials; $g = 2$ appraisers $\times$ 3 items $= 6$; d_2^* equals 1.73 from Table 8.3. Table 8.2 contains the between trial range for each appraiser, each piece. The average range for Joe is 0.0133; the average range for Jill is 0.02. The average range for all appraisers, all trials is the average of these values: 0.0167.

$$\sigma_e = \frac{\bar{R}}{d_2^*} = \frac{0.0167}{1.73} = 0.00965$$

The repeatability standard deviation value can be multiplied by a level of concern factor, stated in sigma units, to obtain the variation due to repeatability. A level of concern of 5.15 sigma units was historically applied to the repeatability standard deviation to provide its 99% confidence level. More recently, a Six Sigma level of concern has been used, prompting the AIAG to revise their definition of repeatability to exclude the level of concern factor altogether, due to the confusion surrounding its use.

TABLE 8.3 Table of d_2^*.

g = # Plotted Groups	\	m = # Samples in Plotted Group												
		2	3	4	5	6	7	8	9	10	11	12	13	14	15
1		1.41	1.91	2.24	2.48	2.67	2.83	2.96	3.08	3.18	3.27	3.35	3.42	3.49	3.55
2		1.28	1.81	2.15	2.4	2.6	2.77	2.91	3.02	3.13	3.22	3.30	3.38	3.45	3.51
3		1.23	1.77	2.12	2.38	2.58	2.75	2.89	3.01	3.11	3.21	3.29	3.37	3.43	3.50
4		1.21	1.75	2.11	2.37	2.57	2.74	2.88	3.00	3.10	3.20	3.28	3.36	3.43	3.49
5		1.19	1.74	2.1	2.36	2.56	2.73	2.87	2.99	43.10	3.19	3.28	3.35	3.42	3.49
6		1.18	1.73	2.09	2.35	2.56	2.73	2.87	2.99	3.10	3.19	3.27	3.35	3.42	3.49
7		1.17	1.73	2.09	2.35	2.55	2.72	2.87	2.99	3.10	3.19	3.27	3.35	3.42	3.48
8		1.17	1.72	2.08	2.35	2.55	2.72	2.87	2.98	3.09	3.19	3.27	3.35	3.42	3.48
9		1.16	1.72	2.08	2.34	2.55	2.72	2.86	2.98	3.09	3.18	3.27	3.35	3.42	3.48
10		1.16	1.72	2.08	2.34	2.55	2.72	2.86	2.98	3.09	3.18	3.27	3.34	3.42	3.48
11		1.16	1.71	2.08	2.34	2.55	2.72	2.86	2.98	3.09	3.18	3.27	3.34	3.41	3.48
12		1.15	1.71	2.07	2.34	2.55	2.72	2.85	2.98	3.09	3.18	3.27	3.34	3.41	3.48
13		1.15	1.71	2.07	2.34	2.55	2.71	2.85	2.98	3.09	3.18	3.27	3.34	3.41	3.48
14		1.15	1.71	2.07	2.34	2.54	2.71	2.85	2.98	3.08	3.18	3.27	3.34	3.41	3.48
15		1.15	1.71	2.07	2.34	2.54	2.71	2.85	2.98	3.08	3.18	3.26	3.34	3.41	3.48
>15		1.128	1.693	2.059		2.534	2.704	2.847	2.970	3.078	3.173	3.258	3.336	3.407	3.472

Practically, the repeatability standard deviation and repeatability variation values are intermediate values used to calculate % Repeatability, which is the pertinent statistic for drawing conclusions about the measurement system. The % Repeatability is the value quoted as "the repeatability" for the measurement system. The % Repeatability compares the repeatability standard deviation to the process sigma, indicating the percent of the process variation due to repeatability error.

Some softwares will also provide the repeatability as a percentage of the tolerance (the difference between the upper and lower specification limits: USL–LSL). When expressed as a percent of tolerance, we need to apply the level of concern discussed earlier, since the specifications apply to the total expected variation at some stated level of statistical significance. For Six Sigma uses, the Six Sigma level of concern is applied, as shown in the calculation above.

If process sigma is provided based on historical data as 0.03, and the process tolerance is stated as 0.2, then:

$$\%\text{Repeatability} = 0.00965/0.03 = 32.2\%$$
$$\%\text{Repeatability (Tolerance)} = (6 \times 0.00965)/0.2 = 29.0\%$$

Repeatability control charts may be constructed by grouping each appraiser's trials for each part into a single subgroup. Therefore, the size of the subgroup is equal to the number of trials per item. The variation within a subgroup is an estimate of the repeatability error inherent to the measurement equipment, so long as the variation is shown to be statistically stable over all parts and all appraisers. This assumption may be proven by observing the range chart for repeatability.

Figure 8.3 provides the repeatability chart based on the data in Table 8.2. Note how the range chart is in control, and the X-bar chart is out of control, with 4 of the 6 subgroups beyond the control limits.

The range chart is in statistical control. If a given item was out of control, the variation observed between the trials was larger than expected. For machined parts, perhaps the part had a burr or some other within part variation or abnormality associated with it. That suspicion increases if out of control is observed on the range chart for the same item/part for other appraisers' measurements.

The X-bar chart for repeatability is analyzed quite differently than most X-bar charts. The plotted statistic, X-bar, is the average of each subgroup (in this case, the average of each appraiser's trials for a given item). These X-bars vary as an indication of item-to-item variation. The control limits, however, are calculated using the average range between trials for each item, which provides

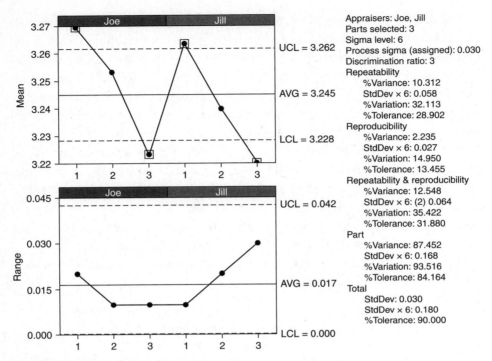

FIGURE 8.3 · Repeatability control chart for Table 8.2 data.

an indication of repeatability error. It is desirable that the measurement system detects real item (or part to part) differences in the presence of this measurement error. For that reason, the variation that is observed from subgroup to subgroup (i.e., part to part fluctuations) should be larger than the measurement errors (i.e., the control limits based on repeatability range), meaning that many subgroups should be out of control on the X-bar chart for repeatability. AIAG recommends that at least half the subgroups exceed the X-bar control limits.

In this example, four out of six of the groups are out of control.

Reproducibility σ_a is calculated using the difference between the appraiser averages:

$$\sigma_a = \sqrt{\left(\frac{\overline{X_{\text{DIFF}}}}{d_2^*}\right)^2 - \frac{\sigma_e^2}{(\#\,\text{parts})(\#\,\text{trials})}}$$

In determining the parameters for d_2^*, the subgroup size, m, for the range estimate equals the number of appraisers; there is only one range estimate used, so $g = 1$.

The average of each appraiser's data is shown in Table 8.2. The difference between these averages (in this case, 3.2489 − 3.2411 = 0.0078) is the $\overline{X}_{\text{DIFF}}$ used to calculate reproducibility.

From Table 8.3, for $m = 2$ and $g = 1$ $d_2^* = 1.41$.

$$\sigma_a = \sqrt{\left(\frac{\overline{X}_{\text{DIFF}}}{d_2^*}\right)^2 - \frac{\sigma_e^2}{(\#\text{parts})(\#\text{trials})}} = \sigma_a = \sqrt{\left(\frac{0.0078}{1.41}\right)^2 - \frac{0.00965^2}{(3)(3)}} = 0.00449$$

$$\%\text{Reproducibility} = 0.00449/0.03 = 15\%$$
$$\%\text{Reproducibility (Tolerance)} = 6 \times 0.00449/0.2 = 13.5\%$$

An $\overline{X}$ chart for reproducibility, which plots the average of each appraiser's measurements, is shown in Figure 8.4. The range chart for reproducibility plots the range between the appraisers' averages.

Sigma charts are used instead of range charts when the subgroup sample size (in this case, the number of appraisers) is more than 10. This is due to the

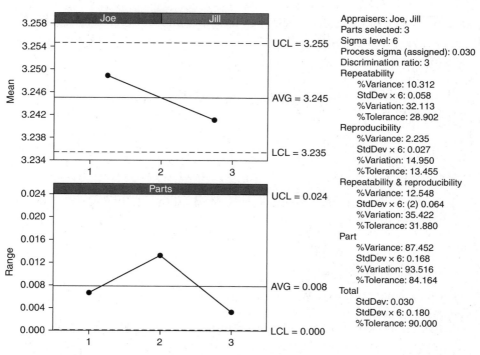

FIGURE 8.4 · Reproducibility control chart for Table 8.2 data.

decreasing efficiency of the range as an estimate of the standard deviation for larger subgroup sizes, as explained in Chapter 5.

The $\overline{X}$ chart for reproducibility analyzes whether each appraiser's average for the selected items is within the expected variability of these averages. In other words, it detects whether the differences between appraisers' averages is an indication of appraiser bias, or an expected variation due to equipment.

If the equipment error, as represented on the repeatability range chart, is in control, then the average repeatability range is an appropriate estimate of the variation from trial to trial. Trial averages, therefore, should fall within this variability, as long as there are no outside influences affecting the trial measurements, such as appraiser bias. This is the basis for the reproducibility $\overline{X}$ control chart.

The range chart for reproducibility analyzes the variability in appraiser averages for each item. As such, it may be used to identify whether the reproducibility is in a state of statistical control. If control is not exhibited, then the estimate of reproducibility may not be valid. Points out of control indicate that the variability in average measurements between appraisers is affected by the bias between parts/items.

The overall R&R statistic is calculated as the square root of the sum of the squares of each of the components: repeatability and reproducibility. It is often reported as either a percent of tolerance or as a percent of the total process variation.

$$\sigma_{RR} = \sqrt{\sigma_e^2 + \sigma_a^2} = \sqrt{.00965^2 + 0.00449^2} = 0.0106$$

$$\%R\&R = 0.0106/0.03 = 35\%$$

$$\%R\&R \text{ (Tolerance)} = 6 \times 0.0106/0.2 = 32\%$$

Typical recommendations for R&R, expressed as ether %Tolerance or %Process Variation, are

- 0% to 10%: Acceptable
- 10% to 30%: Marginal
- Over 30%: Unacceptable

When expressed as %Tolerance, R&R indicates the relative usefulness of the measurement system for determining product/service acceptance. Tolerance, calculated as the upper specification limit minus the lower specification limit, indicates the amount of variation that is permitted between all items produced. As measurement error increases relative to tolerance, the chances increase that:

- The items whose true value is outside specifications are measured as within specifications and accepted for use.
- The items whose true value is within specifications are measured as outside specifications and incorrectly rejected as unfit.

When expressed as %Process Variation, R&R indicates the relative usefulness of the measurement system for control charting and process capability analysis. The calculation of statistical control limits and the estimate of process capability require a sound estimate of the process variation. Subgroups plotted on a control chart are subject to measurement system error. As measurement error increases, so does the chance that:

- Subgroups from a controlled process will be determined out of control.
- Subgroups from an out of control process will be determined in control.

The calculations shown thus far have assumed process sigma is known from SPC analysis of the process, such as through a detailed process capability study. In that case, we can estimate the true standard deviation of the parts or units of service by noting that the process variance consists of the variance between the parts/units, and the variance due to measurement error.

$$\sigma_{part} = \sqrt{\sigma^2_{process} - \sigma^2_{RR}} = \sqrt{.03^2 - 0.0106^2} = 0.028$$

Although this is the preferred method, we may not have reliable estimates of process sigma available. In that case, the part variation may be estimated using the R&R study data. This is a much less accurate estimate of true part variation, due to the limited number of data values, as well as the inability to experience the full range of common cause variations persistent in the process. Using the study data, we calculate an average for each part (using all trials from all appraisers), then use the maximum and minimum part/unit averages to determine the range of part averages. The d_2^* factor will be based on m unique part/units in the study, and $g = 1$ range estimate. For $m = 3$ parts and $g = 1$, $d_2^* = 1.91$; $\sigma_{part} = (3.267 - 3.222)/1.91 = 0.024$, only slightly different in this example from that calculated based on the historical data.

Another useful statistic for R&R analysis is the discrimination ratio, some-times known as the *number of distinct categories*. Discrimination defines the number of distinct categories discernible by the measurement system. The number of classes is obtained by determining the amount of item-to-item varia-tion that is indistinguishable from measurement error.

A discrimination of two, for instance, indicates the measurement method is useful for only attribute analysis, since it can only effectively classify the items as being in one group or the other (for example, good or bad). Typi-cally a value of eight or more is suitable for SPC analysis and product/service disposition (i.e., determining if product/service meet customer requirements).

In the example, discrimination is calculated as:

$$ndc = 1.414 \times (\sigma_{part}/\sigma_{RR}) = 1.414 \times (0.028/0.0106)$$
$$= 3.74, \text{ which is rounded down to } 3.$$

This rather low value is considered unacceptable.

Destructive Testing

Destructive tests are an obvious example of measurements that cannot be repeated for a given sample unit. A tensile strength test results in the destruc-tion of the sample, as do common tests for pH or other chemical attributes. This limitation would seem to prevent both repeatability and reproducibility estimates. In service processes, cycle time estimates cannot be repeated by a single appraiser for a unit of service, although we can have multiple appraisers measure the same instance of service. This would provide an estimate of repro-ducibility, but not repeatability.

Cases such as these require special treatment. For cycle time measurements of observable processes, perhaps videotaping of the activity would allow repeat measurements. We may find through initial reproducibility estimates (which include repeatability error) that the total R&R is insignificant and not worthy of further investigation.

In destructive tests, we often seek to obtain multiple samples in close prox-imity, and assume the sample is homogenous over that region. For example, this approach would be useful in testing the tensile strength of fabric, or the hardness of a steel plate. Likewise, a given chemical sample can be split into multiple samples prior to measurement.

Still Struggling

The control charts for measurement systems analysis is a special case. Don't worry about the calculation of the statistics or the control chart parameters: These are only provided for reference. Software that constructs the charts and generates the statistics is readily available at reasonable cost. Instead, focus on the overall need for the analyses, and the interpretation of the analysis generated: Understand how to interpret the charts; use the %R&R (as percent of process variation and tolerance) as a guide to excessive measurement error; when excessive error exists, use the percent repeatability and percent reproducibility statistics to guide the measurement systems improvement activities.

ANOVA Method

Repeatability and reproducibility can also be estimated using Analysis of Variance (ANOVA) techniques, similar to those used in the scatter diagram and the multiple factor analysis techniques of Chapter 7. ANOVA allows the variation to be split amongst its components:

- Part: the true part to part variation
- Appraiser: the appraiser to appraise variation
- Part × appraiser: the interaction between parts and appraisers, indicative of issues that may be present on some parts that cause appraiser to appraiser differences
- Repeatability: the repeatability error
- Total: all components combined

A properly designed experiment is the most suitable method for obtaining the results for the ANOVA method. Figure 8.5 provides an ANOVA output using the sample data provided earlier.

The "Source of Variation" column of the ANOVA table provides the list of variation components considered for significance. The total variation observed in the response (the measurements) will be split amongst these components

ANOVA					
Source of Variation	SS	dF	MS	F	p-Value
Part	0.0061	2.00	0.0030	30.5	0.000
Appraiser	0.00027222	1.00	0.0003	2.722222222	0.125
Interaction	0.00007778	2.00	0.0000	0.388888889	0.686
Repeatability	0.0012	12.00	0.0001		
Total	0.00765	17.00			
Source	VarComp	% Contribution			
Total Gage R&R	0.000125926	20.06			
Repeatability	0.0001000	15.93			
Reproducability	0.0000259	4.13			
Appraiser	0.0000259	4.13			
Appraiser × Part	0	0.00			
Part-to-Part	0.00050185	79.94			
Total variation	0.00062778	100.00			

FIGURE 8.5 · ANOVA output for Table 8.2 R&R data.

based on the data. For each row, the ANOVA provides the degrees of freedom (DF: related to the information content, based on the number of data values available), the sum of squares (the variation about the mean), the mean square (equals the SS/DF), the calculated F-value (from the F distribution) and the associated p-value.

In practice, the ANOVA table is generated by software, and the analyst concentrates on the p-value, which indicates statistical significance (the other columns are the intermediate statistics required to generate the p-value). A component with p-value of 0.05 or less is generally considered significant (i.e., only a 5% probability that data this extreme could occur by chance alone, so the implication is that the significance is not by chance). For R&R analysis, we may choose to use a less stringent requirement of 0.10 or less, but in this initial analysis of the data we look to see if the part × appraiser interaction is highly insignificant using a threshold of 0.25. Excluding highly insignificant interaction effects will reduce the chance of estimating variance as a negative value.

In this example, the part × appraiser interaction has a p-value of 0.686, far above the 0.25 threshold, so it will be removed from the analysis. This allows the variation and degrees of freedom attributed to the interaction in this initial analysis to be reapportioned to the remaining components. When the interaction is removed, the reproducibility is entirely due to the appraiser variation.

Summary

Measurement system analysis is an important consideration when using measurements for evaluation of a product or service for either fitness for use or statistical control. In some cases measurement error can be a dominant source of either common or special cause variation, in which case measurement system improvement is synonymous with process improvement. Failure to recognize and respond to measurement error can lead to wasteful practices, either by delivering products or services that fail to meet customer requirements, or by responding to perceived errors that do not exist (i.e., tampering).

QUIZ

1. **Gage R&R Studies are best done using:**
   A. calibration standards.
   B. actual samples from the process.
   C. vendor samples.
   D. only the best operators.

2. **When trying to evaluate the error due to a piece of automated test equipment, a Gage R&R Study:**
   A. is usually not worth doing, since the error in the electronics is likely to be small.
   B. should be replaced by a Gage Linearity Study.
   C. can detect differences due to sample preparation or equipment setup.
   D. can only detect variation between the test operators.

3. **When using an X-bar/range chart for evaluating Gage Repeatability:**
   A. the range chart indicates the variation between operators.
   B. the X-bar chart should be out of control.
   C. the X-bar chart is scaled using the process variation.
   D. All of the above.

4. **A criteria for acceptance of Gage R&R is:**
   A. the calculated R&R should be less than 10% of process variation.
   B. the calculated R&R should be less than 10% of process tolerances.
   C. the calculated discrimination should be more than eight or ten.
   D. All of the above.

5. **Gage R&R Studies may be used to:**
   A. understand and reduce common causes of variation in a process.
   B. ensure that process personnel can take process measurements with minimal error.
   C. compare the performance of new test equipment.
   D. All of the above.

6. **Measurement systems analysis is needed because:**
   A. measurements by different personnel using the same equipment on the same sample unit can vary.
   B. measurements by the same personnel using the same equipment on the same sample unit can vary.
   C. calibration will not remove all measurement error.
   D. All of the above.

7. **Gage Linearity Analysis detects:**
   A. measurement error that changes as a function of the size of the measurement.
   B. variation between operators.
   C. variation between different gages.
   D. All of the above.

8. **The control chart for repeatability error shown in Figure 8.6 indicates:**

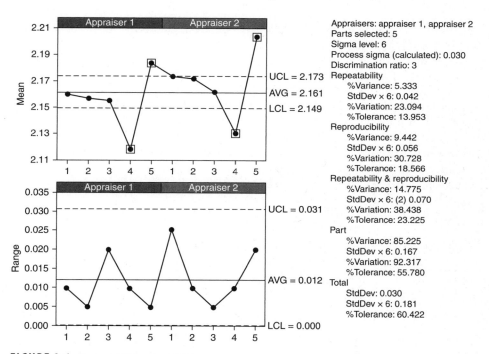

FIGURE 8.6 · Repeatability control chart.

   A. the repeatability is out of control.
   B. the process is out of control.
   C. the repeatability is not quite small enough relative to the process variation.
   D. the repeatability is not statistically stable.

9. **The statistics shown for R&R error in Figure 8.6 indicate:**
   A. the R&R is acceptable relative to process variation, but unacceptable relative to tolerance.
   B. the R&R is unacceptable relative to process variation and tolerance.
   C. the R&R is marginal relative to tolerance and unacceptable relative to the process variation.
   D. the repeatability is not statistically stable, so no estimates can be made of its suitability.

10. **The statistics shown for discrimination error in Figure 8.6 indicate:**
    A. the measurement system's discrimination is acceptable.
    B. the measurement system's discrimination is unacceptable.
    C. the measurement system's discrimination is marginal.
    D. the reproducibility error is not in statistically stable, so no estimates can be made of its suitability.

chapter **9**

Questions and Examples from Practitioners

The material in this chapter appears by permission of www.qualityamerica .com.

Lean Six Sigma/Quality Management Concerns

Importance of SPC to Quality Management System Performance

Q: How important is statistical process control to an organization's quality management system?   *Genevieve D.*

A: That's a great question, because I think it focuses on some key issues that are sometimes forgotten by quality managers. I see this often, because we sell both QMS software as well as SPC software, and I'm always amazed that there isn't more interest in SPC from some of our QMS customers. The short answer is: SPC is extremely important for a successful quality management system; let me explain why.

A quality management system is often focused on a few key areas: CAPA to identify, correct, and prevent the reoccurrence of nonconformances; auditing to ensure processes are using the quality systems effectively; and continuous improvement of the quality system itself. The system encompasses the full supply chain from your suppliers through to customers, as well as training of staff on the systems and processes.

With regard to CAPA, when we talk about preventative action we are referring to actions that will ensure the detected nonconformance will not reoccur. I suspect some practitioners think they can inspect their way out of this problem, that is, they feel by increasing inspection or monitoring of the process output they can prevent nonconformances from being delivered to the customer, or received from a supplier. I discussed the fallacy of this argument in the April 2011 *Quality Magazine* article, as did Deming in his *Out of the Crisis* text nearly 30 years ago. The problem with an inspection-focused approach is that after-the-fact sampling from process output is only credible if the process is in statistical control. In other words, you can't take a sample from a bucket of bolts and expect that sample to be representative of the bolts in the bucket unless the process that generated the bucket of bolts is in statistical control. The problem is, if the process is not in control, the bucket contains multiple distributions of bolts. The statistics of a sample from the bucket will assume the bucket contains a single distribution, not multiple distributions, and provide misleading results.

The fact is, without evidence of process control, you have to apply 100% inspection to the bucket, inspecting each and every bolt in the bucket. So the inspection-focused approach is actually a very costly method for "preventative action." And it's really not preventative at all! At best, it is reactive, at least when a process is out of control. Even for a process that is in control, it shows poor foresight, in that we could predict for the in-control process the percent of product exceeding requirements. Failing to address those issues before shipment is simply an ineffective and inefficient quality system.

The economic approach to preventative action is process improvement to prevent the occurrence of the nonconformance. Here again, Deming's *Out of the Crisis* discussed the need for a control chart to achieve process improvement, since only a control chart can differentiate between a common cause of process variation, which is built into the process, and a special cause of variation. Deming discussed how reacting to common cause variation as if it were a special cause increases process variation. I also discussed this in the April 2011 *Quality Magazine* article. The point is that you can't do meaningful process improvement without a control chart. Failing to recognize that is one of the reasons nonconformances reoccur at some organizations, and their quality department is constantly fighting fires!

Finally, when you talk about improvements to the quality system itself, you're focusing on internal KPIs (key process indicators) that estimate the system's responsiveness to problems. Here again, you need SPC to differentiate between the expected common cause variation in response and the special causes, since the special causes often provide insight into the dynamics of your systems, and thus the potential for improvement. At Quality America, we've developed an interface between our SPC and QMS software to help our customers take quality system's analysis to this next level and improve through system's feedback using effective dashboard display of their KPI.

Importance of SPC to Six Sigma Projects

Q: Many companies now are focusing on a Six Sigma program to achieve improvements. Control charts are a natural for the Six Sigma project's control phase but it seems they make good tools in the Analyze stage as well. Is this a proper use of this tool?   *Brian L.*

A: You are absolutely right. As you suspect, the control charts' ability to distinguish between common and special causes of variation also provides important direction during the Analyze phase. Our response to special causes of variation must be different from the response to common cause variation: For special cause variation, we can determine and remove the cause of instability; for common cause variation, we need to redesign the process.

Actually, control charts are necessary even before the Analyze stage. They are needed in the Measure stage of DMAIC to establish a process baseline.

The process baseline is an essential part of DMAIC, because this baseline is later compared to the improved process to demonstrate the project results. If you are a project sponsor, you should not accept the baseline unless it includes a control chart analysis. Without a sound baseline analysis, there is credible argument that a project may not have achieved its objectives.

For example, consider a baseline analysis of a process using confidence intervals: If the process were out of control during the baseline sample period, the project team will proceed through DMAIC, and try to verify their improvement in the latter part of the Improve stage. If the special cause is no longer present, totally unrelated to any improvement effort of the team, the team would think they had achieved their objective, when in fact that special cause had simply not been present during the Improve stage. The variation they see between the Improve stage and the Measure stage is due to nothing more than random common cause variation. The special cause, unfortunately, will likely reappear at some point in the future, and the team's efforts were essentially wasted!

Unfortunately, there are some Six Sigma training programs that focus on classical statistics in the Measure stage, and that is *simply wrong*. Confidence intervals and hypothesis tests are inappropriate tools for analyzing process data, except in the context of controlled (designed) experiments. The differences between analytical and enumerative statistics were described by Shewhart nearly a hundred years ago and Deming in the 1980s.

Importance of SPC to Lean Six Sigma Projects

Q: SPC is a critical tool within a standard Six Sigma program, but how does it relate to a Lean Six Sigma program?   *Glenn G., Global Director, LSS*

A: First off, there are some general misconceptions about Six Sigma and Lean Six Sigma. These are, in fact, synonymous terms. A proper Six Sigma program is one in which the DMAIC or DMADV approach is applied to projects, sponsored by management and aligned with an organization's strategic objectives related to cost, quality, and schedule. The projects use a variety of tools and techniques to provide measurable and sustainable deliverables to an organization. These tools include general problem-solving tools, statistical tools, as well as lean tools and techniques, as applicable to a given project.

Generally, all Six Sigma projects will focus on one or more of the three basic metric types (Critical to Quality, Critical to Cost, and Critical to Schedule), or some derivation of them such as Critical to Safety. Most projects include cost as a critical deliverable. To be clear, there are perhaps certain types of projects that lend themselves toward emphasis on the lean techniques: A project focused on schedule or any time-oriented metric will likely use lean tools and techniques to achieve improvement.

The point I want to emphasize is that this lean-focused project will still use DMAIC, and will also require the use of general problem-solving, project management, and statistical skills. As in the classic "Six Sigma" project, you'll need to use control charts in the Measure stage to establish a baseline, then again in the Improve and Control stages to verify the results you actually achieved.

It seems odd to me that many people using lean do not realize that many of the core lean concepts assume the process is stable. You cannot implement just-in-time, for example, unless the process is in statistical control. The inventories you are trying to eliminate are necessary because the process is unpredictable. Only the predictable, or in-control, process can consistently meet its takt time.

SPC Three Sigma Limits Relative to Six Sigma Performance

Q: The regular quality control chart usually uses three sigma for upper and lower limits. The chances that the defect falls outside the limits are 0.26%, that is, 99.74% of the output falls inside the limits. But if we look at the theory of Six Sigma, the defect rate at three sigma is 6.68% assuming normal distribution with upper and lower limits. Why such a big discrepancy?   *Ed C.*

A: A standard control chart with plus and minus three sigma limits is designed (assuming normality) to provide for a false alarm rate of 0.27%. That is, over the long run, we'd expect 99.73% of the plotted statistic (i.e., the observations on an individual x chart, or the subgroup averages on an X-bar chart) to lie within the control limits if the process is stable and the normal distribution provides a good fit to the plotted statistic. Conversely, approximately 0.27% of the time (over the long term), subgroups will fall outside these limits when the process is stable (in control), providing our estimate of the false alarm rate of the properly-designed control chart.

However, this false alarm rate cannot be compared to a sigma level for a number of reasons. First, out of control is not synonymous with defective. A defect occurs when an observation exceeds a specification limit, usually defined by the customer. A subgroup out of control implies either a false alarm or a shift in the process. The control chart's limits are calculated based on the statistics of the plotted subgroups, and are not related to the specification limits. When we plot observations on the individual x chart, it is only when the specifications coincide exactly with the calculated control limits that an out of control observation equates to a defect. On an X-bar chart, we plot subgroup averages, so there is even less relationship. When an X-bar chart is used, all of the observations in the subgroup may exceed the specification limits, yet the subgroup falls within the control limits. On an X-bar chart, the control limits must be much narrower than the specification limits to achieve process capability.

In the simple case of an individual x chart where specification limits happen to exactly coincide with the calculated three sigma control limits, the estimated process defect rate for Six Sigma purposes is not 0.27% (or 2700 DPMO), since over the longer term we accept that the process may shift by as much as 1.5 sigma. This 1.5 sigma shift is an "industry-standard" estimate of process sigma levels, as initially developed by Motorola and subsequently adopted throughout general industry applications. Using Appendix Table 8 in the *Six Sigma Demystified* text, we see that the estimated process defect rate for the three sigma process over the longer term is as high as 66,811 DPMO (i.e., 6.68%). Note that a process operating at a 4.5 sigma level of performance is expected to experience 1350 DPMO, which coincides with the one-sided defect rate for the hypothetical process whose specification limits exactly coincide with the three sigma limits.

In this way, the sigma level of a process tells us where the specification limits fall relative to the process distribution, assuming that the process may shift as much as 1.5 sigma over the long term. The 3.4 DPMO quoted for Six Sigma processes reflects a z-value (in a table of the standard normal distribution) of 4.5, since the 1.5 sigma shift prevents the process from experiencing its best estimated performance of 2 parts per *billion* defects (a z-value of 6).

Q: What I don't quite understand is mainly related to the fact that for a process to be "under control," the output is compared with the long-term plus and minus three sigma limits, and, let's say, observing an "out of control" event (beyond these limits) will then call for investigation, possibly stopping the process, troubleshooting, adjusting the process, etc.

However, such an event (beyond plus and minus three sigma) can happen 3 out of 1000 times. This is a fairly high rate which I think can present itself as an "occasional" observation for and in many high-volume production processes (including service companies once their output "opportunities" are considered); right? In other words, I think the three sigma limits are too tight to allow such natural variability, in particular, as will be bound to happen in high-volume processes. This is particularly very critical as occurrence of any point beyond the limits are considered to be indicative of "out of control"/"special cause"/"shift of the process mean" scenarios which, again, will call for strong reaction up to and including adjustment of the process—when it may not be needed at all!

However, to add to that, let's say now, if a process is running at Six Sigma level (being "under control," with a $C_p = C_{pk} = 2.0$), a 2ppb "out of specification" occurrence is considered to be "expected"—and this process is considered to be running fantastically. Of course, for this process, I guess all the parts beyond three sigma and below Six Sigma are also definitely accepted without any problems anyways—process is not considered to have any issues or no investigations/adjustments are called for. This, to me, is contrary with the first principle/test/requirement for a process to be "under control" (as outlined above, any occurrence beyond three sigma means problem!). Of course, this can further create a fallacy working with Six Sigma (as I have seen it here and there) that as long as the process is meeting the DPMO requirement (2ppb or 3ppm depending if the process is centered), it is running great!—without even considering the distribution of the output within plus and minus Six Sigma range!   *Marvin S.*

A: There are a couple issues to consider:

1. Every statistical method involves a balance between two conflicting properties: a false alarm rate and a failure to detect real differences. In the case of a control chart, three sigma levels provide an inherent balance between these issues. Tighter limits (such as two sigma, for example) increase the false alarm rate to unacceptable levels (about 5%). Widening the limits (to four sigma for example) would increase the probability of failing to detect real process shifts. On average, we would expect a false alarm (a subgroup beyond the three sigma control limits when the process has not shifted) about once every 370 subgroups regardless of the performance level of the process. In other words, the false alarm rate of the process is not dependent on whether it is a Six Sigma process or a two sigma process.

2. With respect to its implications on process volume, SPC is typically applied as a means of evaluating *samples* from a process, rather than 100% of the process output. In this regard, the process volume is not inherently linked to the number of subgroups or the resulting number of false alarm signals. The sampling rate should be dictated by consideration of both the economic impact of undetected shifts in the process as well as the physical causes of these shifts, and not a simple reflection of the volume of process output. That is, while high-volume processes may produce a lot of stuff, that in itself doesn't dictate the sampling rate to maintain evidence of process control; nor does it imply that

there will necessarily be many plotted points beyond the three sigma limits of the plotted statistic. As mentioned above, widening the control limits would greatly increase the chance that real shifts in the process will go undetected. In that regard, if you start with a controlled process that has a Six Sigma level of performance, and in widening the control limits fail to detect real shifts in the process, then you have just lost your Six Sigma level of predicted process performance, since you've lost your ability to predict, and you now have a process that has increased levels of variation.

With regard to the assertion that people incorrectly apply these tools "without even considering the distribution of the output within plus and minus Six Sigma range," then I would say they're not doing the analysis correctly. There's plenty of that, no doubt.

Use of SPC to Detect Process Manipulation

Q: I work for an automobile industry in India. We have just started an SPC project with the paint shop. I would like to know the ways to find out if the data has been manipulated, that is, the data is nonrandom.   *Supriya S.*

A: A control chart can detect if the process is in a state of statistical control, which implies that the effects of the various factors that influence the process are fairly consistent. If the process is not in statistical control (aka out of control), then it is being influenced by one or more special causes, whose effect is different than what was seen during the statistically controlled state. Special causes may be due to any of the factors influencing the process, such as the 5Ms & E: manpower, methods, machine, materials, measurement, and environment. A control chart cannot detect which of these factors are special causes, but can indicate approximately when the special cause was introduced. A properly designed experiment would be the correct approach to identify the source of the special cause, once a special cause has been evidenced on the control chart.

Sampling Considerations

Monitoring Batch Variation

Q: We have series of individual voltage measurements taken on our sensors during testing. The sensors can be grouped into batches with varying batch size. How best can we monitor batch to batch variations across batches with varying batch size? All SPC software we find are restricted by fixed subgroup sizes which prohibit the calculation of our batch means.

Richard T., Product Assurance Engineer

A: Generally, SPC control charts used fixed subgroup sizes. Statistically, it's been shown that larger subgroup sizes (greater than ten or so) do not give much more information than the smaller sizes (less than three), so practitioners will generally decide on an economic subgroup size based on the cost of going out of control versus the cost of sampling.

Most SPC software support varying subgroup sizes, for use primarily when observations within particular subgroups must be discarded due to bad data. Once a subgroup size has been specified, the software will properly recalculate the control limits for subgroups having less data than the specified subgroup size. To use this feature when subgroup size is based on batch size, the largest batch size may be input as the subgroup size.

It should be noted that the use of the control charts in this manner must consider the concept of rational subgroups. A control chart's subgroups are rational when the system of causes of process variation within the subgroups is the same system that influences between subgroup variation. The "within subgroup" variation is then a good predictor of the "between subgroup" variation. In the case of "batch to batch" variation, this requirement may not be met. For some processes, such as chemical processes, it is likely that the within batch variation is not a good predictor of between batch variation, since the components (or underlying causes) of variation are different. In cases like these, it is best to use a batch means chart (described in Chapter 5).

Sample Size Selection

Q: How do you choose a sample size? Is there a definite number or does it always depend on the population (# of parts being manufactured)? In the real world, my boss always told me to get at least 30 pieces, and his reasoning was because it makes statistical sense. I think the reasoning doesn't have much weight. However, it seems that everywhere I worked the magic number is 30.

Freddy B., Quality Assurance Engineer III

A: When you work with populations, such as in drawing samples from a homogenous lot to make decisions about lot acceptability, the sample size is determined with consideration to the power of the sample. Generally, you will have greater power to distinguish the deviation of the lot from the acceptability standards when:

- There is a large difference between the lot mean and the acceptability standard.
- The standard deviation of the population is small.

- The sample is large.
- The significance of the test is large. In other words, all else being equal, the power to detect a difference is better when you don't care if you make a false assertion.

You can calculate the sample size to detect a given difference at given significance (alpha) and power using general purpose statistical software. However, the fundamental assumption of this approach is based on the premise that you are sampling from a given (fixed) population, which is rarely the case. Realization of this fundamental fallacy in the analysis of process data as if it were a population leads most practitioners to the use of SPC to properly analyze process data, as Deming popularized in the 1980s.

For process data, where control charts are the optimal tool, the subgroup size is determined with consideration to formation of a rational subgroup. The number of subgroups necessary to properly define the control limits is based on the process dynamics, as well as statistical concerns. For measurement (variables) data, 30 subgroups provide a reasonable estimate of process variation when a subgroup size of 5 is used, but more subgroups are needed for smaller subgroup sizes. As a rule of thumb, I generally suggest 150 to 200 observations, grouped in rational subgroups of size 1 to 5.

Q: What is the minimum number of data points you would recommend for capability analysis?   *Calvin E., Quality Engineer*

A: You may have heard 30 subgroups. Did you ever wonder where that came from?

It comes from the fact that the constants used to define the control limits (A2, D4, D3, etc.) are not really constants, but approach constants for a large number of subgroups. How many subgroups you ask? For subgroups of size 5, you need about 35 subgroups before the second or third decimal place approaches a constant. For smaller subgroup sizes, you need more. When you get down to subgroup size of 1, you may also need to fit a distribution, especially if you want to analyze process capability. Most statisticians would say you need a few hundred data points to fit a distribution. I generally think of 150 to 200 observations minimum for all subgroup sizes, and of course that data must be from a stable process for it to be useful for these purposes. Do I ever make charts with less data? Of course, because it's interesting, easy and I may learn something about the process. But I realize the limitations of the data and don't sell the farm based on the limited data.

Bear in mind that these are only the statistical considerations. If we collect 200 observations over the course of 2 minutes, which we can using automated data collection equipment, would it be useful for estimating the common cause variation we are likely to see from the process? Probably not, so we also have to consider the process dynamics, the consistent sources of variation that we want to measure to fully understand the expected variation from the process if it continues to be stable. This may drive us to collect data over a sufficiently longer period of time, to ensure our initial estimates are meaningful.

Application to Software Projects

Q: In the case of software projects, every data is a single observation. In order not to compare apples and oranges, the software industry tries to group similar projects for measurement and comparison. But, there is no standard in-grouping. I always try to group them by the following:

1. *Size*: dollar value, number of members, or project duration.

2. *Business*: financial, telecommunications, security, etc.

3. *Type*: purely development, testing only, etc.

I wonder, from your experience, if you have any suggestions or any guidelines in this area?   *Ed C.*

A: Plotting results from dissimilar projects on a single control chart can certainly lead to erroneous conclusions. It basically comes down to: What is a process? For the case of software development, if you are tracking the time to complete the coding for each change to the software, and you include all changes to the software on a given control chart, then you're likely to detect some of the larger feature changes as special causes relative to other more minor changes. Constructing separate charts for each type of change, using some classification of the size of the change (lines of code?) can be helpful, or you can also take a short-run approach and look at a standardized deviation from the estimated time for each change. The advantage of this latter approach is it removes some of the subjectivity, and the resulting chart then indicates as special causes those changes where your estimates were very different from the actual time. This may be more useful from a process improvement point of view.

Attribute Chart Examples

p Chart of Prenatal Screening

Q: I've constructed a p chart of the percent of unacceptable prenatal screening requisitions (see Figure 9.1). There were two major process changes (August 2009 and September 2010) during this time period. When do I add new control regions to the chart to reflect these changes? Do I wait until there are 20 points to the new process, or can I define a new region right away since I know the process is different?   *Grace B., Quality Coordinator*

A: Generally, new statistical regions are only applied to the chart when you have statistical evidence of a process shift. The p chart in Figure 9.1 shows no change to the process behavior (as evidenced by out of control or run test violations), in spite of the procedural changes to the process. This suggests the procedural changes had no significant impact on the process dynamics. The variation observed in percent unacceptable requisitions is the expected variation from a stable process.

When a special cause has been detected by the control chart (as an out of control or run test violation), resulting in a sustained process shift, then there

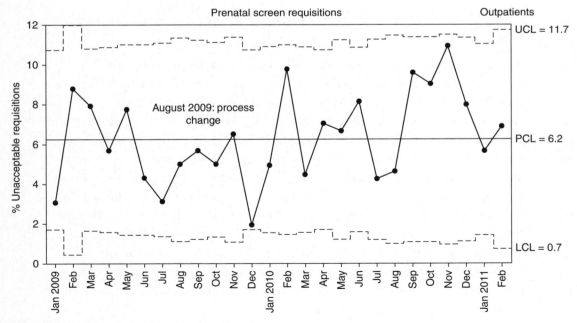

FIGURE 9.1 • Customer-constructed p chart.

is evidence of the process shift and it is appropriate to define a new control region for the process.

Nonetheless, it is possible the control limits in Figure 9.1 are biased by the inclusion of several distinct regions, which makes the chart somewhat insensitive to the differences between the regions. This sometimes happens in a retrospective analysis of a process (as discussed in chapter 2); it's usually best to use control charts in real time to detect these shifts as they occur. To simulate that manually, a control chart was constructed for the base period from January to July 2009 (assuming the process dynamics were relatively stable in that period), resulting in a center line of 5.6698, as shown in Figure 9.2.

The remaining groups are then added back to the chart, whose control limits are preset based solely on the data from January to July 2009, as shown in Figure 9.3. Since the control limits are defined based on the centerline from the initial region, they effectively investigate whether this subsequent data shows any evidence of a process shift relative to the initial baseline process. In this case, there is no evidence of a process improvement relative to the initial base period associated with the procedural change in August 2009; however, there is an out of control group detected

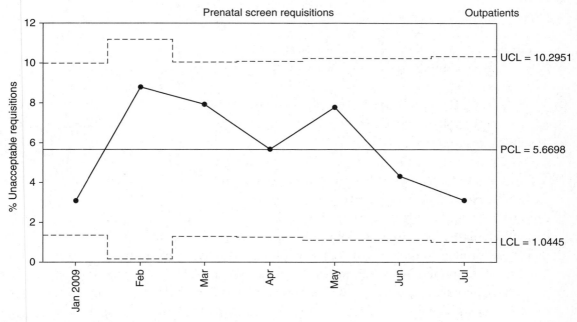

FIGURE 9.2 • Reconstructed p chart for initial base period.

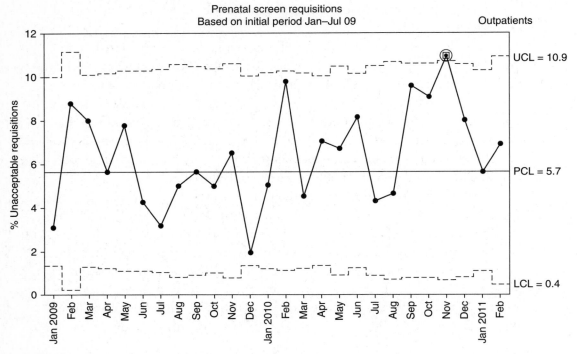

FIGURE 9.3 · p chart with control limits based on initial base period.

in November 2010, which could conceivably have been associated with a change in September 2010. This would appear especially likely given the 3 groups in a row above the centerline (just beyond two sigma even!) beginning in September 2010. On that basis, it is reasonable to assert that the process had shifted in September 2010, but was stable from January 2009 until August 2010.

On the basis of the process shift in September 2010, a final p chart can be constructed as shown in Figure 9.4 with a new region beginning September 2010. Note that, since there was no evidence of a shift until September 2010, the complete data from January 2009 until August 2010 is now used to calculate the initial region's control limits (rather than just the initial "base" period used in Figure 9.3). The process would appear to be in control since September 2010. While it is curious that the initial 3 groups for the new region are above the centerline while the last 3 are below the centerline, there is insufficient statistical evidence at this time to draw any conclusions from the pattern.

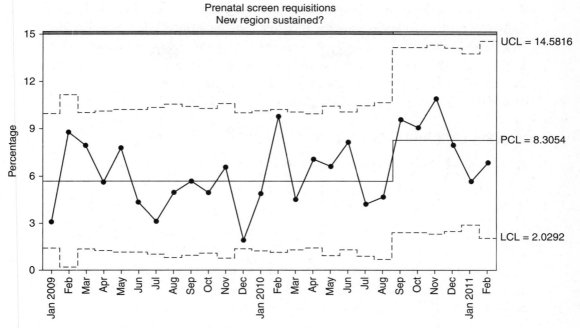

FIGURE 9.4 · p chart showing effect of process shift.

Histograms and Process Capability

Use of Sample Sigma versus Process Sigma

Q: Is it possible to use sample sigma instead of process sigma to determine control limits?   *Ed S.*

A: You do not want to use sample sigma in the calculation of control limits, as this would not then be a control chart. Control charts provide the ability to detect process trends by using the short-term variation as a predictor for the longer-term variation. The short-term variation is measured within the subgroup (or between successive subgroups in the case of subgroup size of 1), and identified by the nomenclature process sigma. Intrinsic to this definition of statistical process control is the time-ordered nature of the process data. The sample sigma calculation ignores the time-ordering of the data, preventing it from being useful for statistical process control estimates.

Q: I am having trouble replicating the capability index calculated by Minitab by hand or with other software. Any ideas?   *Karla W., Quality Specialist.*

A: When you do your six-pack analysis in Minitab, you need to click the *Estimates* button, and select the *R-bar* option for estimating standard deviation. The *pooled standard deviation* option results in an index known industry-wide as process performance. The R-bar and S-bar methods cited are the techniques developed by Shewhart for use in SPC, and specifically differentiates SPC from classical statistical methods designed for fixed populations.

Process Capability for Non-Normal Process

Q: How is process capability (C_p, C_{pk}) estimated for non-normal data?

Andy

A: First, let's discuss some general requirements for process capability indices:

1. You need to know the underlying shape of the process distribution to calculate a meaningful process capability index. The standard calculations apply only to a process whose observations are normally distributed. To properly calculate a capability index for non-normal data, you either need to transform the data to normal, or use special case calculations for non-normal processes.

2. You should never do a transformation, or calculate process capability, until you have determined the process is in the state of statistical control. If the process is not in control, then it is not stable, and cannot be predicted using capability indices. Likewise, an out of control situation is evidence that multiple distributions are in place, so a single transformation for all the process data would be meaningless.

So how do you handle this data?

1. First investigate the process stability using a control chart. We could use an X-bar chart with a subgroup size of 5. Why five? The central limit theorem tells us the average of five observations from even fairly non-normal processes will tend to be normally distributed. You can do a normality test on these averages to verify. You might also go with a subgroup size 3 if that works (it often does). A better approach is to use a moving average chart (cell width of 3 or 5, for same reasons as above) or an EWMA chart with your original subgroup size of 1 (a lambda of 0.4 works well). This chart should handle even non-normal data well.

2. If the process is out of control, stop there and improve the process. Don't bother with a capability analysis or with transformation, as they will be meaningless.

3. If the process is in control, then you can estimate capability. You could either transform the data to normal and use the standard calculations for capability applied to the normalized data, or fit a distribution to the data and calculate the capability using the percentiles of the distribution.

Q: Why do the non-normal process capability analyses max out at a C_{pk} value of 2.500?   *David W., Manufacturing Engineer*

A: When a normal distribution is assumed, the capability indices are conveniently calculated using the algebraic formula (provided in Chapter 3). The arithmetic allows for calculation of any value, down to several decimal places. However, when the Johnson distribution is used, an approximate distribution is fit to the data, and the distribution is interpolated at the specifications. When the specification lie far from the process centerline, in the far tails of the distribution, it is nonsensical to estimate beyond a capability index of 2.5, given that a capability index of 2.5 corresponds to a z-value of 7.5 (beyond the 99.99999999999 percentile of the distribution).

Q: I have a column of 300 numbers that I would like to do a histogram, Johnson bounded curve fit, but the chart that is generated is a normal curve and the software indicates the selected region could not be fit with a Johnson curve fit. What do I have to do to make it fit? I reduced the number of rows to 100 and it worked, but I need all the data if possible.

Wendell W., Manufacturing Engineer

A: When a distribution cannot be fit to data, it is often because the process is out of control, implying that a single distribution can only be fit to a portion of the data. To verify if the process is in control, I used a moving average chart with subgroup size 1 and moving size 3. The process was out of control in this scenario, but I noticed groups 205 to 290 were in control. That's not a lot of data to fit a curve (you'd like 200–300 observations), but it's enough to make it interesting. When I plotted those groups by themselves on the moving average chart, they were in control, as shown in Figure 9.5. Note that the data was separately checked for serial correlation, and none was evident. As a general rule, cycles such as appear in the moving average chart of Figure 9.5 are somewhat common in a moving average chart, and are not indicative of serial correlation in the raw data but rather the serial correlation built into the moving average statistic. (This built-in autocorrelation is the reason that run test rules are not applied to moving average charts.)

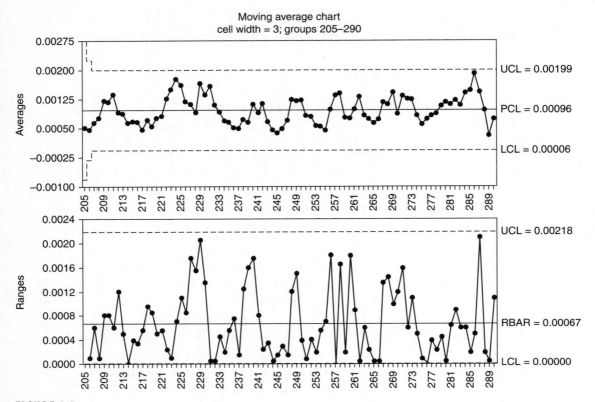

FIGURE 9.5 · Moving average chart for groups 205–290, using *SPC IV Excel* software.

I then plotted all the groups 1 to 300 on the individual x chart and let the software fit the Johnson distribution control limits based on groups 205 to 290, as shown in Figure 9.6. This confirms the process out of control, as evidenced on the moving average chart for all groups.

The key point is that you can't expect to fit a single distribution to an out of control process: If the process is out of control, then (by definition) there is more than one statistical distribution present in the data.

Q: I'm not sure whether I should use a normal or non-normal curve fit for calculating process capability. I've tried both, and compare the K-S statistic, but both K-S are small.

A: Part of the problem you have with fitting curves (normal or non-normal) is that your data is out of control. An extremely small K-S (less than 0.05) is an indication that the data is not well-fit by the chosen distribution. If the

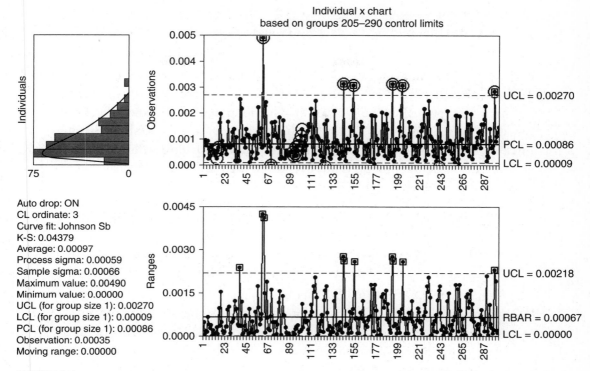

FIGURE 9.6 • Individual x chart for all groups with control limits based on groups 205-290, using *SPC IV Excel* software.

process is out of control, then by definition there are multiple distributions, so it stands to reason that one given distribution may not fit well. I say "may not" since you can get software to fit a good distribution, even a normal distribution, when the process is out of control, if the data just so happens to look not so different than the assumed distribution. So a bad fit may reflect out of control or wrong distribution, and a good fit can still occur if the process is out of control. Technically, a good fit may also occur even when the wrong distribution is chosen, but so long as it works for us in predicting the process, then that's good enough. (George Box said it as: "All models are wrong, but some are useful".)

Start by verifying the process is in control, then worry about capability analysis and curve fitting.

Q: I have C_{pk} data from a supplier and I want to compute a C_{pk} index. For example, one set of data represents a straightness measurement which is bounded by 0 with an upper specification limit of 1.016. The data seems to be centered within the spec limits and is more than three sigma away from the upper specification. Why does my analysis indicate the C_{pk} is only 1.0?

Calvin E., Quality Engineer

A: There's a few things going on here. First and most important, you only have 30 data points, so it can be difficult to fit a statistically relevant distribution. Furthermore, you really should never fit a distribution until you know the process is in control. An EWMA chart (lambda = 0.4) can be used to show that in this case, the process is out of control, so by definition a single distribution is not appropriate. Since the process is out of control, then the process is incapable.

A few other things I might point out:

1. For a straightness measurement, there is no lower specification limit, so that field should be left blank.

2. You should remove out of control data from the calculations of the control limits. This is standard practice. The points should be visible on the chart, but excluded from the analysis.

3. Your comment that the data is more than three sigma from the specification is only pertinent to a normal distribution. Non-normal distributions may require more sigma units on one side or the other of the median to ensure capability.

Variable Chart Examples

Getting Started

Q: Our thought was to begin using SPC for 1 month and then look at the data and decide what the control limits should be from there. For the initial month, the SPC software will automatically calculate the control limits. Is this a recommended approach?

Christy W., Quality Specialist

A: Your overall strategy is generally sound: Let the process run for a period of time, and calculate control limits for the process. However, if your process is initially out of control (as yours is), you need to understand and remove the causes of instability to apply the limits to the future. It would be worthwhile to take a look at the process during the times of instability and try to determine what's different. You can start with brainstorming, and you may even stumble on something that can be corrected immediately, but the best approach usually leads toward some designed experiments. Did I lose you? Some people get nervous as soon as they hear experimental design. DOE doesn't have to be difficult, but it should be planned.

Use of Specification Limits on an X-bar Chart

Q: In several places in your *Six Sigma Demystified* book, you mention to never put specifications on an X-bar chart. Please explain.   *Ed C.*

A: The specifications indicate the desirable values of the process observations, not their actual values. The process itself may be quite different from these recommended levels, so we measure from the process and use the statistics of the measurements to estimate the true process conditions. When we plot values on an X-bar chart, we are not plotting individual measurements: We plot the average of a sample of measurements. For example, the measurements from a process might be 6, 8, 12, and 14. The average of this sample is 10. If the process specification is LSL = 8 and USL = 12 (i.e., desired value is 10, with allowable deviation of plus or minus 2), then the average tells me I'm doing pretty well. Unfortunately, none of the individual measurements satisfy the requirements.

The point is: The specifications apply to the individual measurements, not the average. Think of that the next time your plane is trying to land on the runway: We care if this individual landing is well-centered within the traffic lanes, not whether the average of many flights is within the traffic lanes.

Analysis of Data with Consideration toward Non-Normality of Process

Q: I would like to know how to analyze surface finish. I am attaching a sample of data. The upper specification limit for the finish is 63.   *Cheryl D.*

A: It would appear your data was collected with a rational subgroup size of 1. Given that, we will use one of the charts useful for individuals ($n = 1$) data, such as the individual x chart or the moving average/range chart.

When using an individual x/moving range chart, the choice of distribution (used to define the individual x control limits) is based on the properties of the process. In your case, the process is bounded at zero. The normal distribution, by definition, will place the individual x control limits at plus and minus 3 times the process sigma value from the process mean, without regard to whether your process can logically operate there. Of course, the calculations have no advance knowledge of your process, and in this case assumes that your process approximately follows the conditions of a normal distribution. For some bounded processes this can be a poor assumption, as the process may be skewed. In the case of surface finish [or customer wait time, process cycle time, total indicator reading (TIR), etc.], where the process is physically bounded at zero, process improvement efforts tend to move the mode and median closer to zero. As they move closer to zero, and further from the average, the normal distribution will incorrectly predict a significant amount of the process below zero, a practical impossibility. This induces errors in your capability analysis, as well as your estimation of process control.

Since we need to understand the underlying distribution to define meaningful control limits for the individual x chart, and we can't fit a meaningful distribution without verifying that the process is in control, the individual x chart is not the best tool at this point in the analysis.

Instead, you could use the moving average chart, with subgroup size of 1 and cell width of 3, to verify the process control. If in control, a distribution may be fit to the data for capability analysis or for use in the individual x chart. In your case, there is insufficient data for a complete conclusion, although mathematically we are able to generate the moving average chart shown in Figure 9.7 for an initial estimate of process control. This initial estimate (based on limited data) suggests the process is in control. Viewing the same data on an

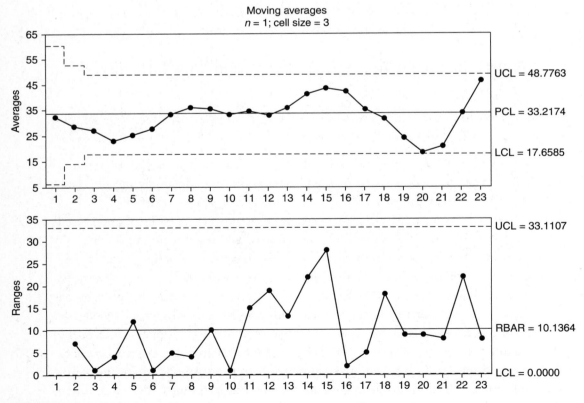

FIGURE 9.7 · Moving average chart.

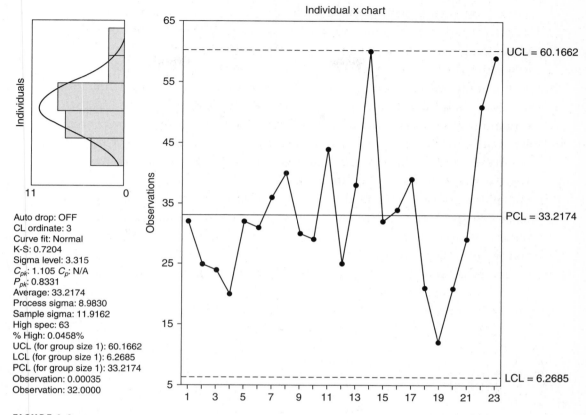

FIGURE 9.8 · Individual x chart.

individual x chart in Figure 9.8 shows that the normal distribution provides a reasonable estimate for the data (note the K-S value of 0.72 and the reasonable fit of the curve to the histogram), with a C_{pk} of 1.105 (a marginal value). Again, this is preliminary information, based on a small set of data (23 data values). For process control purposes, with a moving cell width of 3, we should have 50 or more subgroups to define meaningful control limits. For curve-fitting purposes (such as needed for sound capability estimates), 200 to 300 observations are recommended.

Q: I created a control chart using 23 data points for the time in minutes to achieve small bowel intubation on patients. As you can see the lower control limit is −17.18. Could you please explain how the system could calculate a negative lower control limit when time could not be less than 0 minutes? Also, is an x chart the best chart to be used for this type of analysis?

Tammy W., Quality, Accreditation & Risk Management Dept.

A: The normal distribution, by definition, will place the individual x control limits at plus and minus 3 times the process sigma value from the process mean, without regard to whether your process can logically operate there. Of course, the calculations have no advance knowledge of your process, and in this case assumes that your process approximately follows the conditions of a normal distribution.

Given the physical nature of your process ("time could not be less than 0 minutes"), it's wise to ask what distribution best approximates the process. Keep in mind that a process out of control (by definition) will not be well approximated by a single distribution. Yet, as you saw with your data, we need to understand the distribution to define meaningful control limits for the individual x chart. Since we need to know the distribution for the individual x chart's control limits, and we can't fit a meaningful distribution without verifying that the process is in control, the individual x chart is not the best tool at this point in the analysis.

Instead, I generally recommend the EWMA chart, using a lambda value of 0.4 as shown in Figure 9.9. This chart will allow you to see whether the process is in control. If so, a distribution may be fit to the data for capability

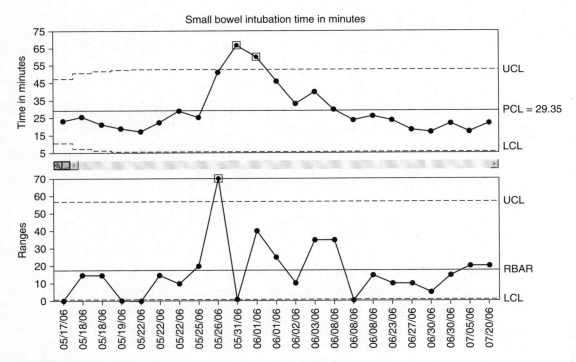

FIGURE 9.9 • EWMA chart.

analysis or for use in the individual x chart. In this case, there is insufficient data for a complete conclusion, but initial analysis indicates it is not in control (groups 9 and 10 are out of control). For fun, we could omit those groups from the analysis. When we repeat the analysis for this limited data on the individual x chart, we use the Johnson distribution with a lower bound defined at 0. This provides a reasonable initial estimate for your control limits, but it is best to collect quite a bit more data to verify the stability and curve fit (using the EWMA to establish control, then the Johnson curve fitting for predicting the distributional properties) before reaching any broad conclusions on the process.

Analysis of Batch Processes

Q: We are a specialty chemical manufacturer that utilizes a batch process to generate our products. From my understanding, SPC charts are basically useless for batch process. Some of our customers require SPC charts anyway. The acceptable range for the C_{pk}, I am told, is 1.33 to 2.00. With the previous software I was using, it was easy to manipulate the C_{pk} by adjusting the control limit. However, with this new program, I can't seem to get the C_{pk} within the acceptable range. Is there any way to manipulate this? Also, which type of chart would be the best for me to use?   *Matt S., QC Chemist*

A: Control charts can be applied to batch processes. However, as in multistream processes, the traditional X-bar chart cannot be used as you might expect. When you select subgroups for the X-bar chart, subgroup observations collected from within the batch provide an estimate of the within batch variation, but do not provide a good estimate of the between batch (or longer-term) variation. As such, subgroups collected as multiple observations from a batch are irrational subgroups, and not useful for defining the control limits on the X-bar chart.

One alternative is to use a batch means chart, which allows you to use the multiple observation subgroup collected from the batch, but corrects the control limits on the X-bar chart to use the variation between batches, such as is done in a moving range chart. One advantage of the batch means X-bar chart controls both the within batch variation (on the range chart) and the between batch variation (on the X-bar chart). The calculated process capability uses process sigma based on the moving range between the batch averages.

The only acceptable method for forcing a capability calculation is to define the control limits based on a predefined estimate, such as from a process qualification/capability study. When control limits are predefined, the capability indices are also predefined, since they are inherently linked. This is one reason why capability indices should never been evaluated without their accompanying control chart: The control chart defines the process sigma and average values applied in the process capability calculation; those estimates are meaningless unless the process is in control relative to the process sigma and average values applied.

When the batch is essentially homogenous, and measurable variation cannot be estimated reliably, then it's only necessary to take a single observation from the batch, and apply it to an individual x/moving range chart or any of the other charts from individuals ($n = 1$) data, such as a moving average or EWMA chart.

Analysis of Sheet Properties (Across Width versus Along Length)

Q: We are analyzing data from production of a polymer sheet. A critical characteristic is the sheet thickness, which we measure at 12 locations across the width (sometimes called web) of the sheet, as well as along its length. Our project objective is to decrease the thickness variation from sheet to sheet as well as within each sheet. Our process is totally out of control! Can you please assist in how we might proceed?   *Toni B., Black Belt*

A: At first glance, your process is certainly out of control, as shown in Figure 9.10; however, the first issue is that your subgroup is irrational: You are creating a subgroup using the 12 measurements across the web, which is not a good predictor of the variation along the length of the sheet, or between sheets. In other words, it is quite likely the sources of variation across the sheet are not the same as those that influence the sheet to sheet variation, or even the variation within the sheet along the feed direction.

I applied the batch mean option for the control limits to produce the control chart shown in Figure 9.11. This removed a great deal of the perceived instability. I then considered the effects of the various process parameters using stratification techniques on the traceability fields provided with the data [product family, extrusion batch, kneader batch, calendar station, orientation (north/south), etc.].

The step change in the control limits noted in both figures is apparently due to a change in the process when switching from product family 77 to product family 71. The instability from groups 211 to 231 is associated with switching to product family 99 then 73. Additional variation is also observed between the

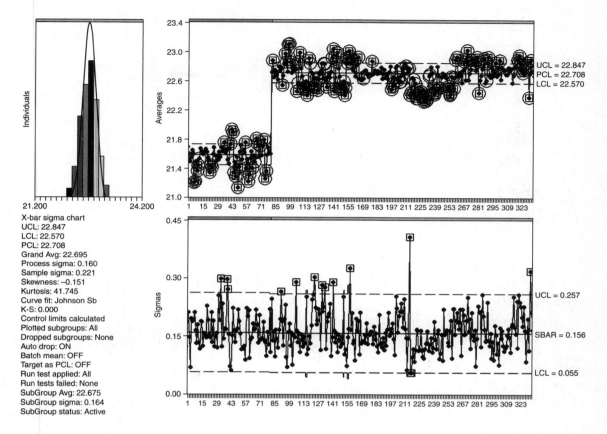

FIGURE 9.10 · Original X-bar/sigma chart of thickness.

north and south orientation (i.e., leading edge versus trailing edge relative to feed direction) of the sheets. If we restrict the analysis to only the north orientation (leading edge), and remove the effects of product families 99 and 73 the resulting Figure 9.12 provides a cleaner template for understanding the special causes of variation.

Referring to Figure 9.12, the instability noted for product 71, from subgroups 107 to 117, occurs immediately after product 73 was switched out. This suggests an issue with process setup when switching between products. I would also verify the data associated with the sigma chart out of control groups. A quick review of the observations in these groups suggests data entry error (e.g., 23.05 instead of 23.5), at least relative to the resolution of other data.

In summary, there are clear issues for the team to consider with respect to both within and between sheet variation. Within sheet variation is largely characterized

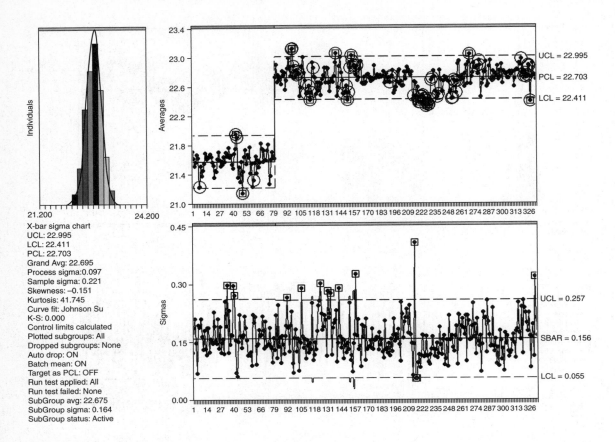

FIGURE 9.11 · Batch means X-bar/sigma chart of thickness.

by the marked difference between leading and trailing edge measurements and the web variation (plotted on the sigma chart). Variation between sheets seems dominated by the instabilities associated with product changeover.

Analysis of Completion Time for Blood Collection Process

Q: I have a series of numbers in the time format that I would like to plot using the individual x chart. Each of these numbers represents the time that the phlebotomist completed the blood collection process. I have 50 data points (collections), and would like to see the mean time for these collections, as well as the UCL and LCL (and would like to set the target time as 07:30 hours). How do I convert the y-axis scale to the standard (24-hour) time format in MS Excel?

Grace B., Quality Coordinator

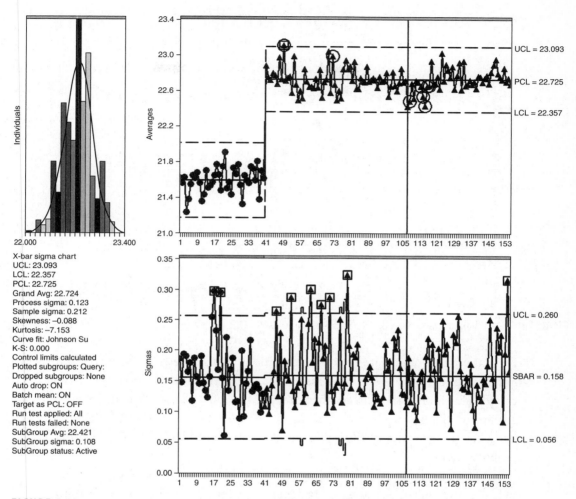

FIGURE 9.12 • Batch means X-bar/sigma chart of thickness for products 77 and 71, north orientation.

A: The time-formatted data in column B on your data tab must be converted to a decimal format, which is necessary for the control chart's centerline and control limit calculations. In MS Excel, convert the time formatted (HH:MM) data in column B to the decimal time using this equation (shown for the data in cell B2):

$$=ROUND((RIGHT(B2,2)/60)+TRUNC(B2/100),3)$$

Nonetheless, the data still violates a basic premise of a control chart, in that the data is autocorrelated (aka serially correlated). A fundamental assumption for the control chart calculations is that the data is independent, yet the

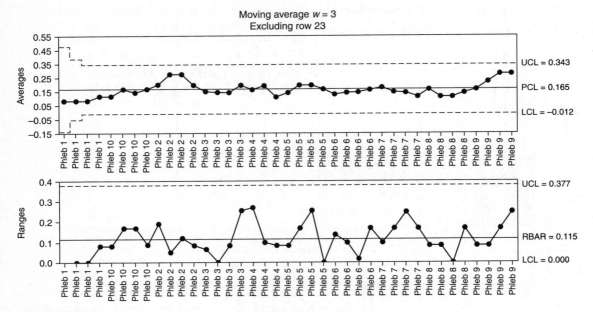

FIGURE 9.13 · Moving average chart of time between samples.

five data values associated with each phlebotomist are serially correlated. Since the times are the end time associated with each of the five samples: The second value is necessarily larger than the first; the third is larger than the second, and so on. This is a natural consequence since the phlebotomist cannot complete (or even start) the subsequent sample until the preceding sample has been completed.

Perhaps a better metric for the process would be the time between samples, such as shown in the moving average chart of Figure 9.13. The moving average chart is a preferred chart for evaluating control for individuals data, since it does not require assumptions about the process distribution. The chart indicated an out of control process, which I guessed resulted from an especially large value in row 23. (Note this affected three plotted groups since the moving size was set to 3.) After removing row 23, the moving average chart indicated a controlled process. An individual x chart with control limits based on the data (omitting row 23) is shown in Figure 9.14, which can be more easily used for process capability estimates.

For example, the Individuals chart using a non-normal curve fit predicts a median time between samples of 0.147 hours (equivalent to 8 minutes, 49 seconds), and an upper limit of 0.849 hours (equivalent to 50 minutes 56 seconds). Note that a normal distribution analysis of the data shows a poor curve fit (K-S value less

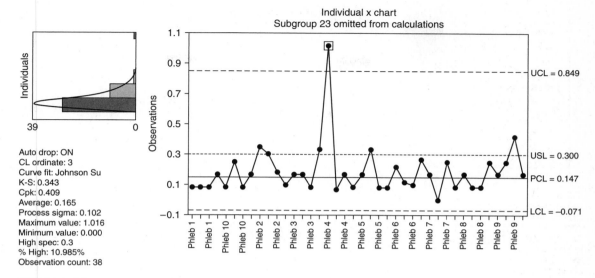

FIGURE 9.14 · Individual x chart of time between samples (excluding row 23).

than 0.05). If the phlebotomist is expected to complete five samples in an hour and a half period, then the upper specification limit is 0.30 hour per sample. Applying this to the analysis provides a C_{pk} of 0.41, or approximately 11% of samples are predicted to exceed the requirement.

Control Chart of Number of Days Between Events

Q: Can you please explain how to create a control chart for the number of days between events using the data provided? I understand you need to transform the data using a Box-Cox transformation.

Sam F., MD, Senior VP, Quality & Safety

A: As background, the Box-Cox transformation is a general transformation technique to convert non-normal data into normal data. The form of the transformation depends upon a lambda value calculated from the data. For example, a lambda near 0 suggests the log transformation; a value near 0.5 suggests a square root transformation. An optimal value of lambda can be determined which minimizes the sum of square error (between the transformed data and a true normal distribution). The idea is that the transformed data is then approximately normally distributed, so the normal distribution can be used to determine control limits of the transformed data on a standard individual x chart.

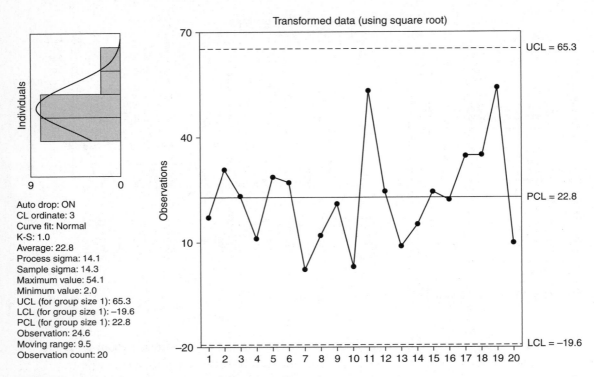

Auto drop: ON
CL ordinate: 3
Curve fit: Normal
K-S: 1.0
Average: 22.8
Process sigma: 14.1
Sample sigma: 14.3
Maximum value: 54.1
Minimum value: 2.0
UCL (for group size 1): 65.3
LCL (for group size 1): −19.6
PCL (for group size 1): 22.8
Observation: 24.6
Moving range: 9.5
Observation count: 20

FIGURE 9.15 · Individual x chart of Box-Cox transformed time between events.

I ran the time between events data provided through Minitab's Box-Cox transformation function, which calculated an optimal value of 0.29. Since this is closer to the value of 0.5 than to 0.0, it suggests a square root transformation. For example, the first observational value of 286 is transformed by taking its square root to a value of 16.911. The resulting individual x control chart, using the normal distribution, is shown in Figure 9.15. Note that neither the control limits nor run tests are violated.

A simpler alternative to this approach uses the Johnson non-normal transformation functions, which Minitab also includes. The Minitab help system explains the Box-Cox transformation is "easy to understand, but is very limited and often does not find a suitable transformation." It recommends the Johnson transformation as the more robust transformation: "The Johnson transformation function is more complicated, but is very powerful for finding an appropriate transformation." Since we are using software to directly transform the data, calculate control limits then plot the data in its native form, the complication is left to the software.

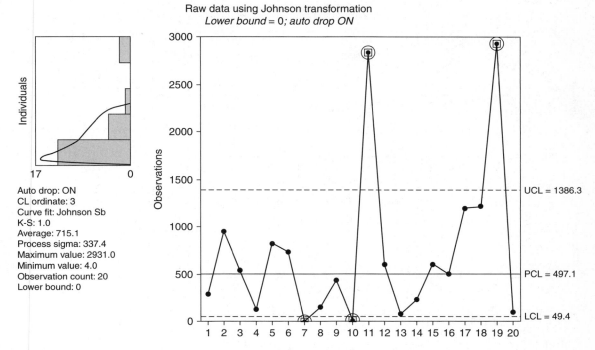

FIGURE 9.16 • Individual x chart of raw time between events using Johnson translation.

An analysis of the raw data using the Johnson transformation option is shown in Figure 9.16. In this case, the lower bound option was set to 0.0, since the time between events data must be positive; the auto drop option was also used to remove the out of control values from the calculation of the control limits. Note that this chart shows the process to be out of statistical control at two values that appear to be somewhat larger than the other values.

I then used a moving average chart of the raw data to determine if the data was really out of control, or if the Johnson transformation was perhaps influencing the analysis. [Note that I used the moving average chart since the plotted points (the moving averages) can be assumed normally distributed via the central limit theorem.] As shown in Figure 9.17, the moving average chart also shows out of control conditions in approximately the same regions as the Johnson analysis.

In summary, the Johnson option provides a superior solution to the Box-Cox transformation. As a rule, you should first verify the process is in control using the moving average or EWMA chart, then fit the distribution by comparing the normal curve fit with the Johnson curve fit.

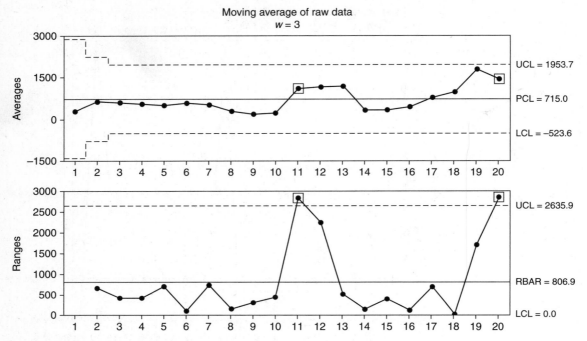

FIGURE 9.17 · Moving average chart of raw time between events.

Understanding Implications and Detection of Serial Correlation

Q: Can you please explain what is meant by "autocorrelation" and why it matters to my control charts? *Dean L., Sales Director*

A: A fundamental assumption of standard SPC charts is the independence of the plotted subgroups (with one another), as well as the observations within each subgroup. When observations are dependant over a short period of time, then the standard control limits are incorrectly calculated: The short-term (within subgroup) variation is not a good predictor of the longer-term between subgroup variation for which the control limits are applied.

Independent processes (discussed throughout this book) are fundamentally different from dependent processes. For independent processes, the latest (most current) observation provides no additional information as to the value of the next observation. For example, using a fair pair of dice, the numbers on any given roll will not provide any indication of the numbers on the next roll, implying that the rolls are independent. Likewise, a given value within the control limits of a stable process provides no additional information on the value of the next observation from the process.

When dealing with processes that are normal and independently distributed (NID), the best guess of the next process observation is always the process mean, regardless of the value of the current observation. (For non-normal, independent processes, the best guess is the process median). The NID process may be modeled as follows, where any value x at time, t, equals the mean of the process plus some (white noise) error:

$$x_t = \mu + e_t$$

For dependent processes, the next observation may be predicted as a function of (i.e., based upon) the value of the current observation or a prior observation, plus some error:

$$x_t = f(x_{t-1}, x_{t-2}, x_{t-3}, \ldots, x_0) + e_t$$

Autocorrelated processes are of two general types: *stationary* and *nonstationary*. Stationary processes are those that remain in equilibrium about a constant mean. Nonstationary processes have no natural mean which can describe the process; the process either wanders or moves in a noticeable direction (over the longer term) of generally increasing or decreasing values. When autocorrelation is present, it is more likely to be nonstationary in nature. (See Chapter 2 for examples of autocorrelated processes.)

Autocorrelation can be positive or negative: In positive autocorrelation, large data values tend to follow large values, and small data values tend to follow small values, in a trending fashion. This is often the case for service wait times, as well as the slowly changing properties of chemical batches. In negative autocorrelation, there is a cyclical nature to the data, where large data values alternate with small data values. In manufacturing operations, negative correlation may result from process tampering, as the process moves one direction then the other as a result of over-adjustment.

Fortunately, the presence of autocorrelation can be detected through statistical analysis. In linear regression analysis (see Chapter 7), the correlation coefficient R is used to estimate the linear relationship between two variables. Similarly, we can use an autocorrelation function to estimate the correlation between observations k samples apart, where k is referred to as the lag.

For example, lag 5 autocorrelation refers to correlation between data values 5 time periods (or samples) apart, so sample 1 will be compared with sample 6, sample 2 will be compared with sample 7, sample 3 will be compared with sample 8, and so on to estimate lag 5 autocorrelation.

The scatter diagram in Figure 9.18a was created by comparing observations of queue time for a sales process at lag 1 (i.e., one sample apart): It indicates a

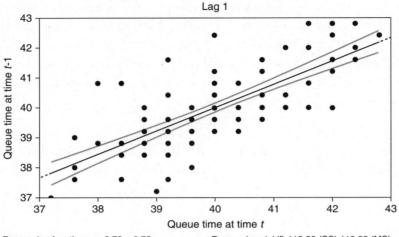

Regression function: $y = 8.78 + 0.78 \times x$
Correlation coefficient: 0.77
Function explains 58.56% of variation

Regression: 1 (df) 118.28 (SS) 118.28 (MS)
Residual: 117 (df) 83.69 (SS) 0.72 (MS)
F: 165.36
Prob F: 0.00

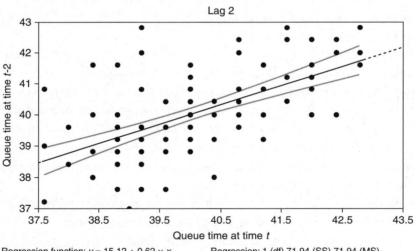

Regression function: $y = 15.12 + 0.62 \times x$
Correlation coefficient: 0.60
Function explains 35.66% of variation

Regression: 1 (df) 71.94 (SS) 71.94 (MS)
Residual: 116 (df) 129.82 (SS) 1.12 (MS)
F: 64.28
Prob F: 0.00

FIGURE 9.18 • a-d Scatter diagrams of time in queue data for lag 1 (a), lag 2 (b), lag 5 (c), and lag 10 (d).

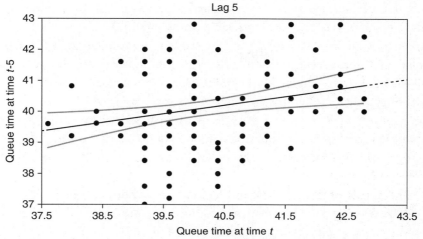

Regression function: $y = 28.83 + 0.28 \times x$
Correlation coefficient: 0.26
Function explains 6.84% of variation

Regression: 1 (df) 13.52 (SS) 13.52 (MS)
Residual: 113 (df) 184.25 (SS) 1.63 (MS)
F: 8.29
Prob F: 0.00

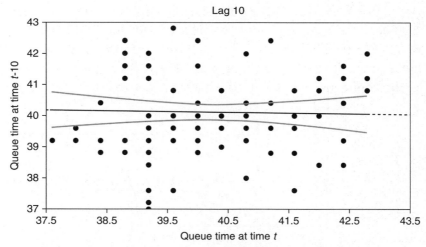

Regression function: $y = 41.03 + 0.02 \times x$
Correlation coefficient: −0.02
Function explains 0.05% of variation

Regression: 1 (df) 0.09 (SS) 0.09 (MS)
Residual: 108 (df) 194.66 (SS) 1.80 (MS)
F: 0.05
Prob F: 0.83

FIGURE 9.18 · (*Continued*)

very high correlation between the data and the most recent data value preceding it. (This data was previously presented in Figure 5.9.)

As we move to lag 2 (Figure 9.18b), we see that the correlation between data 2 samples apart is much less, but still fairly strong; at lag 5 (Figure 9.18c) correlation is still evident. A check at lag 10 (Figure 9.18d) shows negligible autocorrelation.

Although scatter diagrams are relatively simple tools to interpret, it can be cumbersome to generate a multitude of them to check for autocorrelation. Instead, an autocorrelation function can be defined using the correlation coefficient at each lag m, such as shown in Figure 9.19 for the queue data of Figures 9.18a–d.

A general rule of thumb (Box and Jenkins) is to check autocorrelation to lag $n/4$, where n is the total number of data points. In the queue data, there were 120 observations, so the autocorrelation is tested out to lag 30 in Figure 9.19.

Confidence intervals can also be calculated for the autocorrelation function to test the hypothesis of zero correlation at each lag. If the correlation coefficient is non-zero, then the correlation coefficient will be greater than z divided by the square root of n, where n is the number of observations and z is the ordinate of the normal distribution at a stated confidence level. For example, a 95% confidence level corresponds to a z value of 1.96; for the 120 observations analyzed in Figures 9.18 and 9.19 the confidence interval for the autocorrelation function is calculated as 0.179. Note in Figure 9.19 that lags 1 through 5 exceed the confidence interval. In this case, each observation was recorded a

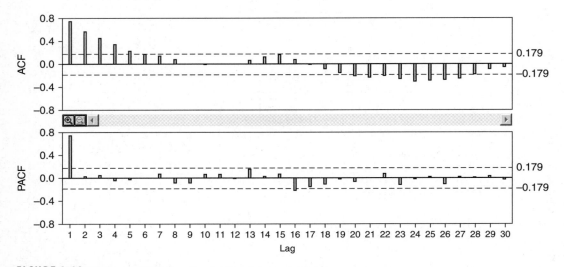

FIGURE 9.19 · Autocorrelation function for time in queue data.

minute apart, so independent data can be obtained by analyzing samples 6 or more minutes apart.

Many times software will also provide a plot of the partial autocorrelation function (PACF), which is similar in appearance to the autocorrelation function. The PACF removes the effect of the shorter-term autocorrelation from the calculation at larger lags. In many cases, a significant autocorrelation at low lag causes the autocorrelation function to be inflated at higher lags. For example, when lag 1 correlation is significant, then the observation at time $t = 3$ is strongly correlated to the observation at time $t = 2$; likewise, the observation at time $t = 2$ is strongly correlated to the observation at time $t = 1$. This strong lag 1 correlation can make it appear that the observation at time $t = 3$ is strongly correlated to the observation at time $t = 1$, which inflates the lag 2 correlation. By removing the effect of the short-lag autocorrelation, we can better estimate the effects over longer lag periods. The PACF plot in Figure 9.19 indicates the correlation is largely due to lag 1 autocorrelation, also known as first-order autocorrelation.

Once autocorrelation has been detected, the easiest remedy is to use restrictive sampling to chart only the independent data. Use the autocorrelation function to determine the time interval between samples needed for data independence; then apply a standard control chart for individuals data (see Chapter 6) to the independent data, and do not plot the data between the independent samples.

The obvious disadvantage of the restricted sampling approach is that some data is ignored. If data is automatically collected, perhaps even a fair amount of data would need to be discarded. Most troubling is that the time periods between the independent data could be large, so that there is a period of time for which the process may be unmonitored with the control chart. Recall that control charts do not always detect assignable causes as soon as they occur, so it may be several plotted subgroups before an assignable cause that is present is detected by the control chart. If the cost associated with this risk is significant, then this restricted sampling approach may not be the best method for dealing with autocorrelation.

A batch means chart (see Chapter 5) provides an alternative to the restricted sampling approach, and uses all the data: Use the autocorrelation function to determine the time interval needed between samples to attain independence; then calculate the average of the data within the time interval, and treat the average as individual data value. The variation within the subgroup is plotted on a range or sigma chart, the same as if we were dealing with

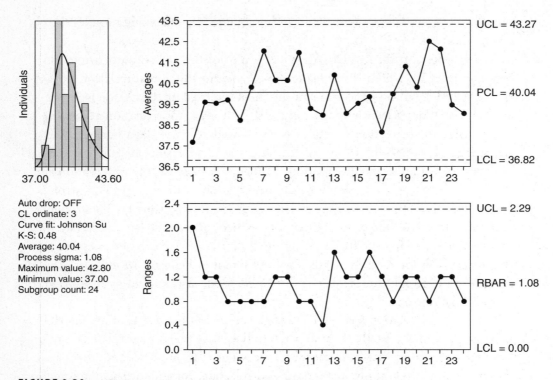

FIGURE 9.20 · Batch means chart of time in queue data using *SPC IV Excel* software.

rational subgroups on the X-bar chart. The queue data analyzed as above for autocorrelation, and shown in the X-bar chart of Figure 5.9 is plotted as a batch mean chart in Figure 9.20. Some software includes the batch means chart as a direct option, removing the need to construct a special chart. (Note that Minitab refers to this as their Between/Within chart.)

When data is significantly autocorrelated in nature, a time series model may also be developed for prediction.

Final Exam

1. **Control limits indicate:**

   A. the expected variation in the process statistic, assuming the process remains in control.

   B. the acceptable variation in the process statistic.

   C. the error in measurements.

   D. the uncertainty in process data.

2. **Control charts are designed to analyze:**

   A. data sampled from a process or population.

   B. only data sampled at random from a process.

   C. data sampled from a process that retains its time-order.

   D. data sampled from a process that retains its time-order and is normally distributed.

3. **A control chart provides a direct estimate of the:**

   A. ability of the process to meet requirements.

   B. stability of the process over time.

   C. capability of the process.

   D. conformance to requirement, or overall quality of the process.

4. A process produces 500 pieces per hour. A process operator checks 5 pieces every hour to verify the process is meeting the dimensional specifications defined by the customer. On the latest 5 piece sample, one of the pieces exceeds the upper specification limit. To ensure that all pieces sent to the customer conform to their requirement, the operator should:

A. Remove the one sample piece found defective and ship the remaining pieces.

B. Remove the one sample piece found defective; adjust the process; and take an additional 5 piece samples immediately to ensure process is properly targeted.

C. Adjust the process and sample 100% of the process output since the last 5 piece sample.

D. Stop the process and sample 100% of all process output in inventory and in the process flow, since there is no way to know when the process actually shifted.

5. A process produces 500 pieces per hour. A process operator checks 5 pieces every hour to verify the process is meeting the dimensional specifications defined by the customer. The measurement from each piece is plotted on a chart which uses the upper and lower specifications as decision points. On the latest 5 piece sample, one of the pieces exceeds the upper specification limit on the chart. The prior 5 piece sample was also above the centerline, suggesting a possible upward trend. To ensure that all pieces sent to the customer conform to their requirement, the operator should:

A. Remove the one sample piece found defective and ship the remaining pieces.

B. Remove the one sample piece found defective; adjust the process; and take an additional 5 piece sample immediately to ensure process is properly targeted.

C. Remove the one sample piece found defective; adjust the process; take an additional 5 piece samples immediately to ensure process is properly targeted; and sample 100% of the process output since the prior 5 piece sample.

D. Stop the process and sample 100% of all process output in inventory and in the process flow, since there is no way to know when the process actually shifted.

6. A process produces 500 pieces per hour. A process operator checks 5 pieces every hour to verify the process is in statistical control. The measurement from each piece is plotted on a chart which uses statistical control limits as decision points. The statistical control limits were defined in a process capability study, and verified to provide a capability relative to customer specifications of 1.3. On the latest 5 piece sample, one of the pieces exceeds the upper control limit on the chart. To ensure that all pieces sent to the customer conform to their requirement, the operator should:

A. Remove the one sample piece found defective; adjust the process; and take an additional 5 piece samples immediately to ensure process is properly targeted.

B. Remove the one sample piece found defective; adjust the process; take an additional 5 piece samples immediately to ensure process is properly targeted; and sample 100% of the process output since the last 5 piece sample.

C. Stop the process and determine the source of the special cause variation, which is likely to have occurred since the last 5 piece sample. Sample 100% of all process output since the last 5 piece sample (or since the special cause was introduced, whichever is earlier). Remove the source of the special cause and continue the process operations.

D. Stop the process and sample 100% of all process output in inventory and in the process flow, since there is no way to know when the process actually shifted.

7. Process stability is evidenced when:

A. The process is in statistical control.

B. The short-term variation in an independent process metric provides a good indicator of longer-term variation.

C. The process is influenced by only common cause variation.

D. All of the above.

8. A process histogram is a preferred tool for showing:

A. process stability.

B. process shape and location.

C. process distribution.

D. the shape, location, and distribution of a set of sample data that may or may not reflect the process from which it was sampled, depending on the method of sampling and whether the process is in statistical control.

9. **On an X-bar chart, an out of control subgroup is evident that:**

A. One or more samples in the subgroup are defective.

B. All of the samples in the subgroup are defective.

C. The process mean has shifted.

D. Both B and C.

10. **On an individual x chart, an out of control subgroup is evident that:**

A. The sample is defective.

B. The process mean has shifted and the sample is defective.

C. The process is out of control but might be capable.

D. The process mean has shifted; there is no information provided on specifications or capability, so it is unclear if the sample is defective or not.

11. **The control limits represent:**

A. the expected variation in the process, until the process is influenced by a special cause.

B. the sum of all variation the process will ever experience.

C. the maximum variation allowed by the customers.

D. All of the above.

12. **A special cause is defined through:**

A. brainstorming by process personnel.

B. brainstorming by process operators, support staff, and other process experts.

C. analysis of how often each source of variation occurs.

D. the occurrence of an out of control condition on a control chart.

13. **Control charts will generally detect:**

A. all shifts as soon as they occur.

B. smaller shifts quicker than larger shifts.

C. larger shifts quicker than smaller shifts.

D. sporadic shifts quicker than sustained shifts.

14. **A control chart using a subgroup size of 4 is referred to as a(n):**

A. individual x chart.

B. X-bar chart.

C. u chart.

D. c chart.

15. **When seeking to reduce the errors in a process, the preferred method for control charting is to:**

    A. Construct a p chart of the percent defective to detect the defect as soon as it occurs.

    B. Construct a u chart of the number of errors per sample to analyze how prevalent the error is.

    C. Construct a chart of a measured parameter that determines whether the sample is good or bad. This will allow prevention of the error, as the metric trends toward the defect condition.

    D. Construct a scatter diagram to determine the source of all errors.

16. **A rational subgroup in one in which:**

    A. All sources of variation are included.

    B. No special causes of variation are included.

    C. Common causes of variation are excluded.

    D. Process personnel agree make sense for the process.

17. **A control chart using a subgroup size of 3 will detect a two sigma shift in the process mean:**

    A. on the first subgroup after any and all shifts in the process mean

    B. on average, on the first subgroup after a shift in the process mean

    C. on the second subgroup after the shift in the process mean

    D. as soon as the shift in the mean occurs

18. **A control chart using a subgroup size of 1 will detect a two sigma shift in the process mean:**

    A. on the first subgroup after the shift in the mean

    B. on average, on the sixth subgroup after the shift in the mean

    C. on the second subgroup after the shift in the mean

    D. as soon as the shift in the mean occurs

19. **Where possible, an X-bar chart with a subgroup size of 3, 4, or 5 is preferred since:**

    A. It provides reasonable sensitivity to respond quickly to process shifts.

    B. The plotted subgroup averages can be reasonably assumed to follow the normal distribution.

    C. The relatively small size of the subgroup limits the risk for special causes of variation occurring within the subgroups.

    D. All of the above.

20. **As subgroup size increases above 10:**

    A. The sensitivity of the chart to moderate process shifts (1.5 sigma or larger) is greatly improved.

    B. The chart provides an improved estimate of the process mean.

    C. Each subgroup has an increased risk of becoming irrational by including special causes.

    D. The estimate of subgroup variation using the range statistic is improved.

21. **In designing a control chart for a process that is unfamiliar:**

    A. Collect one large subgroup (15 or more observations) each day, spreading the data collection over the entire period of operation.

    B. Collect one large subgroup (15 or more observations) each shift, spreading the data collection over the entire shift.

    C. Collect small subgroups (3 to 5 observations) frequently over the entire period of operation, perhaps starting at one subgroup every 20 minutes or so and loosening the frequency after sufficient data is collected to gauge process stability.

    D. Collect random samples over the entire period of operation (each shift or each day) and group the observations into a single subgroup.

22. **When control limits are fixed based on an initial sample or study:**

    A. The control chart will define special causes as causes that were not present during the initial study.

    B. The process may be held to tighter limits than if the control limits are recalculated based on new data, especially if the study data was over a limited time frame or excluded many sources of variation inherent to the process.

C. The initial study data can be used to estimate process capability, and any shifts in process capability will be detected as special causes using the predefined control limits.

D. All of the above.

23. If a process is frequently modified to enable processing of different products, each with unique operating levels, such that there is limited data available at a given operating level to define the process control limits:

A. Use short-run techniques to standardize the data.

B. Use Western Electric run test rules to standardize the data.

C. Construct separate control limits for each unique operating level.

D. Use confidence intervals.

24. A stable process has an average of 60 and an average within subgroup range of 5, using subgroups of size $n = 4$. The specification requirements are 50 ± 8. The process standard deviation is approximately:

A. 2.43

B. 16

C. 2.67

D. 2.15

25. Using an X-bar chart with a subgroup size of 4, the overall process mean is calculated as 60, and the average within subgroup range is 5. The lower control limit for the X-bar chart is approximately:

A. 63.6

B. 57.1

C. 56.4

D. 45

26. Which of the following is the correct control chart for the waiting time for customers in a bank; each individual customer's waiting time will be plotted?

A. u chart

B. Individual x/moving range

C. X-bar and s

D. Np chart

27. **A control chart for individuals data is necessary when:**
    A. The rational subgroup size is 1.
    B. There is only one characteristic to be monitored.
    C. It is always the best choice for control charting.
    D. All of the above.

28. **A disadvantage of control charts for individuals data is:**
    A. There is less data to collect.
    B. The chart is less sensitive to process shifts than larger subgroups.
    C. It only works for autocorrelated processes.
    D. All of the above.

29. **When process data occurs infrequently, subgroups containing more than one observation:**
    A. might include special causes of variation.
    B. generally are not rational subgroups.
    C. are poor indicators of short-term variation.
    D. All of the above.

30. **It is appropriate to use the sample standard deviation to define control limits on an individual x chart in which of the following cases?**
    A. Never
    B. Always
    C. When the process may drift
    D. When the process is highly capable

31. **When using process capability estimates:**
    A. The process must be in control or the estimate is misleading.
    B. Always estimate the process using sample sigma.
    C. Sort the data by size prior to analysis.
    D. All of the above.

32. The cycle time of a process (the time taken from beginning to completing the process) is in statistical control, with an average of 7 days and a process standard deviation of 0.75 days. Assuming a normal distribution, if the customer requires the process be completed in 10 days, then process capability C_{pk} is approximately:

   A. 2.22

   B. 1.33

   C. 4.0

   D. cannot be determined with the information provided.

33. When using process capability estimates:

   A. A C_{pk} value of 1.0 is perfect.

   B. A C_{pk} value greater than 1.3 is usually preferred.

   C. Smaller values of C_{pk} are best.

   D. C_p values must not exceed the C_{pk} value.

34. All of the following statements regarding process histograms are true EXCEPT:

   A. The data is ordered by value, with the smallest observations appearing on the left, and values increasing in magnitude as you move horizontally to the right.

   B. The height of each bar indicates the number of data values within a specific range of data values.

   C. The time history of the data is shown in the horizontal axis.

   D. The number of bars should be based on the number of data values in the analysis.

35. If a probability plot shows that a set of data does NOT fit a normal distribution, then:

   A. The process is out of control.

   B. The normal distribution may not be a good assumption for the data.

   C. The measurement process is certainly flawed.

   D. All of the above.

36. **When a process is not in control:**

    A. The process capability index provides a reasonable estimate of the process expectations relative to the customer requirements.

    B. The process capability index provides a reasonable estimate of the process expectations relative to the customer requirements, but only over a limited time frame.

    C. The process capability index provides a reasonable estimate of the process expectations relative to the customer requirements, but only for a normal distribution.

    D. The process capability index should not be used.

37. **If C_p is calculated as 1.0, and C_{pk} calculated to be .75, then:**

    A. The process variation should be reduced.

    B. The process mean should be relocated closer to the midpoint of the specifications.

    C. Both of the above.

    D. More information is needed.

38. **When calculating the process capability indices C_p and C_{pk}, use:**

    A. sample sigma such as provided by Excel's STDEV function.

    B. process sigma calculated using a control chart.

    C. either process or sample sigma.

    D. neither process nor sample sigma.

39. **A customer requires that inventory replenishments be received within 10 days of due date, but no earlier than the due date. The number of days from due date to shipment receipt is in statistical control, with an average of 7 days and a process standard deviation of 0.75 days. Assuming a normal distribution, the process capability C_p is approximately:**

    A. 2.22

    B. 1.33

    C. 4.0

    D. cannot be determined with the information provided.

40. **The process performance index:**

   A. Indicates whether the process is expected to meet customer requirements in the future.

   B. Indicates whether the process is currently meeting customer requirements.

   C. Indicates whether a batch of material that has been randomly sampled meets customer requirements.

   D. Indicates whether a sample of observations from a process or a batch of material meets customer requirements.

41. **The standard calculation for process capability (USL-LSL/6σ) assumes:**

   A. normality of the process observations

   B. statistical control of the process

   C. standard deviation calculated using the short-term control chart estimates

   D. All of the above.

42. **When only a single specification exists, such as "no larger than…":**

   A. C_p cannot be calculated.

   B. C_p will be greater than C_{pk}.

   C. C_p will be less than C_{pk}.

   D. C_p should be based on the physical limitations. For example, if surface roughness cannot exceed 5 microns (the upper specification), no lower specification is provided because it is assumed the lower specification is zero.

43. **A capability index C_{pk} of 1.0 indicates a one-sided process error rate of:**

   A. less than 1 parts per million.

   B. 0.135%.

   C. three sigma.

   D. Six Sigma.

44. **The minimum recommended C_{pk} value for most processes is:**

   A. 0

   B. 1.0

   C. 1.33

   D. 3

45. A negative C_{pk} value indicates:

A. The statistic was incorrectly calculated.

B. The process mean is less than the lower specification or greater than the upper specification.

C. A non-normal curve fit should be used.

D. The process is well-designed to meet customer requirements.

46. A process is in control. A given batch is collected for shipment to a customer, and a 100 piece sample is taken from the batch; its average and sample standard deviation are calculated and used to estimate process capability.

A. This is the preferred approach for calculating process capability.

B. This is a suitable approach since it is based on a large sample and the process is in control.

C. This is an unsuitable approach since the sample standard deviation is used; the better estimate of the process variation is obtained using the process sigma value from the control chart.

D. Both A and B.

Questions 47–50 use Figure F.1.

47. The process histogram, shown in Figure F.1 with an upper specification limit of 90 and a lower specification limit of 10, provides evidence that:

A. The process is in control and capable.

B. The normal distribution well models the data, with less than 0.01% of the process exceeding the limits.

C. Both A and B.

D. None of the above.

48. The process capability index C_p is calculated as:

A. 1.38

B. 2.76

C. 1.3

D. cannot be determined with the information provided.

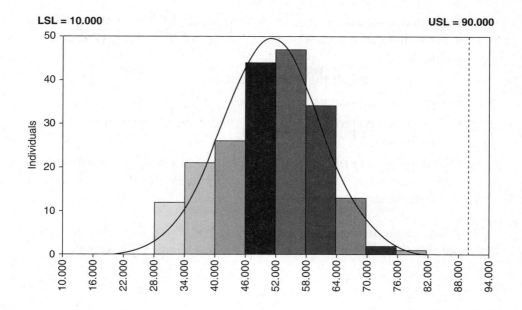

LSL = 10.000   USL = 90.000

Smallest value = 28.400   Sample sigma = 9.655
Largest value = 76.200   High spec: 90
Average = 50.709   Low spec: 10
Skewness = −0.217   % Above high spec: 0.002%
Kurtosis = −0.395   % Below low spec: 0.001%
Standard error of mean = 0.683   % Out of spec: 0.004%
K-S Test: 0.699
Curve fit: Normal

FIGURE F.1 • Histogram.

49. The process capability index C_{pk} is calculated as:

   A. 1.36

   B. 1.41

   C. 1.38

   D. cannot be determined with the information provided.

50. The K-S value of 0.699 provided for the normal distribution is evidence that:

   A. The process is normally distributed.

   B. The process is not well-modeled by the normal distribution.

   C. The standard capability indices can be used.

   D. The sample data is normally distributed.

51. Each day a shipment is sent to a customer, and with the shipment a capability estimate is provided. The capability estimate should be recalculated:

    A. each day based on the most current data.

    B. with each new data point.

    C. if new raw material is used in the process, or any other major changes are introduced.

    D. only when the process has undergone a special cause of variation as evidenced by the control chart; otherwise the capability is unchanged.

52. A marketing department is interested in tracking the number of visitors per day to a page on their website. The best chart to use is the:

    A. c chart.

    B. p chart.

    C. Np chart.

    D. X-bar chart.

53. A marketing department is interested in tracking the relative percentage of visitors per day that come from a particular website. The best chart to use is the:

    A. c chart.

    B. p chart.

    C. Np chart.

    D. u chart.

54. A marketing department is interested in tracking the average number of web pages visited each day per visitor on their website. The best chart to use is the:

    A. c chart.

    B. p chart.

    C. Np chart.

    D. u chart.

Questions 55–59 refer to the p chart in Figure F.2, which shows the error rate for a process.

55. **The p chart shown in the figure indicates:**

   A. The error rate for the process is stable.

   B. The error rate is not influenced by any special causes over the time period shown.

   C. The error rate is reasonably estimated to be between approximately 8.4% and 14.5%.

   D. All of the above.

56. **The control limits in Figure F.2 vary because:**

   A. The sample size varies.

   B. The expected error rate varies.

   C. The confidence interval is influenced by the sampling statistics.

   D. None of the above.

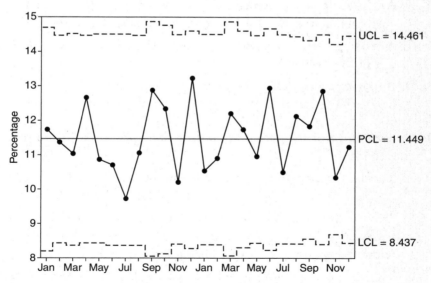

FIGURE F.2 • p chart.

57. **A supervisor uses the control chart to monitor the process, and notices that the last 2 months (November & December) are below the average line, while the 3 months preceding (August–October) were above the average line. This is evidence that:**

   A. Process improvements made in October have had a positive impact on reducing errors.

   B. The next sample will also be below the average line, so that the three below the average will offset the three above the average.

   C. The error is stable but may still be excessive. The variation seen on the chart is random, inherent to the process, and not indicative of any changes to the process.

   D. The error is not stable; it fluctuates rather unpredictably.

58. **If the error plotted in the chart represents the percentage of time when a customer waits more than 10 minutes in line, an alternative to the chart is:**

   A. An X-bar chart plotting the average time in queue for five customers in a row within one of the cashier lines.

   B. An X-bar chart plotting the average time in queue for a single customer from each of five cashier lines at a specific time.

   C. A moving average chart of the time in queue for every customer in one of the cashier lines.

   D. A moving average chart of the time in queue for a sample of customers in one of the cashier lines, where the sample is taken every half hour.

59. **An advantage of the variables control chart proposed in the previous question is:**

   A. The data is easier to collect than the number of errors (i.e., number of people who waited more than 10 minutes).

   B. The control chart for the variables data will provide the expected behavior of the process (and estimated error rate for the process) even without any customers experiencing the error.

   C. The control chart for variables could be used to prevent the errors from occurring.

   D. Both B and C.

Questions 60–64 refer to the $\bar{X}$ chart based on subgroup size of 5 shown in Figure F.3, whose process specifications are USL = 11.0 and LSL = 8.5.

60. If the process specifications are USL = 11.0 and LSL = 8.5, the control chart indicates:

   A. The process is in control.

   B. The process is capable of meeting the requirements.

   C. There are no values exceeding the specifications, and none is expected (so long as the process remains in control).

   D. All of the above.

61. The process standard deviation estimated from the figure is:

   A. 0.968

   B. 0.416

   C. 0.403

   D. 0.919

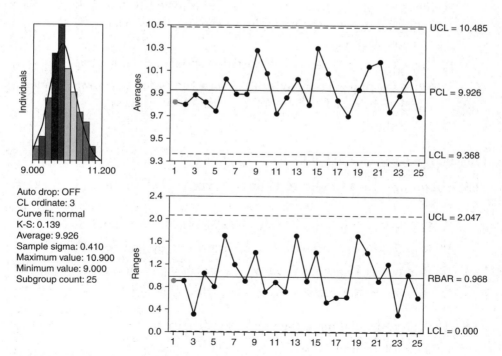

FIGURE F.3 • Example $\bar{X}$ chart based on subgroup size of 5.

62. If the process specifications are USL = 11.0 and LSL = 8.5, the process capability C_p is estimated as:

A. 1.00

B. 0.45

C. 1.03

D. 0.43

63. If the process specifications are USL = 11.0 and LSL = 8.5, the process capability C_{pk} is estimated as:

A. 0.37

B. 0.40

C. 0.86

D. 0.90

64. If the process specifications are USL = 11 and LSL = 8.5, the process capability C_{pk} can be improved by:

A. Since $C_{pk} < C_p$, if the process can be adjusted to move the process centerline toward the midpoint of the specifications (9.75) then C_{pk} can approach C_p.

B. Since $C_p < 1.33$, the process variation should be reduced.

C. Since the process is in control the variation is due to common causes, which requires a fundamental redesign of the process.

D. All of the above.

Questions 65–68 refer to Figure F.4.

65. Subgroups 16–44 indicate failure of which of the following run test rules?

A. Run test 2: 9 groups in a row on same side of centerline.

B. Run test 4: 14 successive groups alternating up and down.

C. Run test 7: 15 groups in a row within one sigma of center line.

D. Run test 8: 8 successive groups not within one sigma of centerline.

66. The run test violation in the figure is indicative of:

A. a multistream process.

B. an irrational subgroup.

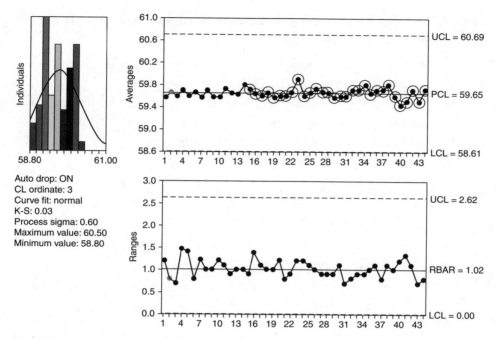

Individuals

58.80   61.00

Auto drop: ON
CL ordinate: 3
Curve fit: normal
K-S: 0.03
Process sigma: 0.60
Maximum value: 60.50
Minimum value: 58.80

Averages

61.0
60.6 - UCL = 60.69
60.2
59.8
59.4 ————————————————————————— PCL = 59.65
59.0
58.6 - LCL = 58.61
    1   4   7   10 13 16 19 22 25 28 31 34 37 40 43

Ranges

3.0
2.5 - UCL = 2.62
2.0
1.5
1.0 ————————————————————————— RBAR = 1.02
0.5
0.0 - LCL = 0.00
    1   4   7   10 13 16 19 22 25 28 31 34 37 40 43

FIGURE F.4 • X-bar chart with run test violation.

C. a situation where the within subgroup variation is much larger than the variation between groups.

D. All of the above.

67. **An example of a process that might produce data such as shown in the figure include:**

A. A bottle filling operation where the subgroup is obtained by sampling from each of six filling heads.

B. A service operation where people are waiting in queue and the subgroup is obtained by selecting successive people in the same line.

C. A manufacturing operation where a process controller adjusts the process based on prior measurements.

D. All of the above.

68. **The remedy for correcting the run test violations observed in the figure include:**

    A. Take samples less frequently.

    B. Create separate control charts for each subprocess.

    C. Use a batch means chart, which uses the range chart to plot the variation within the subgroup and an individual x chart for the subgroup averages to monitor the subgroup averages.

    D. Choices B and C.

Questions 69–71 refer to Figure F.5.

69. **The special causes in the figure are indicative of:**

    A. serial correlation within each subgroup.

    B. an irrational subgroup.

    C. a situation where the within subgroup variation is much smaller than the variation between groups.

    D. All of the above.

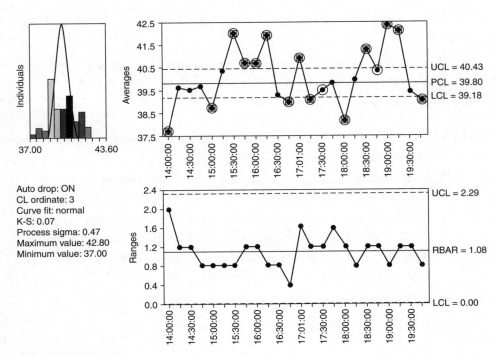

FIGURE F.5 • X-bar chart of process.

70. **An example of a process that might produce data such as shown in the figure include:**

    A. A bottle filling operation where the subgroup is obtained by sampling from each of six filling heads.

    B. A service operation where people are waiting in queue and the subgroup is obtained by selecting successive people in the same line.

    C. A manufacturing operation where a fixture contains multiple parts, and the fixture may not be square such that parts are consistently ground to different sizes depending on their position on the fixture.

    D. All of the above.

71. **The remedy for correcting the special causes evident in the figure include:**

    A. Take samples less frequently.

    B. Create separate control charts for each subprocess.

    C. Use a batch means chart, which uses the range chart to plot the variation within the subgroup and an individual x chart for the subgroup averages to monitor the subgroup averages.

    D. Choices B and C.

Questions 72–75 refer to the individual x chart shown in Figure F.6, which is applied to a process having an upper specification of 1.75 (and no lower specification).

72. **Using only the information provided in Figure F.6, it is clear the data is from a process that is:**

    A. in control.

    B. out of control.

    C. influenced by special causes of variation that are reflected in the odd distribution.

    D. cannot be determined for the process given the information provided.

73. **The process capability index C_p based on the analysis is:**

    A. 0.805

    B. 1.33

    C. 1.0

    D. cannot be determined for the process given the information provided.

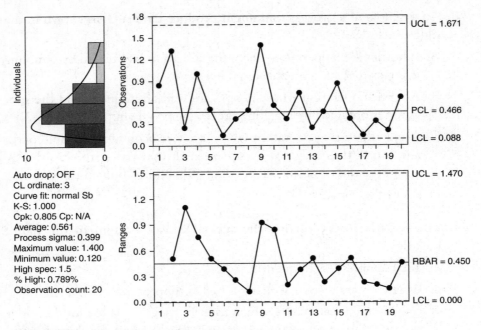

Auto drop: OFF
CL ordinate: 3
Curve fit: normal Sb
K-S: 1.000
Cpk: 0.805 Cp: N/A
Average: 0.561
Process sigma: 0.399
Maximum value: 1.400
Minimum value: 0.120
High spec: 1.5
% High: 0.789%
Observation count: 20

FIGURE F.6 • Individual X chart of a sample process.

74. The process capability index C_{pk} based on the analysis is:

    A. 0.805

    B. 1.33

    C. 1.0

    D. cannot be determined for the process given the information provided.

75. The distribution of the process is:

    A. normal.

    B. non-normal, with an excellent curve fit provided.

    C. it is suspected to be non-normal, but the statistics indicates a poor fit.

    D. cannot be determined for the process given the information provided.

Questions 76–78 refer to the moving average chart shown in Figure F.7, which is applied to a process having an upper specification of 1.75 (and no lower specification).

76. The process data shown in Figure F.7 is from a process that is:

    A. in control.

    B. out of control.

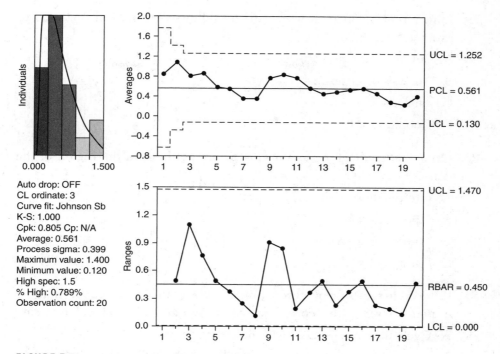

FIGURE F.7 • Moving average chart for analysis.

    C. influenced by special causes of variation that are reflected in the odd distribution.

    D. in violation of run test rules.

77. The process capability index C_{pk}, provided in the analysis as 0.805, is:

    A. acceptable.

    B. unacceptable.

    C. marginal.

    D. meaningless since the process is not in control.

78. The distribution of the process is:

    A. normal.

    B. suspected to be nonnormal, with an excellent curve fit provided, albeit with limited data.

    C. suspected to be non-normal, but the statistics indicates a poor fit.

    D. undeterminable given the information provided.

79. **Linear regression uses which of the following statistical methods to estimate correlation?**

    A. Failure modes and effects.

    B. Analysis of means.

    C. Analysis of variance.

    D. Goodness of fit.

80. **On a Scatter diagram, attempting to predict beyond the region of the data is known as:**

    A. Interpolation.

    B. Bipolarization.

    C. Multiple regression.

    D. Extrapolation.

81. **If the cycle time of a process is predicted by cycle time = 5.25 × (number of items) + 4.3, with a correlation coefficient of 0.7, then it is fair to say:**

    A. Cycle time is predicted with no error.

    B. Cycle time is only influenced by the number of items.

    C. Cycle time is definitely influenced by the number of items.

    D. For the data analyzed, cycle time is statistically correlated with the number of items.

82. **In constructing a scatter diagram, it is customary to put the dependent variable on:**

    A. the x-axis.

    B. the y-axis.

    C. All of the above.

    D. None of the above.

83. **Negative correlation implies:**

    A. The dependent variable gets worse as the independent variable increases.

    B. The dependent variable decreases as the independent variable increases.

    C. The dependent variable increases as the independent variable increases.

    D. The independent variable decreases as the dependent variable decreases.

84. **In estimating correlation and the parameters of a linear regression model, we should vary the independent variable over a sufficient range so that:**

   A. A sufficient amount of variation in the dependent variable is experienced.

   B. We can predict the dependent variable over a wide range.

   C. We don't need to extrapolate.

   D. All of the above.

85. **Weak correlation implies:**

   A. The dependent variable is not well-predicted by the model.

   B. There is one or more unexplained sources of variation, preventing good prediction of the response as the dependent variable increases.

   C. It might be useful to stratify the data.

   D. All of the above.

86. **Residuals are:**

   A. the error between the actual y-value and the predicted y-value at each x-value.

   B. the difference between the x-value and the regression line for each of the predicted y-values.

   C. due to measurement error.

   D. All of the above.

87. **If the cycle time of a process is predicted by cycle time = 5.25 × (number of items) + 4.3, with a correlation of 0.8, then the slope of the line is:**

   A. 5.25

   B. 4.3

   C. 35.8

   D. 0.8

88. **If the correlation coefficient R is 0.9, then:**

   A. 90% of the variation in y is explained by the regression model.

   B. 81% of the variation in y is explained by the regression model.

   C. 90% of the variation in y is explained by the variation in x.

   D. Approximately 95% of the error is explained by the variation in x.

89. In the interaction plot below, it is evident that:

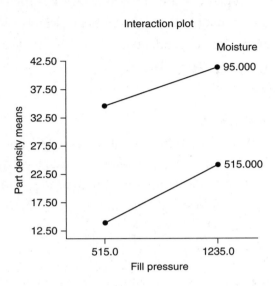

A. There is a strong interaction between moisture and fill pressure.

B. There is a weak to negligible interaction between moisture and fill pressure.

C. The effect of fill pressure on part density changes drastically as we change the moisture.

D. None of the above.

90. In the expression cycle time (in minutes) = 3 + 1.4 × (number of orders) − 2.1 × (number of clerks) − 0.034 × (process distance):

A. Removing one clerk will increase the cycle time by 2.1 minutes.

B. Removing one clerk will decrease the cycle time by 2.1 minutes.

C. Adding one clerk will increase the cycle time by 2.1 minutes.

D. None of the above.

91. **Considering only the interaction plot below, it is evident that:**

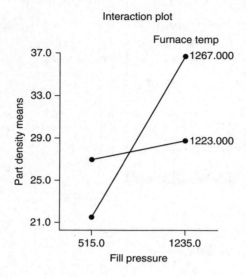

Interaction plot

A. If furnace temperature is difficult to control, we should run the process at high fill pressure to minimize the variation in part density.

B. If fill pressure is difficult to control, we should run the process at low furnace temperature to minimize the variation in part density.

C. Running the process at low furnace temperature and high fill pressure gives us the best conditions.

D. None of the above.

Questions 92–95 refer to the repeatability control chart shown in Figure F.8.

92. **The repeatability chart indicates:**

A. The process is out of control.

B. The repeatability is out of control.

C. The repeatability is in control, but the repeatability error is larger than desired.

D. None of the above.

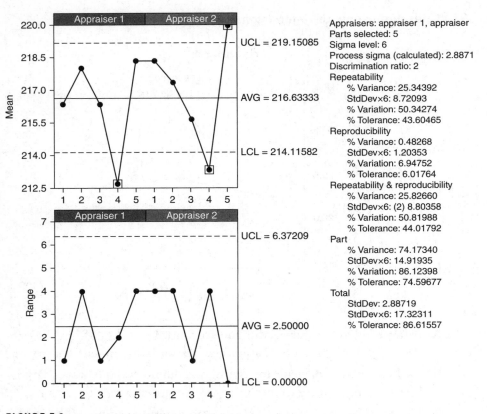

FIGURE F.8 • Example repeatability control chart.

93. **In Figure F.8, the R&R is shown to be approximately 50% of process variation and 44% of process tolerance, which indicates:**

    A. The R&R is acceptable relative to process variation, but unacceptable relative to tolerance.

    B. The R&R is unacceptable relative to process variation and tolerance.

    C. The R&R is marginal relative to tolerance and unacceptable relative to the process variation.

    D. The repeatability is not statistically stable, so no estimates can be made of its suitability.

94. **Figure 8.6 provides a discrimination ratio of 2 for the measurement system, which indicates:**

    A. The measurement system's discrimination is acceptable.

    B. The measurement system's discrimination is unacceptable.

C. The measurement system's discrimination is marginal.

D. The reproducibility error is not statistically stable, so no estimates can be made of its suitability.

95. **Figure F.8 provides a repeatability error for the measurement system as 50% of process variation (44% of tolerance) and a reproducibility error of 7% of variation (6% of tolerance), which indicates:**

A. The variation associated with the measurement equipment is unacceptable.

B. The variation between appraisers is unacceptable.

C. Both A and B.

D. Neither A nor B.

Questions 96–98 refer to the reproducibility control chart shown in Figure F.9.

96. **The reproducibility chart indicates:**

A. There is no discernible difference in the appraisers' measurements on a part by part basis.

B. There is a significant difference in the appraisers' average measurements.

C. Both A and B.

D. Neither A nor B.

97. **Figure F.9 provides an Appraiser × Part interaction of 9.5% of process variation (8% of tolerance). If the analysis also indicates the p-value of the interaction is 0.04, then:**

A. There is interaction between the appraisers and parts.

B. There is no interaction between the appraisers and parts.

C. The appraisers' error does not vary depending on the parts inspected.

D. None of the above.

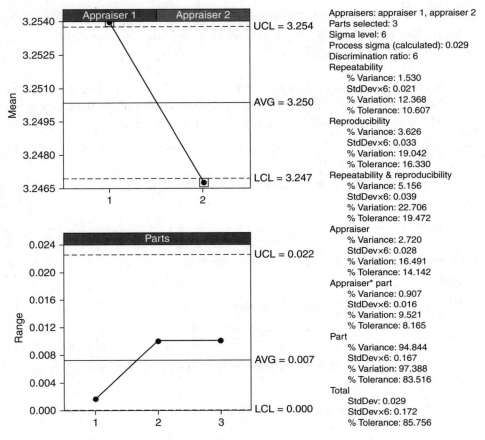

FIGURE F.9 • Example reproducibility control chart.

98. In addition to the information provided in the last question, Figure F.9 also provides a reproducibility error of 19% of process variation (16% of tolerance) and a repeatability error of 12% of process variation (11% of tolerance), which indicates:

    A. The variation between appraisers is significant and exceeds 10% of process variation and/or tolerance.

    B. The measurement equipment error is significant and exceeds 10% of process variation and/or tolerance.

    C. The appraisers' error varies somewhat dependent on the parts inspected, which is a clue to be investigated.

    D. All of the above.

99. **The effect of the measurement error on the current operations include:**

   A. Defective product may be incorrectly considered acceptable for use.

   B. Acceptable product may be incorrectly considered unacceptable for use.

   C. Estimates of statistical process control may be in error.

   D. All of the above.

100. **SPC charts were invented by:**

   A. Walter Shewhart

   B. W. Edwards Deming

   C. Ronald Fisher

   D. Lloyd Nelson

Answers to Quizzes and Final Exam

Chapter 1
1. A
2. B
3. D. There is no guarantee that all process shifts are detected. The charts are designed to minimize false alarms.
4. C. Tampering, which increases process variation, results from responding to random variation as if it were a special cause. Choice D is incorrect unless perhaps there is 100% sampling (assuming inspection were 100% accurate, which is rare).
5. A
6. D. Choice D describes a control chart.
7. D
8. A
9. D
10. C. By itself, a histogram can only indicate the properties of the sample.

Chapter 2
1. B
2. D
3. C. Choices A and B are not related to measurement resolution.
4. B. Suggested business level dashboards are necessarily broad to address needs of its audience.
5. D

6. **C.** Subtle shifts will not be readily detected in individual stream of a multistream processes.

7. **D**

8. **C.** Using Table 2.2, the first row shows the number of subgroups needed (on average) to detect a shift using subgroup size of 1. The column labeled "2" provides the number of groups needed to detect a two-sigma shift in the process mean.

9. **B**

10. **B.** This is a multistream process with an irrational subgroup.

Chapter 3

1. **D**

2. **D.** The customer requires the process be completed in 10 days (the upper specification limit), but no lower specification is provided so C_p cannot be calculated.

3. **D**

4. **A.** The histogram will not indicate if the process is in control. It may provide the shape of the process distribution, but only if used in conjunction with a control chart to verify the process is in control. Generally, the histogram only provides information on the sample data.

5. **A**

6. **B**

7. **B.** In this case there is an upper specification (10) and a lower specification (0).

$$Z_l = \frac{\bar{\bar{x}} - \text{low spec}}{\sigma_x} = \frac{7 - 0}{0.75} = 9.33$$

$$C_{pl} = \frac{Z_l}{3} = \frac{9.33}{3} = 3.11$$

$$Z_u = \frac{\text{high spec} - \bar{\bar{x}}}{\sigma_x} = \frac{10 - 7}{0.75} = 4$$

$$C_{pu} = \frac{Z_u}{3} = \frac{4}{3} = 1.33$$

8. **C.** The histogram is not useful for determining if the shipment meets requirements unless it is also known that either the process is in control or that the histogram includes 100% inspection of the sample shipment.

9. **D**

10. **B**

Chapter 4

1. **D.** The average count of errors must be 5 or higher for use of an attribute control chart to determine if the process is in control.

2. **D**

3. **A.** The data is binomial, since each patient either dies or does not die. Since the sample size (number of surgical patients) varies each month, the Np chart cannot be used.

4. **C.** Since each sample (a patient) may report multiple instances of the condition of interest, the data is poisson distributed. Since the number of patients is likely to vary month to month the u chart is preferred.

5. **B.** The sample has a p-value of 25/125 = 0.2. Since that is above the centerline of 0.14, we only need to calculate the upper control limit as

$$UCL = \bar{p} + 3\sqrt{\frac{\bar{p}(1-\bar{p})}{n_j}} = 0.14 + 3\sqrt{\frac{0.14(0.86)}{125}} = 0.23$$

6. **A.** The sample has a p-value of 25/88 = 0.28. Since that is above the centerline of 0.14, we only need to calculate the upper control limit as

$$UCL = \bar{p} + 3\sqrt{\frac{\bar{p}(1-\bar{p})}{n_j}} = 0.14 + 3\sqrt{\frac{0.14(0.86)}{88}} = 0.25$$

7. **A.** The historical percent error is 7/100 = 0.07. For a sample size of 88:

$$UCL_{np} = \overline{np} + 3\sqrt{\overline{np}(1-\bar{p})} = (88 \times 0.07) + 3\sqrt{(88 \times 0.07)(1-0.07)} = 13.3$$

8. **B.** The new sample has a u-value of 125/88 = 1.42. For a sample size of 88:

$$UCL = \bar{u} + 3\sqrt{\frac{\bar{u}}{n_j}} = 1.14 + 3\sqrt{\frac{1.14}{88}} = 1.48$$

9. **A.** The new sample has a u-value of 125/80 = 1.56. For a sample size of 80:

$$UCL = \bar{u} + 3\sqrt{\frac{\bar{u}}{n_j}} = 1.14 + 3\sqrt{\frac{1.14}{80}} = 1.50$$

10. **B**

Chapter 5

1. **D.** When the process is in control, the subgroup averages will plot within the control limits; the distribution of the subgroup averages is estimated by plus or minus $3 \times \bar{R}/d_2$. The observations within the subgroups have a much wider distribution, estimated by plus or minus $3 \times \bar{R}/(d_2 \times \text{SQRT}(n))$.

2. **B.** The average of the sample (45.25) is less than the lower control limit on the $\bar{X}$ chart; its range (7) is within the control limits of the range chart.

3. **B.** The average of the sample (51.75) is within the control limits on the $\bar{X}$ chart; its range (9) is within the control limits of the range chart. The observation value 57 is larger than the upper specification.

4. **D.** The average of the sample (50.5) is within the control limits on the $\bar{X}$ chart; its range (9) is within the control limits of the range chart.

5. **D.** From Appendix, c_4 for $n = 5$ is 0.94; $\sigma_x = \bar{S}/c_4 = 5/0.94 = 5.32$.

$$\text{UCL}_{\bar{x}} = \bar{\bar{x}} + 3\left(\frac{\sigma_x}{\sqrt{n}}\right) = 100 + 3\frac{5.32}{\sqrt{5}} = 107.1$$

6. **C.** From Appendix, d_2 for $n = 5$ is 2.326; $\sigma_x = \bar{R}/d_2 = 5/2.326 = 2.15$.

$$\text{UCL}_{\bar{x}} = \bar{\bar{x}} + 3\left(\frac{\sigma_x}{\sqrt{n}}\right) = 100 + 3\frac{2.15}{\sqrt{5}} = 102.9$$

7. **A.** From Appendix, D_3 is 0 for $n \leq 6$.

8. **C.** This is an example of tampering.

9. **A.** The range chart should not be used for subgroups larger than 10.

10. **A.** Using a larger subgroup size risks including special causes of variation within the subgroups.

Chapter 6

1. **B**
2. **D**
3. **D**
4. **D**
5. **B.** Choices A and C require additional samples at significant cost.
6. **D**
7. **C**
8. **B**
9. **D**
10. **C**

Chapter 7

1. **D**
2. **C**
3. **B**
4. **D**
5. **C.** For six units, cycle time $= 5.25 \times (6) + 4.3 = 35.8$
6. **B.** Strong correlation does not necessarily imply a large coefficient for the independent variable (choice C).
7. **D**
8. **B.** A low p-value (usually less than 0.05) is used to determine statistical significance.
9. **D.** The number of orders and number of clerks are two independent variables that are independently varied to achieve a change in the response (cycle time).
10. **D.** On the low furnace temperature line (labeled 1223), there is little change in the part density response as fill pressure varies from min (515) to max (1235). Thus if fill pressure is difficult to control then running the process at low furnace temperature will reduce the influence of fill pressure variation. Conversely, at high furnace temperature (line labeled 1267), there is a large variation in part density as fill pressure varies between its min and max condition. In this way, fill pressure and furnace temperature interact.

Chapter 8

1. **B**
2. **C**
3. **B**
4. **D**
5. **D**
6. **D**
7. **A**
8. **C.** The repeatability control chart provides no indication of the process stability. It is not interpreted as a classic control chart: The range chart, which in this case is in control, indicates the repeatability is stable; the X-bar chart indicates the amount of repeatability error relative to the process variation. An acceptably small amount of repeatability error will have at least 50% of the subgroups out of control. In this case, 40% of the groups are out of control, so repeatability error is a bit larger than desired.

9. **C.** Using the recommendations shown in the text, the R&R as a percent of variation (38%) is unacceptable (>30%); as a percent of tolerance (23%) is marginal (15%–30%).

10. **B.** The calculated discrimination (3) is unacceptable. Values of 8 or higher are recommended.

Final Exam

1. **A.** Choice B refers to specifications. While control limits include the effects of measurement error, they also include other sources of variation in the process data. The term uncertainty in a statistical context generally refers to measurement error.

2. **C**

3. **B.** Choices A, C, and D require knowledge of customer requirements. The control chart is not used to determine conformance to requirement, but to estimate the process stability. Once stability is attained, conformance to requirement can be estimated.

4. **D.** The operator is sampling from the process, and by chance happened across a non-conforming item. There may be many more non-conforming items that were not sampled, at the current time as well as in the past. There is no evidence the process is now stable (i.e., in control), or has ever been stable. The ability to detect the non-conforming part was luck of the draw. The only way to verify that all pieces are within specification is by 100% inspection.

5. **D.** See answer to Question 4, above.

6. **C.** Since the process was in control and capable when the control limits were established, then an out of specification condition can only occur if the process is also out of control. A subgroup size of 5 is likely to detect most process shifts in the first subgroup (see Table 2.2), so a search for special causes should be initiated to look for sources of change since the last subgroup, or perhaps two subgroups prior. Once the special cause is determined, process output since its occurrence should be 100% sampled for non-conformity to specification.

7. **D.** Choices A through C imply statistical control, as does the term stability.

8. **D**

9. **C.** The control limits do not directly indicate conformance to requirement. Capability analysis is required to make assertions regarding conformance to specifications.

10. **D.** Choice C is incorrect since an out of control process cannot be capable (control is prerequisite for capability).

11. **A.** The control limits represent common cause variation. Total variation also includes special cause variation. Control limits are not based on the customers' requirements.

12. **D.** The control chart provides the operational definition of a special cause.

13. **C**

14. **B**

15. **C.** The variables chart can detect trends or process shifts before the defect occurs.

16. **B**

17. **B.** See Table 2.2.

18. **B.** See Table 2.2.

19. **D**

20. **C.** Larger subgroups provide little advantage. See Table 2.2 for sensitivity to shifts. The estimate of process mean is not greatly improved with increased sample size, and even the short-term process variation is adequately estimated using smaller groups.

21. **C.** Small subgroups taken frequently provide the best information on process stability.

22. **D**

23. **A**

24. **A.** From Appendix, d_2 for $n = 4$ is 2.059; $\sigma_x = \overline{R}/d_2 = 5/2.059 = 2.43$.

25. **C.** From Appendix, d_2 for $n = 4$ is 2.059; $\sigma_x = \overline{R}/d_2 = 5/2.059 = 2.43$.

$$\text{LCL}_{\bar{x}} = \overline{\overline{x}} - 3\left(\frac{\sigma_x}{\sqrt{n}}\right) = 60 - 3\frac{2.43}{\sqrt{4}} = 56.4$$

26. **B**

27. **A**

28. **B**

29. **D**

30. **A.** Sample sigma is never used for calculating control limits for an individual x chart.

31. **A**

32. **B.** There is only an upper specification (10), so $C_{pu} = C_{pk}$

$$Z_u = \frac{\text{high spec} - \overline{\overline{x}}}{\sigma_x} = \frac{10 - 7}{0.75} = 4$$

$$C_{pu} = \frac{Z_u}{3} = \frac{4}{3} = 1.33$$

33. **B.** A C_{pk} of 1.0 provides no margin for a process shift or any other errors in estimation.

34. **C.** There is no time axis in a histogram.

35. **B.** The probability plot can only provide information on the data sampled. It provides no information on the process itself unless the process is also known to be in control.

36. **D**

37. **C**

38. **B**

39. **A.** The upper specification is 10; the lower specification is 0 (since the shipment must be received no earlier than the due date).

$$C_p = \frac{\text{high spec} - \text{low spec}}{6\sigma_x} = \frac{10 - 0}{6 \times 0.75} = 2.2$$

40. **D.** The process performance index is used when the process is out of control. When the process is not in control, a sample of observations (i.e., anything short of 100% inspection) will NOT provide a reasonable estimate of the process or even the batch of material from which the sampled was obtained. By definition, a process that is out of control consists of multiple process distributions, which cannot be evaluated as a single distribution using statistical estimates. The process performance index provides information only on the specific pieces that were sampled from the process or batch.

41. **D**

42. **A.** Choice D is incorrect because a specification must be related to a customer need. If a lower specification is set at 0 for the surface finish, then the C_p calculation will estimate the optimal condition for the process as midway between the specifications. Yet, the optimal condition for surface finish is zero. Zero is clearly not a customer limit to be avoided to please the customer but instead a physical limit that cannot be crossed due to the physical world.

43. **B.** The error rate associated with the closest specification is indicated in Table 3.1.

44. **C**

45. **B**

46. **C**

47. **D.** There is no evidence provided that the process is in control, so process capability cannot be estimated, nor can a meaningful distribution be fit to the data.

48. **D.** There is no evidence provided that the process is in control, so process capability cannot be estimated.
49. **D.** There is no evidence provided that the process is in control, so process capability cannot be estimated.
50. **D.** There is no evidence provided that the process is in control, so the histogram provides information only about the sample data.
51. **D.** Process capability estimates are linked to the control charts from which the statistics are derived. The capability estimate is only revised if the process undergoes a shift, as evidenced by a special cause on the control chart.
52. **A.** The process is poisson, with a fixed sample size of 1 (day). The statistic plotted is the count of visitors to that page each day.
53. **B.** The process is binomial, since each visitor either comes from that specific website or doesn't. Since the total number of visitors to the website (the denominator of the percentage) is likely to vary each day, the p chart is used.
54. **D.** The sample size is the number of visitors per day, which varies. Each sample (i.e., visitor) can visit multiple pages, so the process is poisson.
55. **D**
56. **A**
57. **C.** The process is in control. The variation within the control limits is due to the combined effects of common cause variation inherent to the process. There is no evidence that any process changes have had any meaningful impact on the process performance.
58. **D.** Choices A and C are very likely to collect data that is serially correlated; choice B is likely to be a multistream process. The half-hour time between samples in choice D provides some protection against the serial correlation.
59. **D**
60. **A.** The process is not capable, as calculated in Question 63. The fact that the upper and lower control limits are within the specification limits is not necessarily indicative of capability. Recall that the distribution of the plotted subgroup averages (indicated by the control limits) is much smaller than the distribution of the observations from which the averages are calculated.
61. **B.** Process sigma is calculated as $\overline{R}/d_2 = 0.968/2.326 = 0.416$, where d_2 is from Appendix for $n = 5$.
62. **A.** Using the process sigma value calculated in Question 61:

$$C_p = \frac{\text{high spec} - \text{low spec}}{6\sigma_x} = \frac{11 - 8.5}{6 \times 0.416} = 1.00$$

63. **C.** Since the process average is closer to the USL:

$$C_{pu} = \frac{\text{high spec} - \bar{\bar{x}}}{3\sigma_x} = \frac{11 - 9.926}{3 \times 0.416} = 0.86$$

64. **D**

65. **C**

66. **D**

67. **A**

68. **D**

69. **D**

70. **B.** Choices A and C are examples of multisteam processes (shown in Figure F4) rather than serial correlation evidenced in Figure F5.

71. **A**

72. **D.** There is no independent confirmation that the process is in control, so the curve fit could be misleading. As such, the chart cannot be used to establish process control.

73. **D.** There is no independent confirmation that the process is in control, so the curve fit could be misleading. In addition, C_p cannot be calculated because there is only one specification.

74. **D.** There is no independent confirmation that the process is in control, so the curve fit could be misleading.

75. **D.** There is no independent confirmation that the process is in control, so the curve fit could well be misleading.

76. **A**

77. **B**

78. **B.** Note the K-S value greatly exceeding 0.05.

79. **C**

80. **D**

81. **D.** With a correlation coefficient of 0.7, approximately 49% (0.7^2) of the total variation in the cycle time is predicted by the regression equation. As such, there are obviously other variables that influence cycle time. Yet, statistical significance does not mean physical significance, so there is no guarantee regardless of the correlation coefficient that "number of items" actually influences cycle time (it may well be coincident with one or more other factors). All regression functions, as such, only explain the data from which they are derived. Their ability to explain the physical world must be tested, such as in a designed experiment.

82. **B**

83. **B.** Choice A is not correct in that the term "negative" has nothing to do with good or bad or the desired direction of the dependent variable.
84. **D**
85. **D**
86. **A**
87. **A**
88. **B**
89. **B.** Choices A and C are equivalent statements.
90. **A.** The coefficient on the "number of clerks" term is −2.1. Adding one clerk would decrease the cycle time by 2.1 minutes; removing a clerk would increase the cycle time by 2.1 minutes.
91. **B.** On the low furnace temperature line (labeled 1223), there is little change in the part density response as fill pressure varies from min (515) to max (1235). Thus if fill pressure is heard to control then running the process at low furnace temperature will reduce the influence of fill pressure variation. Conversely, at high furnace temperature (line labeled 1267), there is a large variation in part density as fill pressure varies between its min and max condition. In this way, fill pressure and furnace temperature interact.
92. **C.** The range chart shows the repeatability error is stable. It is desirable for the $\overline{X}$ for repeatability to show out of control (recommended is at least half the plotted values beyond the control limits). In this case, only 3 of the 10 plotted values (30%) exceed the limits, indicating excessive repeatability error.
93. **B.** R&R is 50% of the process variation and 44% of the tolerance. Acceptable values are 10% or less.
94. **B.** The discrimination ratio is 2. Recommended values are 8 to 10 or larger.
95. **A.** The repeatability error is 50% of the process variation and 44% of the tolerance. The reproducibility error is 7% of the process variation and 6% of the tolerance. Acceptable values are 10% or less.
96. **C**
97. **A.** Choices B and C are equivalent statements; the presence of interaction is indicated by the p-value being less than 0.10 (or better yet 0.05).
98. **D**
99. **D**
100. **A**

appendix

Control Chart Constants

Observations in Sample, n	Chart for Average			Chart for Standard Deviations					
	Factors for Control Limits			Factors for Central Line		Factors for Control Limits			
	A	A_2	A_3	c_4	$1/c_4$	B_3	B_4	B_5	B_6
2	2.121	1.880	2.659	0.7979	1.2533	0	3.267	0	2.606
3	1.732	1.023	1.954	0.8862	1.1284	0	2.568	0	2.276
4	1.500	0.729	1.628	0.9213	1.0854	0	2.266	0	2.088
5	1.342	0.577	1.427	0.9400	1.0638	0	2.089	0	1.964
6	1.225	0.483	1.287	0.9515	1.0510	0.030	1.970	0.029	1.874
7	1.134	0.419	1.182	0.9594	1.0423	0.118	1.882	0.113	1.806
8	1.061	0.373	1.099	0.9650	1.0363	0.185	1.815	0.179	1.751
9	1.000	0.337	1.032	0.9693	1.0317	0.239	1.761	0.232	1.707
10	0.949	0.308	0.975	0.9727	1.0281	0.284	1.716	0.276	1.669
11	0.905	0.285	0.927	0.9754	1.0252	0.321	1.679	0.313	1.637
12	0.866	0.266	0.886	0.9776	1.0229	0.354	1.646	0.346	1.610
13	0.832	0.249	0.850	0.9794	1.0210	0.382	1.618	0.374	1.585
14	0.802	0.235	0.817	0.9810	1.0194	0.406	1.594	0.399	1.563
15	0.775	0.223	0.789	0.9823	1.0180	0.428	1.572	0.421	1.544
16	0.750	0.212	0.763	0.9835	1.0168	0.448	1.552	0.440	1.526
17	0.728	0.203	0.739	0.9845	1.0157	0.466	1.534	0.458	1.511
18	0.707	0.194	0.718	0.9854	1.0148	0.482	1.518	0.475	1.496
19	0.688	0.187	0.698	0.9862	1.0140	0.497	1.503	0.490	1.483
20	0.671	0.180	0.680	0.9869	1.0133	0.510	1.490	0.504	1.470
21	0.655	0.173	0.663	0.9876	1.0126	0.523	1.477	0.516	1.459
22	0.640	0.167	0.647	0.9882	1.0119	0.534	1.466	0.528	1.448
23	0.626	0.162	0.633	0.9887	1.0114	0.545	1.455	0.539	1.438
24	0.612	0.157	0.619	0.9892	1.0109	0.555	1.445	0.549	1.429
25	0.600	0.153	0.606	0.9896	1.0105	0.565	1.435	0.559	1.420

	Chart for Ranges							x Charts
Observations in Sample, n	Factors for Central Line			Factors for Control Limits				
	d_2	$1/d_2$	d_3	D_1	D_2	D_3	D_4	E_2
2	1.128	0.8865	0.853	0	3.686	0	3.267	2.660
3	1.693	0.5907	0.888	0	4.358	0	2.574	1.772
4	2.059	0.4857	0.880	0	4.698	0	2.282	1.457
5	2.326	0.4299	0.864	0	4.918	0	2.114	1.290
6	2.534	0.3946	0.848	0	5.078	0	2.004	1.184
7	2.704	0.3698	0.833	0.204	5.204	0.076	1.924	1.109
8	2.847	0.3512	0.820	0.388	5.306	0.136	1.864	1.054
9	2.970	0.3367	0.808	0.547	5.393	0.184	1.816	1.010
10	3.078	0.3249	0.797	0.687	5.469	0.223	1.777	0.975
11	3.173	0.3152	0.787	0.811	5.535	0.256	1.744	0.945
12	3.258	0.3069	0.778	0.922	5.594	0.283	1.717	0.921
13	3.336	0.2998	0.770	1.025	5.647	0.307	1.693	0.899
14	3.407	0.2935	0.763	1.118	5.696	0.328	1.672	0.881
15	3.472	0.2880	0.756	1.203	5.741	0.347	1.653	0.864
16	3.532	0.2831	0.750	1.282	5.782	0.363	1.637	0.849
17	3.588	0.2787	0.744	1.356	5.820	0.378	1.622	0.836
18	3.640	0.2747	0.739	1.424	5.856	0.391	1.608	0.824
19	3.689	0.2711	0.734	1.487	5.891	0.403	1.597	0.813
20	3.735	0.2677	0.729	1.549	5.921	0.415	1.585	0.803
21	3.778	0.2647	0.724	1.605	5.951	0.425	1.575	0.794
22	3.819	0.2618	0.720	1.659	5.979	0.434	1.566	0.786
23	3.858	0.2592	0.716	1.710	6.006	0.443	1.557	0.778
24	3.895	0.2567	0.712	1.759	6.031	0.451	1.548	0.770
25	3.931	0.2544	0.708	1.806	6.056	0.459	1.541	0.763

References

AIAG (1995). *MSA Reference Manual.* Automotive Industry Action Group.

Boggs PB (1996). "Peak expiratory flow rate control chart: A breakthrough in asthma care." *Ann Allergy Asthma Immunol.* Dec;77(6):429–432. PubMed PMID: 8970429.

_____, Hayati F, Washburne WF, Wheeler DA (1999). "Using statistical process control charts for the continual improvement of asthma care." *Jt Comm J Qual Improv.* Apr;25(4):163–181. PubMed PMID:10228909.

_____, Wheeler D, Washburne WF, Hayati F (1998). "Peak expiratory flow rate control chart in asthma care: Chart construction and use in asthma care." *Ann Allergy Asthma Immunol.* Dec;81(6):552–562. PubMed PMID: 9892027.

Box GEP, Jenkins GM (1970). *Time Series Analysis, Forecasting and Control.* San Francisco: Holden-Day.

Burr, Irving W. (1969). "Control charts for measurements with varying sample sizes." *Journal of Quality Technology*, 1.3 (July), pp. 163–167.

Deming WE (1986). *Out of the Crisis.* Cambridge, MA: MIT.

Duncan, Acheson J. (1986). *Quality Control and Industrial Statistics.* 5th ed. Homewood: Richard D. Irwin, Inc.

Johnson NL (1949). "Systems of frequency curves generated by methods of translation." *Biometrika*, 36, pp. 149–176.

_____, Kotz S (eds 1983). *Encyclopedia of Statistical Sciences.* 303–314. New York: John Wiley & Sons.

Keller, Paul (2011). *Six Sigma Demystified.* 2nd ed. New York: McGraw-Hill.

Massey, Frank J., Jr. (1951). "The Kolmogorov-Smirnov Test for Goodness of Fit." *Journal of the American Statistical Association*, 46, pp. 68–78.

Montgomery, Douglas C. (1991). *Introduction to Statistical Quality Control*. New York: John Wiley & Sons.

Nelson, Lloyd S. (1988). "Control charts: Rational subgroups and effective applications." *Journal of Quality Technology*, 20.1 (Jan.), pp. 73–75.

Nelson, Lloyd S. (1984). "The Shewhart control chart—Tests for special causes." *Journal of Quality Technology*, 16.4 (Oct.), pp. 237–239.

Pignatiello, Joseph, and Ramberg, John. *Process Capability Indices: Just Say "NO."* ASQ 47th AQC.

Pyzdek, Thomas (1992). "Process capability analysis using personal computers." *Quality Engineering*, 4.3, pp. 419–440.

Western Electric Company, Inc. (1958). *Statistical Quality Control Handbook*. 2nd ed. New York.

Index

Note: Page numbers followed by *f* denote figures; page numbers followed by *t* denote tables.